Also available at all good book stores

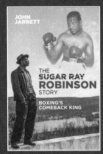

9781785315350

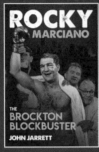

9781785313813

9781785312960

9781785310317

9781785316272

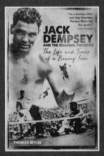

9781785316371

9781785316425

9781785314919

9781785315404

THE GREAT
BENNY LEONARD

THE GREAT
BENNY LEONARD
MAMA'S BOY TO
WORLD CHAMP

JOHN JARRETT

First published by Pitch Publishing, 2021

Pitch Publishing
A2 Yeoman Gate
Yeoman Way
Worthing
Sussex
BN13 3QZ
www.pitchpublishing.co.uk
info@pitchpublishing.co.uk

ISBN 978 1 78531 786 6

Typesetting and origination by Pitch Publishing
Printed and bound in India by Replika Press Pvt. Ltd.

CONTENTS

This book is for my daughter Glenda,
my gracious thanks for getting me
through the rough spots

INTRODUCTION

IN HIS 1997 book *When Boxing Was a Jewish Sport,* Allen Bodner wrote, 'On the surface, it seems unlikely that Jews ever participated in such a brutal sport. It is assumed that Jewish pursuits were traditionally more cerebral and that education played an overriding role in the Jewish culture. "How was it possible?" they would ask. "It is so contrary to Jewish tradition … It is astounding. Who would box when he could go to college and become a professional?" But going to college and becoming a professional were not necessarily options for the vast majority of Jewish youths in the 1920s and 1930s.

'During the years 1910–1940, there were 26 Jewish world champions. This was an impressive achievement, particularly in an era when there were only eight weight classes. But this success must be viewed in the context of overall Jewish participation in boxing. Throughout the 1920s and 1930s approximately, 16 per cent of the champions were Jewish, but nearly one-third of the fighters were also Jewish. In boxing at least, Jews could be average, a possibility that was not available in other sports.

'The boxers knew of no fabled Jewish worship of education. To them and their families the choice was not boxing or college, but boxing or work. In the depression days of the 1930s, college was a remote luxury, even for second-generation Jews such as the boxers.

The boxers did, however, for the most part value education, and once they could afford it, a great number of their children became doctors, lawyers and teachers.

'Jews in boxing encountered virtually no anti-Semitism either in the ring or outside it. So many of the fighters, trainers, promoters and managers were Jewish that it would have been difficult for anti-Semitism to obtain a foothold. Was the pre-eminent position of Jews in boxing during its "Golden Era" really so astonishing? Boxing was part of the urban Jew's effort to get ahead. It provided opportunity, and had Jews not played such an important role in boxing during those years, it would have been even more surprising.

'Benny Leonard was among the first of the modern era Jews. From 1917 to 1925, he was world lightweight champion. Eight years was an exceptionally long period of time to retain a title, especially since the lightweight division had so many talented fighters. Leonard had a truly remarkable record. He was knocked out only four times in over 200 fights. He never lost a decision, and except for the loss by foul to Jack Britton in 1922 did not lose a fight from 1913 to 1932.'

* * *

In 1997, when the American publication *Sporting News* published its 75th anniversary issue, Benny Leonard was named 'Best Boxer of the Last 75 Years'. In 1990, Leonard was inducted into the International Boxing Hall of Fame.

Meet the great Benny Leonard ...

CHAPTER ONE

BENJAMIN LEINER was born in Manhattan's East Village district on 17 April 1896. His mother, Minnie, was German, born in Berlin, while his father, Gershon, was a Hebrew who first saw the light of this world in Austria-Hungary. Benny had four brothers and three sisters and Gershon toiled 72 hours a week in a sweatshop to support his family.

In the sectioned-off Jewish turf around Eighth Street and Second Avenue where Benny grew up, violence was an integral part of every boy's daily education.

'I was a skinny, puny youngster and apart from my legs, very underdeveloped,' he would tell Leo Fuller of the *Topical Times* many years later. 'I was the butt of the fierce Irish "Micks" the Italian "Wops" and the hoodlums of a dozen different races. On Eighth Street, I was free to play on the sunbaked cobbles for 200 yards. Outside of that distance was No Man's Land and running an errand for my mother was a journey fraught with real danger. One day I was trying to sneak to the grocer's with a quarter clutched in my hand when about a half-dozen members of the Sixth Street Boys appeared and grabbed me. They bounced me around and kicked me all the way home. I was limping badly and minus the quarter.'

Benny's mother consoled him but there was little sympathy from his Uncle Max, who took him by the shoulders and asked the frightened boy, 'Why is it the other kids always wipe the street with you? I'm going to take you to the Silver Heel Club on Saturdays and you'll get a little boxing instruction there.'[1]

Uncle Max was a member of the club and every Saturday afternoon he and his fellow members would have a bunch of kids in off the street to fight in the back yard. Young Benny learned quickly and by the time he was 11 years old he was boxing kids older than himself. Before he was much older he was champion of Eighth Street and Uncle Max fixed him up to fight a tough little Irish kid named Joey Fogarty, the Sixth Street champion.

Benny had developed good boxing skills and was able to handle Joey, a stronger, heavier boy. It was in the corner between rounds that he suffered punishment, from his enthusiastic seconds, and when 'time' was called he was glad to get back to the action. The bout ended with Benny proclaimed the winner. His purse of 60 cents soon evaporated when his pals dragged him to the hot dog stand at the corner of the street.

In 1911, Benny was 15 and working in a printing plant. He became friendly with a guy named William Areton, who ran a billiards parlour on the East Side. Known as 'Buck' Areton, he would later have a few fights as Joe Malone and go on to become a trainer, eventually working with Max Schmeling. They would work out together and Areton encouraged Benny to think about having a professional bout for which he could receive five dollars. The kid finally agreed and told his pal to make the fight. Areton took Benny to the old Fordon Athletic Club, where Moe Smith was the matchmaker.

Smith looked the pair over, then said, 'OK, you're on next Saturday against a kid called Mickey Finnegan, four rounds.' Benny was delighted, but he was also worried. He feared his parents would

---

1   Ken Blady *The Jewish Boxers' Hall of Fame* 1988

find out he was going to fight for money and told Areton what was bothering him.

Joe Leslie, a friend who had accompanied the pair to the club, suggested the name of Leonard. Leslie was on the stage at the time with Eddie Leonard, the minstrel, and that's why he made the suggestion. Benny and Areton agreed and thereafter it was Benny Leonard instead of Benny Leiner. Benny outpointed his man by a mile in the first round but in the next, Finnegan landed one on the nose and the claret from Benny's beezer flowed freely. They came out for the third round when Leonard slugged his opponent all over the ring but with the blood streaming down Benny's face, the referee became scared and halted the fight, awarding the bout to Finnegan. As no decisions were rendered in those days, Leonard insisted that he had won and so his record shows, though actually he was stopped.[2]

'Benny was a wonder right off the reel,' Areton told boxing writer Ed Van Every. 'He was just about the fastest thing in the way of a boxer I had ever looked at. He sure was the class from the start and could soon lick any kid his size. Benny would have won easily had he been permitted to continue. The truth is that the decision went to Mickey Finnegan and Benny Leonard lost his first fight. For this fight Benny received the sum of five dollars, but you never saw a more downhearted kid. All he could keep on saying was, "Why did they stop the fight?"'[3]

Areton soon got his boy back in the ring and Benny went through nine fights, winning five by knockout. New York was still in the no-decision era and Benny was considered a winner in the other four contests. But in March 1912, young Leonard struck a bad patch. Coming home from a fight one night, Benny was unable to hide his black eye, much to the distress of his mother. She was still weeping when her husband came home from the sweatshop.

2   Nat Fleischer *Leonard the Magnificent* 1947
3   Ed Van Every *Charleston Gazette* West Virginia 30 January 1925

Gershon was not so upset, especially when his son handed him 20 dollars, his purse for the fight. 'All right, Benny, keep on fighting,' he said. 'It's worth getting a black eye for 20 dollars. I am getting blackened for 20 dollars a week!' But there was more distress for Mama Leiner, caused by a Jersey City Irishman named Joe Shugrue.

Nat Fleischer recorded, 'Shugrue, an aggressive battler, tore into Benny from the start. He didn't give Leonard a chance to get set and Benny, to avoid punishment, kept back-pedalling. Joe had a sort of rolling action and hit from a crouch like Jim Jeffries. This made him a tough target. Shugrue forced the action for two rounds and in the third he caught Benny with a beautiful solar plexus wallop that knocked the wind out of Leonard and made him gasp for breath. The bell came to Benny's rescue.

'Then came a hectic fourth round. One of Benny's blows caught Joe on the chin and put him to the canvas. When Shugrue got to his feet, he set after Benny like a tiger after its prey. A right to Benny's eye almost blinded him. He kept rubbing the optic and retreating but Shugrue gave him no rest. A crushing right to the chin dropped Leonard to his knees. He dragged himself to his feet when a smash from Joe's left hand landed on Benny's mouth and knocked him against the ropes. A tattoo on the jaw sent Benny down again. The referee thought Benny had suffered sufficiently and halted the bout.

'Benny sobbed. He thought the knockout, the first he suffered, would put an end to his career. But Shugrue walked to his corner, patted Benny and remarked, "Kid, you've got it. Other fighters were kayoed and came back. You'll do the same."'

Legendary former heavyweight champion James J. Corbett was writing a column for the newspapers some time later, and he recalled the Shugrue and Fleming defeats. 'When Leonard and Shugrue met in what was the fourth or fifth fight of Leonard's career, the bout was halted in the fourth round. Earlier in the fight, Shugrue's glove had touched the floor and become covered with rosin. Every time after that when he hit Leonard's face the rosin dust flew into the youngster's eye. In the fourth he was in a blinded condition and the contest was stopped.'[4]

Two months later, young Leonard crashed to another knockout defeat. Boxing Frankie Fleming at the Madison AC in New York, the young Canadian smashed a left to the chin in the third round and Benny fell into the ropes. He was still dazed in the fourth and Frankie took the points. Round five and a series of body punches followed by a left hook to the jaw finished Benny for the evening. 'They won't get me any more,' he said to Areton as they walked to the dressing room. He insisted on meeting Fleming again and held his own through the ten rounds. It was a better fight but with no winner, a no-decision bout. Fleming thought that he had won and claimed to have newspaper clippings supporting his claim. 'I may say that Benny Leonard was one fighter I think I owned.' He was the only fighter to beat Leonard twice.

Billy Areton, following the knockout defeats suffered by Leonard at the heavy hands of Shugrue and Fleming, questioned his ability to move Benny in the right direction. There was no misunderstanding between them as they broke their partnership, and Benny was for a short period working with Louis Wallach, brother of the better-known Leach Cross. But Wallach decided to accept an invitation from another fighter, Patsy Cline, to handle him in a Californian campaign. Wallach figured he would make more money with Cline than he could get working with Leonard, a decision he would live to regret in the years ahead as Leonard rose through the ranks to become a world champion.

'The true story of how Billy Gibson became the manager of Leonard was told by Benny to me on a trip we made to Billings Hospital at Fort Harrison,' wrote Fleischer in his book. 'Benny had

---

4   James J. Corbett *Chicago Examiner* 28 August 1917

engaged in close to 50 fights before he ever met Gibson. Gibson had never seen Leonard in action but consented to give him a tryout at the request of Billy's matchmaker and partner, Tom McArdle, provided Benny would accept a bout with tough Teddy Hubbs, at the time an excellent attraction at the Fairmont Club and popular with the fans. Gibson also informed Benny that he would be given $50 for the fight and, as was customary in those days, 25 per cent of whatever tickets he sold. Both Benny and his manager were eager for the opportunity to show at the club and signed.'[5]

When Benny told Uncle Max his good news, they formed a club with the neighbourhood boys and together they sold about 400 tickets for Benny's fight with Hubbs at $1.50 per head. Benny cut in for about $150, with the Fairmont receiving $300 for staging the fight. Billy Areton was also delighted that Gibson was taking charge of Benny's affairs. In the fight with Hubbs, Leonard gave Teddy a lesson and was given the newspaper decision after ten rounds.

Benny was developing into a fine boxer but in his 48 bouts up to when he joined Gibson, he had only scored 14 knockouts. It was troubling the young boxer and he asked his new manager what he could do to increase his punching power. Gibson advised heavy training and slower footwork. Billy also handed his new boy over to George Engel, a trainer and manager of top fighters such as middleweight champions Harry Greb and Frank Klaus, featherweight Eddie Campi and California light-heavyweight Bob McAllister. He would later train heavyweight champion Gene Tunney for Gibson.

There are several versions of how Leonard developed the knockout punch that sparked many of his later victories. Training in the gym one day, Benny explained his problem to veteran fighter Willie Lewis. 'I don't understand it, Willie,' he said. 'I think I'm punching right but something is missing.'

---

5   Nat Fleischer *Leonard the Magnificent* 1947

16

Lewis offered to look Benny over in the gym and try to find the answer. He found it. After watching the youngster in a training session, Willie offered his advice. 'You're doing everything right,' he said, 'but you're not getting the proper leverage behind your punches. Try rolling on the ball of your right foot, like this,' and Willie demonstrated. Leonard tried it, and it was the answer.

Leading American trainer Mannie Seamon worked with Leonard through seven of his eight championship years from 1917 to 1925. 'Clever as he was, Benny wasn't a great hitter. I worked on him for months trying to correct all the little things which make the difference, and then one day it came to him in a flash. It was all a matter of hitting properly. His well-directed punches at one time wouldn't have cracked an egg – and then as a result of all his gym work, suddenly, without warning, he started hitting like a sledge-hammer.

'It was just a matter of acquiring the knack and once he'd got it, he never lost it. Had I tried to alter his style to cause him to find that punch, it might never have worked. But it came, and I was happy. Benny had four brothers, Willie, Charlie, Murray and Joey. Charlie was a very good puncher, the type who could knock a guy out with a single punch, and when the two of them got going in the gym there were no hard measures – it was a real fight every time. They just looked as if they were going to kill each other. Those gymnasium bouts did him more good than it's possible to estimate, and were a contributory cause to his development of an analytical mind which led him always to live his fights over again, to make sure he never repeated a mistake.'[6]

Benny had previously been trained by Doc Robb and George Engel, and Engel was never shy of telling of his work with Leonard. Talking to Nat Fleischer, he said, 'One fighter I made a champion

---

6   Mannie Seamon *Sunday Empire News* London 3 October 1978

was Benny. A few weeks after Gibson became the manager of Leonard, Benny made a poor showing in one of his fights. Gibson always liked a puncher and he realised that Leonard was clever but couldn't sock. He got disgusted and believe it or not, he wanted to give Benny away. When I heard this, I went up to Billy and remarked that I would be happy to assume full management of the lad and pleaded with Billy to give Leonard to me.

'He replied, "George, if you like that kid so much, there must be something to him. You don't go after any but the good ones. No, I'll keep him but I'm going to ask you to train him into a puncher."

'We made a deal on that and I was with Benny for some time. I learned that Benny hadn't had anyone to teach him anything. He didn't go on the road and seldom punched the bag. Well, I changed all that. With proper training he became a real hitter and in a little more than a year under my supervision, he knocked out Freddie Welsh to win the world lightweight title.'[7]

Corbett wrote in this 1917 column, 'When the natives began to call him "The Powder Puff Kid" it hurt Leonard a bit and he asked Gibson to let him loose with his punches. "Not yet – not for a year or two," answered the wise Gibson. "First of all, you are going to learn how to box better than any man at your weight. After that, you can begin to learn the knockout tricks." So he began to school him and quickly did Benny learn the knack of sending crashing blows to head and body. A few months ago, Gibson was satisfied that Benny Leonard had learned every trick of the trade – that the boy he had discovered in 1912 and nursed along for five years was a ring master.

'"Now, Benny," said Gibson a few months ago, "go out and knock 'em out as fast as you feel like. They can't hurt you. Let loose."'[8]

---

7   Nat Fleischer *Leonard the Magnificent* 1947
8   James J. Corbett *Chicago Examiner* 28 August 1917

Benny became one of the best punchers in the business, racking up 71 knockouts in winning 91 fights, with many more in no-decision bouts.

So who taught Benny Leonard how to punch? Willie Lewis? Mannie Seamon? George Engel? Billy Gibson? Maybe all four? Or maybe just Benny himself.

CHAPTER TWO

'AT THE Westchester Biltmore,' boxing writer Robert Edgren was writing in 1925, 'where W. Gibson is now one of the noted golfers, they call him "William" … Other places he is "Billy", except to his friend Benny Leonard, who calls him "Gib". Billy Gibson is one of the few born New Yorkers still decorating the map of the Bronx. He is noted as the manager of Benny Leonard and Gene Tunney, a couple of champions who make an ordinary gold mine look like a hole in the ground.

'In his early sporting days, Billy ran the Fairmont A.C. in the Bronx for several years. This was a matter of philanthropy with Bill, for he never got a real stake with the Fairmont, and most of the time the gate receipts went to pay the ushers and ticket takers and some of the fighters, while Bill dug into the bank roll to make up the balance. Bill made a reputation for honesty at the old Fairmont, which was a club run on the "membership plan" in the days when New York had no boxing law, when promoters were skating on thin ice and in great luck the nights they weren't raided.

'Billy's chief claim to fame was his discovery of Benny Leonard. After seeing him two or three times, Gibson suggested that he'd act as Benny's manager and make his matches. That was all the contract Billy Gibson ever needed with Benny Leonard. When Benny became famous many other managers tried to steal him away, but he always stuck to "Gib" and Billy Gibson always stuck to Benny.'[9]

'The son of a Bronx butcher, Billy was known all over New York. He ran the Criterion Restaurant, a popular bar and grill at East 149th Street and Third Avenue which soon became one of the Bronx's "in" places. It catered to judges, lawyers, politicians, athletes, newspaper-men and show people. Gibson was one of the city's best-known political power brokers and toyed with boxing mostly as a hobby. One day, his pal, Chief of Police Surgeon Edward T. Higgins, came in and gave him a heavyweight. It turned out to be Jim Coffey, the famous Roscommon Giant.'[10]

The big Irishman (6ft 3½in) won 36 of 43 fights from 1911 through 1921, 34 by knockouts, and fought Carl Morris, Battling Levinsky and Fireman Jim Flynn. In April 1914, Gibson staged the inaugural show of the New Stadium A.C. at St Nicholas Arena, New York, where Coffey knocked out Flynn in four rounds of a brawl. Gibson also handled Paulino Uzcudun, Louis 'Kid' Kaplan and the ill-fated Frankie Jerome, a Bronx bantamweight who was knocked out by Bud Taylor in 12 rounds at the old Garden in January 1924 and died two days later.

Gibson's stars were Benny Leonard and Gene Tunney, two all-time greats of fistiana. 'Gibson did a great deal for me,' Benny would recall, 'and I always will be grateful to him. I used to hang around the Fairmont even on nights when I wasn't fighting, and he was always talking to me and advising me. I can see us now, just like it was yesterday. I'd pull out the lower drawer in his big desk and sit on it, and Gib would sit in his chair and talk to me, waving his long fingers in my face, and I'd sit and listen to him and try to remember everything he was saying. I was just a little Jewish boy listening to a wise Irishman who had been through the mill.

---

9 Robert Edgren *Salt Lake Telegram* 13 January 1925
10 *Sheboygan Press*, Wisconsin 26 July 1947

'I never had any other manager than Mr Gibson. He just put me on at the Fairmont for a long time, and then matched me with Eddie Wallace at the Broadway Sporting Club. I won in ten rounds. Tommy Houck had never been knocked out. I met him at White Plains and knocked him out in seven rounds. That was the first time I showed a real knockout punch, although I won some of my first fights with knockouts. It was a different thing with Houck. He was good, and it's hard to knock out a good man.'[11]

Talking to John Reed in June 1917, Benny said, '"Up to two years ago, I was so light that I couldn't knock a guy out if he leaned against my fist with his chin." Then it was that he suddenly began to grow, to take on power and heaviness. He described to me how, after fighting Tommy Langdon in Philadelphia on 15 February 1915, he woke up next morning "feeling like a king," with his muscles harder than they had been. Afterward, after every fight he felt himself grow perceptibly heavier and stronger.

'It was about this time that his father began to get reconciled to Benny's fighting, for he was taking care of himself as no other son of his was doing, going to bed early, exercising, avoiding bad habits and at the same time making more money than any of his brothers or even Papa Leiner himself. Mr Leiner was at that time eking out a scanty living as foreman in a cloak and suit sweatshop down on the East Side, and breaking his health into the bargain. But as soon as Benny began to get real money for his bouts he took the whole family and moved uptown to Jewish Harlem, providing for his father and mother and younger brothers and lovingly forbidding his father ever to work again.'[12]

'Like most great fighters,' wrote Fleischer in his biography, 'Benny was of the opinion that his earliest battles were his most trying. "I'll bet you never heard of a fellow named Willie Jones," he

11   Robert Edgren *New York Evening World* 8 April 1916
12   John Green *Boston Evening Globe* 15 June 1917

remarked to me one day. I acknowledged my ignorance whereupon Benny continued. "What a tough bird he was. He could hit like a mule and take it till the cows came home. And I mean hit. He could fight. He showed me a few things I'll never forget when I tackled him in my early fighting days [October 1913]. And there was a chap named Kid Black. He almost made me quit the ring shortly after I got started [January 1914]. He murdered me with body punches that left their mark for a week. I was afraid to let on at home what hurt me when my mother asked me why I kept holding my hand to my stomach."[13]

Towards the end of 1915, Benny was beginning to feel he was ready for the best and asked manager Gibson to test him against a tough lightweight. Billy did better than that; he went out and signed Benny to fight *two* tough lightweights, Gene Moriarty and Joe Mandot. They were saying that Moriarty had an iron jaw. Well, he needed more than that against young Mister Leonard. It was all over in round three, with Moriarty hanging on the ropes after two knockdowns, and the referee stopped the bout. Gibson was delighted as he hugged Benny, saying, 'You've got it now. You've got the punch I've been looking for. You'll soon lick any man in the division.'

A couple of weeks later, Benny entered the ring at the Harlem Sporting Club to go ten rounds with Joe Mandot. Joe was known as the Orleans Wildcat, but Benny was confident he could tame the Southerner. In the early rounds, Mandot tested Benny's boxing skills to the limit, forcing the action three minutes every round. But from the fourth round, Leonard went on the attack and coming out for round seven he knew he had solved Joe's style and he went in for the kill. A smashing right to the jaw dropped Mandot to the canvas and brought the crowd to its feet. Joe rose at the count of nine but

---

13   Nat Fleischer *Leonard the Magnificent* 1947

Benny was on him in a flash, landing a savage left to the head followed by a solid right to the chin and Mandot dropped again. By the time he got up, it was all over and young Benny Leonard was the talk of the boxing world.

'He actually found the punch when boxing Joe Mandot, from New Orleans,' trainer Mannie Seamon recalled. 'Joe had the reputation, not only of being a good fighter, but also of having the best pivot punch in the world. If he missed, he would swing round and hit his opponent with a vicious back-hand punch. Knowing this, Benny realised he had to move in and hit. He did so and knocked Mandot flat out. And from that moment, many others had to take the same medicine. Mandot announced that he was through with boxing, after this loss to Leonard. He later changed his mind.'[14]

A few weeks after the Leonard–Mandot fight, an interesting item was published in *The Boston Globe*. 'Tommy Walsh, manager of Joe Mandot, is another one of the great makers of alibis. In trying to square Joe Mandot for being defeated by Benny Leonard in New York a short time ago, manager Walsh writes, "Mandot is like all great athletes that hail from the South. The balmy, semitropical air seems to breed a degree of temperament which finds expression in the great blaze of glory which sometimes characterises their work: at other times it finds them performing in a listless manner, far below their true form. They are affected by certain conditions of time, of surroundings, of outside interests, even of friendly faces at the ringside or the track.'[15]

Shortly before Benny fought Mandot, he faced Al (Doc) Schumacher in New York, scoring a knockout in seven rounds. Fast forward to a December day in 1967. Writer George Girsch was working in the New York office of *The Ring* magazine when,

---

14 Mannie Seamon *Sunday Empire News* London 3 October 1948
15 *The Boston Globe* 21 January 1916

'a couple, both somewhat beyond middle age, came into the office, "sight-seeing", as they explained it. They deplored the fact that thieves had cleaned out most of *The Ring* Museum.

"'I guess I should introduce myself," the husband half of the team chuckled. "I am Dr S. Albert Scimeca, head of the Scimeca Clinic at Caney, Kansas. This is Mrs Scimeca, who is a dentist. Why am I telling you all these details? Well, I used to be a lightweight boxer around New York. I fought under the name of Al Schumacher. On 19 June 1915, in New York, I met the greatest of all lightweights, Benny Leonard. I was knocked out in seven rounds. Leonard was tough. He was crafty. He could take it and he sure could dish it out. I will never forget the right to the chin which laid me out. However, it was a trick to go seven with Benny, the greatest lightweight of all time." Now *The Ring* knows what became of Al Schumacher, who fought Leonard.'[16]

In 1916, Benny Leonard was starting to look like a championship contender and Gibson matched him with Johnny Dundee. Born in Sicily, the kid named Giuseppe Carrora was taken to New York to grow up in 'Hell's Kitchen', where his family ran a fish market. In a street fight one day, the kid caught the eye of fight manager Scotty Montieth, who took him in hand and taught him all about boxing. Scotty even gave his boy a new name, Johnny Dundee, and in fight circles he became known as 'The Scotch Wop'. He was soon known as a helluva fighter and in 1913 he battled world featherweight champion Johnny Kilbane. The referee stopped the bout in the 20th round and declared a draw, with many observers thinking the kid had the best of it.

Benny knew he had been in a scrap when he fought Dundee over 15 rounds in a New York bout. It was the first of eight fights between the two and every one was a battle. Leonard was adjudged

---

16   George Girsch *Ring* December 1967

to be the winner of five of them, with Dundee taking the newspaper decision in the other three. Half the time, it depended on which newspaper you bought. A good example was the Dundee–Leonard scrap in March 1915, with a headline in *The Boston Globe* reading, 'Guess Who Won? – That's What Gotham Has to Do.' The *Associated Press* reported Johnny Dundee was given a newspaper decision over Benny Leonard, while readers of the *New York World* were informed that Benny Leonard added Johnny Dundee to his list of victims.

With a smile on his face, Benny used to say he fought Johnny so many times he learned to speak Italian. After eight fights with the 'Scotch Wop', Leonard told columnist Robert Edgren in a 1921 interview, 'I've found the Italians the hardest to knock out. They can fight all the time and not tire. Their vitality is astonishing. Fellows like Johnny Dundee are tireless and can stand an immense amount of work without going stale. That's because their ancestors for a thousand years back have been workers and have lived on plain food and little of it. A loaf of bread was a feast to those birds.' Dundee later displayed his admirable fighting qualities when he beat Frenchman Eugene Criqui over 15 rounds for the world featherweight title, with 40,000 fans looking on at the Polo Grounds in New York.

In September 1916, Benny met Frankie Conifrey, Harlem's Fighting Fireman, at the Star A.C. in a bout that paired his Jewish fans against Frankie's Irish followers. 'In the early rounds, Benny was really "putting the hurt" on Frankie. Having no other way to escape punishment, Frankie began mauling and butting in the clinches. Benny was incensed. If Frankie wanted a real fight, Benny would give it to him. Resorting to damaging uppercuts and blood-producing hooks, Benny cut Frankie to ribbons. It was such an obvious mismatch that Frankie's brother jumped into the ring and called a halt to Part I of the great fight.

'Now the real action began – it was Part II. Frankie's partisans, who had much money and even more pride riding on him, were furious. In the balconies, all hell broke loose; half an hour passed before the riot squad arrived. Benny, wrapped in a bathrobe and with a towel draped over his head, was hustled out the back door into a waiting cab. "The fight I can never forget," is the way Benny described it.'[17] He was credited with a knockout in seven rounds.

In 1916, Benny twice fought a New York Irishman named Shamus O'Brien, a rough and tough fellow whose square name was Michael Joseph Hogan. They boxed a no-decision bout in Syracuse with Benny getting the newspaper verdict, much to O'Brien's disgust. So when they clashed in New York a month later, Leonard made no mistake. 'Benny flattened Shamus so violently in a seven-round knockout that the manager of Shamus sent out a loud and vociferous claim that Benny had a piece of lead pipe in his glove – or something like that. Needless to say, the only thing Benny had in his glove was his good right hand. He seldom puts on even a soft bandage. His four knuckles are well developed and good enough for his purpose.'[18]

Jack Dempsey's nemesis, black heavyweight Harry Wills, was a keen student of boxing and a great admirer of Leonard. 'I will always say that good as he was, Benny Leonard would have been even better if he hadn't got such a kick out of showing his skill. Benny had what few men ever have, a natural right hand, but he enjoyed fancy boxing so much he held it back and only let it go in emergencies. I remember his fight with Leo Johnson.

'I warned Leo just to go along with Benny and not make him mad. Back in those days they used to say that nobody could muss Benny's hair, he was so clever. That night, when the referee called Leo and Benny out to the centre of the ring, Leo reached over and

17   Ken Blady *The Jewish Boxers' Hall of Fame* 1988
18   Robert Edgren *The Syracuse Herald* 29 April 1917

rumpled Benny's hair. When he did this, Benny forgot his boxing and the fight was over in a minute.'[19]

By the spring of 1916, 19-year-old Benny Leonard was one of the leading contenders for the world lightweight championship, having mixed it up with such stars as Phil Bloom, Patsy Cline, Pal Moore, Frankie Conifrey, Johnny Drummie, Jimmy Duffy, Johnny Dundee, and Johnny Kilbane, who had taken the featherweight title from the legendary Abe Attell in a 20-round upset. Manager Billy Gibson had set his sights on lightweight champ Freddie Welsh, who was not getting any younger. The veteran Welshman was 29 and had boxed his way through 69 fights against the finest in the division since beating Willie Ritchie over 20 rounds in London on 7 July 1914.

Welsh was certain that he could hold the New York youngster in a ten-round bout. It was 1916 and no-decision contests were the only ones allowed in New York. The only way Welsh could lose his title was if he was knocked out, or otherwise unable to complete the ten rounds. He had never been knocked out and he could not see Leonard putting his lights out. He told manager Harry Pollock to make the match with the stipulation that he receive 50 per cent of the purse …

---

19   John Jarrett *Champ in the Corner The Ray Arcel Story* 2007

CHAPTER THREE

'BILLY GIBSON was right,' Frank G. Menke wrote in his syndicated column. 'Six months ago he said that he had under his wing the greatest lightweight battler since the days of Joe Gans. "His name is Benny Leonard. I've been sending him along slowly during the past year. Now, he's ready. Watch him go."

'New York watched him against several ordinary battlers – and Leonard showed up his adversaries. It watched him fight Johnny Dundee and voted him a higher ranking. And then came the real test – the battle with Freddie Welsh.

'Some of the natives figured that Leonard, after meeting Welsh, would make his departure from the ring under the auspices of the Red Cross. But what a surprise that fight occasioned! Leonard outpunched, outgeneralled, outboxed and outpointed the champion in practically every one of the ten rounds. The young Jewish boy stands out today as the greatest all-round boxer and fighter the ring game has produced in many years. The old-timers insist that Joe Gans was a bit shiftier, but they admit that if Leonard improves at the rate he has shown during the past six months, he will become the superior of Gans in his prime.

'Benny Leonard will be the next lightweight champion of the world – if Freddie Welsh ever gives him a chance over the decision route.'[20] Jimmy Johnston of Madison Square Garden was ready to guarantee Welsh a purse of $12,500 for a fight with Benny Leonard and the news generated great excitement in New York. Welsh was beginning to tire of the criticism in the newspapers that he was on the way out, and he took it out on Frank Whitney in a fight at the Harlem Sporting Club. After five rounds, Whitney quit on his stool with a badly cut left eye. Maybe the champion was putting out his best stuff to impress young Benny Leonard, at ringside to assess his next job.

Benny's fight with the world champion took place in the old Garden, with advance ticket sales hitting $16,000. There were more than 10,000 in the place that night of 31 March 1916, the biggest crowd for a lightweight fight since the Frawley Law took effect, banning boxing to a decision. If Benny wanted the title, he would have to knock Welsh out or cause a stoppage inside the ten rounds. The young New Yorker was sure he could do just that and set about the veteran Welshman from the opening bell.

'Benny Leonard, who has been coming along like the flash of a meteor for the last few months, gave Welsh the beating of his career tonight in a ten-round contest at the Madison Square Garden. It was Welsh's ring generalship that saved him from falling an easy prey to the New York lightweight sensation. In the seventh round it did seem that he must succumb, but he was not found wanting on this occasion. Smashes rained in upon the champion from all angles and caught him everywhere allowed by the boxing rules. To many it looked that Welsh must be beaten, but he weathered the storm and at the bell was fighting back. Leonard won practically every round despite the fact that Welsh was carrying the fight as well as he could.'[21]

---

20   Frank G. Menke *Logansport Pharos Reporter* 8 April 1916
21   *Washington Post* 1 April 1916

'It was a case of youth charged with fight from his toes to his head pitted against a veteran ringmaster whose long sojourn in the ring is counting against him, and the old-time skill of Welsh is plainly on the wane.'[22]

Veteran Charley Rose had been Welsh's trainer and cornerman since he took the title from Willie Ritchie in London on 7 July 1914. 'Freddie first took on Leonard in the old Garden on 31 March 1916,' he recalled for Daniel M. Daniel in *Ring* in March 1960. 'Freddie was in no condition to fight the 20-year-old puncher. There was no question as to the winner. Benny took the champion handily. But it was a no-decision, no title fight. Then they were matched for 28 July in Brooklyn.

'I warned Welsh that to go into the ring again with Benny, in poor shape, would invite disaster. I said, "Freddie, you have got to take this one seriously. You have got to put in a few weeks of hard work. I am going to ask Bill Brown to let you train at his health farm at Garrison, New York. When I put the proposition to Brown, who ran a fight club on West 23rd Street as well as his health farm, Bill refused. He said that some of his wealthy patrons would not want to have a professional fighter around the place. Of course, Bill was wrong. I kept working on him, and finally Brown gave in.

'Welsh trained faithfully and went into the ring at Washington Park in fine shape. I felt that Welsh beat Leonard that time. But the newspapers gave it to Benny. It was a close fight. I said to myself, "Welsh never again will be in such fine shape. If, in that condition, he failed to win decisively, what will he be likely to do if they meet a third time? Leonard could stop him."'[23]

Washington Park in Brooklyn was an old baseball park but it was boxing that drew the crowds this night in July 1916. 'It was a typical New York boxing crowd. The night was perfect for an open

22 *New York Times* 1 April 1916
23 Daniel M. Daniel *Ring* March 1960

air fisticuffs carnival, and it seemed as if all Broadway had motored over. Cars filled the streets for several blocks around the venue. There was a 15-minute delay in getting the two men into the ring. Leonard insisted on entering second because he'd beaten Freddie in their previous fight. The champion, who came in last according to custom, gave in and marched into the enclosure. Freddie stepped through the ropes looking lean and muscular and obviously feeling pleased with himself.'[24]

'Freddie Welsh showed several thumping good reasons why he is champion lightweight of the world when he licked Benny Leonard at Washington Park last night. There wasn't a sign of a tango step in any one of the ten rounds. It was a stand-up and drag-out from the start. Excepting one round, the third, Welsh won all the way.

'But he showed a little of Abe Attell, Battling Nelson and Joe Gans combined to turn the trick. Benny was no slouch. It was the old story of science, punch, condition and experience against science, punch, condition and a younger vigour. There is not one man or woman of the thousands who saw the battle who doesn't believe Benny Leonard will wear the lightweight championship crown some time in the future. If he does not spoil it by thinking he's good enough to quit learning.

'For the first time in a decade of moons New York's fight experts agreed on the result, the quality of the fight put up by both men, the titleholder's championship ability and the challenger's championship possibilities. Leonard had been using a whale of a slam to Welsh's left kidney. He placed it beautifully six or eight times in the first three rounds. Every time it brought the champion up with a jolt.

'Then Welsh used several of his ubiquitous arms and fists to cover his kidneys as well as his face. He was foiling off blows like a fencer. But he showed at least a double track fighting brain by

24   Andrew Gallimore *Occupation: Prizefighter The Freddie Welsh Story* 2006

leaping out from behind his defending arms with sufficient jabs and swings and uppercuts to give him a good edge at the finish.'[25]

After fighting Welsh twice, Benny Leonard knew there would come a third meeting, and there had to be no mistakes in that one. If he wanted to be champion, he would have to knock Freddie Welsh out, a tough one as the Welshman had never been knocked out. But as Benny figured, there had to be a first time for everything.

In the meantime, Billy Gibson looked over the field. Benny had already beaten Frankie Conifrey and after taking a couple of easy ones in Philadelphia, Gibson signed Benny to meet a guy named Ever Hammer in Kansas City on 18 October 1916. Billy McCarney, who dabbled in managing and seconding fighters, was the promoter. He and Billy Gibson were very friendly and as a favour Gibson accepted his offer for a Leonard–Hammer fight.

'When Gibson and Benny arrived in Kansas City the day before the fight, they were astonished to see the posters plastered all over the city announcing the contest as a 15-rounder. Gibson almost went into hysterics as he cornered McCarney and argued against the length of the bout. He threatened to take the next train back to New York, but McCarney was obdurate. He told Billy that in Kansas the fans would not pay to see a ten-round bout, and since it was his money that was supplying the funds, it would have to be for 15 rounds.

'The fight was staged in Convention Hall and the advance sale was excellent. Benny was working on a good percentage and guarantee, and as Gibson was about to call the fight off, Benny stepped into the argument. "Look here, Billy. What's the use of all this commotion? If this is a 15-round town and the people won't go to a show unless they get the main event at that distance, let's forget it and we'll fight 15 rounds."

---

25   *La Crosse Tribune* Wisconsin 29 July 1916

'Gibson didn't expect that from Leonard, who never had gone more than ten rounds, and with a gesture of resignation he replied, "If it's OK with you, Benny, it's all right with me. That settles it."[26]

'Gabe Kaufman, Kansas City promoter, expects to pack them in at his Convention Hall arena tonight. He probably will not be disappointed. Gabe is offering the glove bugs of his neighbourhood the most attractive card of the indoor lightweight season to date – a 15-round encounter between Ever Hammer and Benny Leonard at 135 pounds, the men to climb on the scales at three in the afternoon. These are two of the most quarrelsome lads in that division, and because of their respective aggressive styles there is certain to be plenty of action once they get under full headway.

'The Bristling Blond of this town is tackling the most dangerous party he ever has met. This is true because Leonard is a much harder hitter than Johnny Dundee, the classiest foe Ever has faced up to this time and whom the blond gave two very close arguments. Leonard comes West with a reputation as a deadly right-hand puncher who is noted for his accuracy with the KO wallop. As Hammer never has been very difficult to locate, it is figured he is taking more of a chance with Leonard that he was with Dundee, who is not famous for his punch.

'Inasmuch as both Leonard and Dundee are leading candidates for a Freddie Welsh match, it may be gathered that the fuss this evening means much to Hammer. If he can beat Leonard or even get a draw, they will want him in New York as soon as he can get there.'[27]

With that in mind, Kid Howard, Hammer's manager, sent his man out to go for broke and he did just that. 'Leonard would recall, "Hammer bounded from his corner at the bell, and before I knew what was up the fellow shot a hard left hook to my mouth. I didn't

---

26   Nat Fleischer *Leonard the Magnificent* 1947
27   Sam P. Hall *Chicago Examiner* 18 October 1916

even see it coming and before I could compose myself the Swede was whaling me about with both hands. I was badly rattled and didn't know just how to handle the matter. I tried to sprint, but Hammer caught up with me. Then I tried boxing him, and then slugging. I was second best all the way. My mouth was badly gashed and I was already as dizzy as a ginny sailor. That first round with Hammer was the worst I ever encountered, either before or after the winning of the lightweight title.'[28]

'The second was Hammer's best round,' reported Ed Cochrane from ringside. 'He sent two left hooks to the face and Leonard complained to the referee that Hammer was hitting in the clinches. Hammer sent several lefts to the face and Leonard was kept busy blocking and ducking to avoid punishment. The round was so much in favour of Hammer that Billy Gibson jumped to the ropes to caution his lightweight to be careful. 'Hammer rocked Leonard's head with a stiff left hook, which he landed while in a clinch, and forced Leonard to hold on and cover up. In the seventh, he fought Leonard from rope to rope and landed some stiff left hooks. That spell and the second were the only rounds in which the Chicago boy had a chance.'[29]

'I don't know how I ever got through that second round,' said Benny. 'It must have been an accident that I ever got to my corner. Gibson was still lashing me. "What are you trying to do? You're a boxer – not a catch-all. Will you pull yourself together. You're breaking my heart. If you lose to this fellow, it will put you back a whole year." Well, I kept taking a hammering from both Hammer and Gibson until along about the sixth round.

'Then a curious thing, a psychic touch developed that helped me a lot. Hammer began kidding to me, "So you're from *Noo Yark*, hey? Say, are you the best they've got down in that dump?" Stuff

28 Benny Leonard *Hobbs Daily News* New Mexico 29 January 1939
29 Ed Cochrane *Chicago Examiner* 19 October 1916

like that, and all accompanied by grins and other side remarks to the ringside. Now I always had a lot of pride, and it made me hot to hear this fellow give me the razz, and then I began to fight. I boxed better, avoided many of his blows and began to get in a good dig now and then. Hammer began to slow up a bit himself.

'In the ninth, I figured myself strong enough to let out. I took my time, still letting Hammer push the fighting until the right moment arrived. That was when Hammer started a left hook. I beat him to the punch with as cruel a right hook under the heart as any fighter ever got. His knees sagged till they almost touched the floor, but he managed to grab me and tumble into a clinch. That blow was the winner. Hammer was easy for me after that and I punished him thoroughly. The same punch dropped him like a sack of cement in the 12th, but the tough fellow got up at nine. I appealed to the referee to stop it, for Hammer was helpless, both arms dangling at his sides. The referee refused to act, however, and I was obliged to start another punch. Luckily, Hammer toppled over before it reached him and the fight was over.'[30]

For *The Chicago Examiner*, Ed Cochrane reported, 'Leonard danced about his opponent and completely bewildered him with a shower of lefts and rights to the face in the ninth, tenth and 11th rounds. It was believed Hammer would stand a better chance against Leonard after the tenth round because Leonard had never gone 15 rounds before. But by the time the tenth had arrived, Hammer had stopped so many vicious punches that his stamina was sapped, and it was plain that the end was in sight.'[31]

'Then came the 12th,' wrote Nat Fleischer. 'Hammer rushed from his corner and drove Benny against the ropes, where they mixed it. The referee separated them and in a flash Benny saw the Swede's unguarded chin. He leaped forth, jabbed Ever with his left,

---

30   Benny Leonard *Hobbs Daily News* New Mexico 29 January 1939
31   Ed Cochrane *The Chicago Examiner* 19 October 1916

knocking him off balance, and followed with a murderous right that carried all the force behind Benny's weight. It was an accurate punch that carried everything and Hammer was knocked out. He lay on the canvas without a muscle moving.

'The fans yelled as the referee started the count and to their amazement they saw Hammer get to his feet at nine. How he did it, no one will ever know! But he did. He stood with hands dangling at his side, a helpless battler for whom one more such blow by Leonard might bring a fatality. Benny stood eying his opponent and also the referee. He didn't know whether to take another swipe at his man or let the third man in the ring intercede. Neither had to be done, for Hammer, body quivering, crumpled to the canvas again and this time the referee counted him out. Thus he went down twice from the effects of one punch! It was a great victory for Benny and it was heralded all over the country.

'Benny Leonard had now reached a point where he couldn't be denied a shot at the top men of the lightweight division.'[32]

---

32 Nat Fleischer *Leonard the Magnificent* 1947

CHAPTER FOUR

TRAINER MANNIE Seamon would recall, 'Benny often went to the gym even when he wasn't fighting. Because boxing was his life. He said he discovered more tricks and new moves watching other fighters work out. He was a thorough student of boxing. Benny wasn't strong and he knew it. He was easily hurt with good punches. That's what made him such a great boxer. He knew he had to be clever to keep out of trouble. He learned to change his style in the middle of a round. Leonard made the closest study of feinting of anyone I've ever dealt with. He was a fast boxer so to keep up his speed I used to put two boys in the ring with him together. He either jabbed one and watched for the other or he feinted one and jabbed the other. If one missed him, as they often did, he knew he could take care of the other.

'One of the reasons he worked so hard on defence, he was a good son. His mother was a long-time invalid and did not want him to fight. Benny saw to it that he did not come home bearing marks of contest.

For the first time, Seamon started looking at diets. Leonard was always making weight and had the ability to get as much satisfaction from a light meal as others would from a heavy meal. He would sit down to one lamb chop, half a head of lettuce, half a grapefruit, a cup of tea with lemon and two slices of toast.

He would cut his food into very small bites and chew them thoroughly.'[33]

A month after his sensational fight with Ever Hammer, Leonard stepped out with one of his contemporaries, Johnny Dundee, with whom he shared a ring no less than eight times. Dundee always gave Benny a good scrap, all in no-decision bouts, with Leonard generally adjudged the winner. Dundee was favoured in three of their bouts, with one of those three taking place in Philadelphia on 15 November 1916. A crowd of 5,000, packing the local Olympia, were stunned by the clear-cut victory of the little Italian, who never gave the New York sensation a chance to get set and land his knockout wallop.

'Dundee's lightning attack started at the close of the first round and he never let up. He was like a bulldog, sticking out his jaw and taking Leonard's heavy punches just to get his own across. He landed three punches to Benny's one after the first session, which was Leonard's by a narrow margin. It was a terrific right-hand smash to the left cheekbone in the fourth round that really gave Dundee the big edge. He caught Leonard flush on the jaw with the smash and the Gotham entry staggered back several steps.'[34]

A week later Benny was in St Louis, where Harvey Thorpe stood up gamely for 12 rounds. Well, almost. Harvey was knocked out ten seconds before the final bell, by which time he had had enough. 'The bout itself was a murder. After five rounds Thorpe was bleeding from his mouth, nose and left eye. The ring resembled a slaughterhouse. No boxer ever displayed more gameness than the Kansas City boy did in going the 12 rounds.'[35]

Death stalked the ring at the German Hall in Albany, New York. Stephen McDonald, a young middleweight engaged in his

---

33 Mannie Seamon Series in *Sunday Empire News* London September-October 1948
34 *New Castle News* Pennsylvania 16 November 1916
35 *East Chicago Times* 23 November 1916

first professional venture in the prize ring, was instantly killed by a blow over the heart in the first round. A number of legislators saw the fight in which McDonald was knocked out by Teddy Hicks. Hicks, his second Claude Tibbetts, referee O.H. Stacey and H.G. Goldman, promoters of the bout and the matchmaker, were held by the police on charges of second degree manslaughter. It was asserted by Hicks' seconds that McDonald might have been killed by breaking his neck when he fell against the ropes. McDonald's death was due to 'a shock occasioned by a blow over the solar plexus,' according to the decision of Dr Fred Myers, who performed an autopsy.[36]

'Benny Leonard was giving Phil Bloom a one-handed beating in New York when McDonald met his death in Albany. With an injured left hand, Leonard had Bloom all but out on three occasions. If Leonard shows as well in his meeting with Frankie Callahan, there probably will be a loud and insistent clamour for a return bout for Leonard with champion Freddie Welsh.'[37]

It was at this time that several boxing promoters in New York expressed fears that the game would suffer further restrictions at the hands of the state legislature. It was reported that Governor Whitman intended to ask the legislature to repeal the present law, which permitted ten-round bouts without a decision. This was the Frawley Law, which came into being in New York on 29 August 1911 and would be repealed on 15 November 1917.

'The Frawley Law provided for ten-round no-decision fights,' wrote Al Buck in *Ring* in April 1949. 'Supposed to discourage gambling, it didn't. People will always bet and they left it to the newspapers to give the decision to decide their wagers. According to Francis Albertanti, veteran sports scribe, it was customary to make the wager payable on the majority opinion arrived at by the

---

36   *Salt Lake Telegram* 31 January 1917
37   *Lima Daily News* Ohio 31 January 1917

boxing writers on the *Evening World, The Globe,* and *The Mail.* There were no-decisions permitted in New York. The same was the case in most other cities. About the only places where the referee was allowed to decide were Boston, New Orleans, and California …

'The *Associated Press* paid little attention to fights out of town in the no-decision years. The managers usually made their own decisions, wiring the results to the New York newspapers. Frequently their thrilling stories of ten-round battles were written long before the men entered the ring. More often than not, they were filed before the fight was over! Al McCoy was the only champion to win and lose a title in New York under the Frawley Law. McCoy, Mike O'Dowd and Benny Leonard were the only champions crowned in New York rings during the six years the Frawley Law was in existence.'[38]

Before Benny could be crowned champion he had to beat Welsh, and the contest was arranged for 28 May 1917 in the Manhattan Casino.

'Can Leonard score such a decisive victory?' mused a writer for the *Lincoln Sunday Star* on the eve of battle. 'It seems improbable but it is not impossible. Any fighter who has the punching power of Leonard is likely to upset Welsh at any minute. Leonard is hitting more viciously than ever. He has shown this in his last four matches, all of which ended in knockouts. He started flattening his opponents on 22 March.'[39]

Leonard gave Packy Hommey a lacing for ten rounds, flooring him in the ninth for nine seconds. Hommey did not come out for the tenth round, his seconds throwing up the sponge. Benny followed this up with a journey to Milwaukee, where he was matched with local favourite Ritchie Mitchell. 'The beginning of the end for the Brewery City star was seen shortly after the start of

---

38   Al Buck *Ring* April 1949
39   *The Lincoln Sunday Star* Nebraska 27 May 1917

the seventh when Leonard, evidently intent on a knockout, fought Ritchie halfway across the ring to the ropes and during a mix-up on the hemp shot a terrific right cross to the jaw. The blow sent Mitchell sprawling on the canvas and he was nearly gone then. At nine, wobbly but game, he regained his feet. Leonard shot a hard left hook to the body. Down came Mitchell's guard and the instant it fell the easterner tore loose with a relentless fire of lefts and rights to the head. The furious attack shook Mitchell from head to toe. He slipped to one knee, then got up, but a Leonard right to the jaw sent him crashing into the ropes and to defeat. There is only one term that tells adequately why Leonard beat Mitchell, and that term is class.'[40]

Benny kept his tools sharp with a short trip to Philadelphia, where he knocked out local Charlie 'Kid' Thomas in six rounds. At the end of the bout, both of Thomas's eyes were nearly closed and his mouth and nose were badly swollen. Pacific coast lightweight champion Eddie Shannon came to Brooklyn three days later and suffered the same fate as Kid Thomas, a knockout in six rounds.

'Benny Leonard will be the favourite when he faces Freddie Welsh in a ten-round bout in New York, 28th of May. There are two reasons why the little New Yorker will enter the ring with the balance of sentiment on his side. The first of these is the fact that he carries a knockout punch in his right hand, and the second lies in the belief that Welsh is fast going back. Welsh's poor showing against Johnny Kilbane, regardless of alibis that have been made for him…Welsh's latest declaration to the effect that he will meet any title aspirant over the 20-round route has been taken with a grain of salt by Leonard and his followers. Leonard does not believe he can entice Welsh into the ring for more than ten rounds, so the coming battle is his big chance.'[41]

---

40 *Winnipeg Tribune* 20 April 1917
41 *Oakland Tribune* 25 May 1917

Leonard was training hard with brother Charley at the New Polo Club in the city, while champion Welsh was working at his farm in Summit, New Jersey. Freddie was anxious to beat Benny as he was already matched to fight Johnny Kilbane over 15 rounds in Cleveland on Independence Day, 4 July. There were words from Freddie's long-time trainer Charley Rose. After the second fight with Leonard, Charley told reporters, 'I don't want to see a third fight and if they meet, I won't be in Freddie's corner.'

Betting odds out of New York had Leonard a 7 to 5 favourite to win on points, and 5 to 9 that he would win by stoppage. There was a last-minute wrangle over the appointment of Billy Roche as referee. Billy Gibson, as Leonard's manager, protested the decision. Roche had been involved in Welsh's defence against Charley White at the Ramona Athletic Club in Colorado Springs, which saw a large section of the makeshift arena fall, killing two spectators and injuring hundreds. Moving past the horror the two men fought, with White getting the better of the action according to most, yet Roche awarded the decision to Welsh.

Both parties compromised, choosing former lightweight title challenger Kid McPartland … Charley Rose reported, 'As for the weights, at 9.45pm on the night of the fight, they were right – Leonard 133 pounds, Welsh 134¾.'

On fight night, the fans made their way to the Manhattan Casino in the shadow of the Polo Grounds. Main event, scheduled for ten three-minute rounds, was between Freddie Welsh, lightweight champion of the world, and the guy the crowd had come to see, Benny Leonard, the young Jewish boy from Harlem. Leonard was 21, Welsh was 31. Benny took fine care of himself, Freddie had become careless about training and condition.

Freddie's veteran trainer Charley Rose would later tell *The Ring* magazine, 'As to the reason for my not being in Welsh's corner the night Benny took him – well, I knew what was going to happen. Welsh had not been taking of himself. He was older than his accepted age. I begged him not to take the match. I said, "Freddie, this boy is a great fighter. I think that you can outbox him in ten rounds. But there also is the chance of getting beaten." I pleaded with Harry Pollok, his manager, not to take the match. But you remember Harry. He was a hungry manager. Pollok and Billy Roach begged me to train Welsh for this fight, but I insisted that I did not want anything to do with it.'[42]

'Leonard was the first to land when the timekeeper got them away, sending two rights to the champion's jaw. Welsh went into close quarters and banged Leonard's wind with a few short rights. Leonard backed away and hooked two lefts to the mouth. He ducked a right swing. The lads were boxing carefully. Leonard sent a hard right to the jaw which made Welsh wince. Leonard's round. In round two, Leonard began by sending three lefts to the face and hooked two rights to the jaw. He blocked Welsh's leads. Leonard then began to play for the body, not giving Welsh a chance to get set. Then followed a mix-up and the champion came out of it with a smile, although he appeared wobbly. Leonard's round.

'Round three and Leonard began again to force matters. He sent two rights to the jaw and an uppercut to the mouth. Then Welsh came back and poked four blows to Leonard's wind. He followed this with two blows to the face. A furious mix-up in the centre of the ring followed. Honours were even.'[43]

'As the fight went on, Welsh began to depend more and more upon his blocking,' wrote veteran scribe Robert Edgren from ringside. 'He gave a wonderful exhibition of defence. Leonard tried and tried and could find no hole large enough to drive a glove through. But in the fourth he broke loose and began hitting so fast that Welsh couldn't block everything. Many blows were caught on

---

42 *Ring* March 1960
43 *Syracuse Herald* 29 May 1917

forearm or elbow, but a few went through and these had Freddie reeling a little and looking in serious trouble when the bell rang.'[44]

'Beginning with the fifth round,' Benny would recall, 'I could feel that Welsh's holding tactics were beginning to slacken, and I knew then that he was weakening. Then Gibson and Engel reminded me that I already had outpointed Welsh in two previous ten-round bouts and if I didn't knock him out before the finish of this, I probably never would get another opportunity to win the title. I wanted that championship, yes, craved it. Every boxer is anxious to become a titleholder. And Gibson and Engel's pleadings for me to score a knockout became more and more insistent, while my frantic efforts became harder and harder.'[45]

'Welsh seemed tired when he came up for the sixth. He jabbed several times with his left, but Leonard straightened his rival up with a right to the side of the head. Both missed wicked rights. Welsh covered and worked in closer, but the East Side lad kept a right uppercut working. He scored heavily in the third attempt. Welsh landed a stinging left to the face, beating Leonard's attempt to counter with a right. Leonard put several good rights to the face just before the bell.

'They mixed it in the seventh. Welsh showed his wonderful defence to the best advantage. He kept himself as well guarded as a turtle in the shell. His arms, gloves or elbows were usually in the way of Leonard's torrent of blows. Welsh drove Leonard to the ropes with left jabs to win the round.

'Round eight and Welsh jabbed with a left, but Leonard rushed and after three gallant attempts brushed Freddie's jaw with a left. Leonard danced about and went after Welsh's stomach with three lefts. Welsh fought in close and raked Leonard's body with short left and right jolts. Welsh jabbed a left to the face at the bell.

44   Robert Edgren *Boston Evening Globe* 29 May 1917
45   Benny Leonard *Davenport Democrat and Leader* Iowa 8 June 1922

'Round nine. They worked in close. Welsh was smiling a sardonic smile, in which was far more apprehension than confidence. Welsh feinted and tried with his right after the left fell short. Benny danced away out of danger. He side-stepped and after feinting with his right, put all he had in a left swing that landed flush on the jaw. That was the punch that started Welsh on the road to the down-and-out club. Quick as a tiger, Leonard sprang in. He shot the right that landed above Welsh's ear with such force that the Briton spun like a top and slipped to his knees in Leonard's corner. Referee Kid McPartland came to the rescue and pried Leonard away from his prey. The lightweight championship had come back once more to America. Leonard was the new king of the division.'[46]

'So badly had Welsh been whipped,' wrote Fleischer, 'that the referee, Kid McPartland, had stopped the fight without taking the trouble to give the champ the count and because of this, Welsh refused for a time to recognise Leonard as the new champion. Freddie went down from a right to the jaw – the third time he had been felled in the ninth frame. He was in danger of serious injury. The right crumpled Welsh on the lower ropes and as he hung there, dazed, defeated, McPartland chased Benny away and propped Freddie up in his corner.

'After McPartland had propped Welsh up in his corner, Freddie had slipped down to the floor. He fell on his hands and knees. His mind must have cleared that split second, for he tottered to his feet. He tried to stand, spun round like a whirling dervish and almost went through the ropes. If ever a man had been knocked out, that man was Welsh. But Pollok set up a yammer. He insisted that the referee had no right to halt the bout and that the title couldn't change hands that way. But his protests were in vain. Neither referee nor the fans were in sympathy with him in his claim.

---

46 *Winnipeg Tribune*, Manitoba, Canada 29 May 1917

'When Welsh regained his senses, he turned to McPartland and said, "I never heard of a champion being licked for the title without a count. That doesn't go where I come from." Crafty Harry Pollok chirped in, "Nor I. Never heard of such a thing." Pollok, of course, knew better but he was doing his utmost to protect his man and his meal ticket. He knew that had McPartland counted 30, Welsh would still have remained on the canvas. The kayo came 1.15 after the bell had sent the boys on their way in that fatal round for Welsh.'[47]

When he was 13 years old, Thomas Aloysius Dorgan lost the last three fingers of his right hand in a factory machine. While recuperating, he drew a lot of cartoons as therapy. A year later he found himself a job as staff artist on the *San Francisco Bulletin*, moved to *The Chronicle* then was hired away by newspaper tycoon William Randolph Hearst and put to work at the *New York Journal* as a sportswriter/cartoonist. He signed his work TAD. He was ringside when Benny Leonard knocked out Freddie Welsh to become champion.

'With his right hand still clinging to the upper rope in his opponent's corner, Freddie Welsh, beaten and helpless, tried to lift himself up in the ninth round of his championship fight at the Manhattan Casino. Before the toppled titleholder stood Benny Leonard. Kid McPartland, the referee, had just pushed Leonard away, automatically making him the champion, the first New York boy to claim such a distinction in any class. Welsh was not on the floor, and there had not been a count of any sort over him, yet he was in such a helpless condition that to allow the quarrel to go further would have been more than brutal.'[48]

'Seldom has the winning of a boxing championship created a state of frenzied excitement such as attended the Benny Leonard

---

47 Nat Fleischer *Leonard the Magnificent* 1947

48 TAD *The New York Journal* 29 May 1917

victory over Freddie Welsh. When the crowd realised that Welsh was beaten it surged toward the ring, shattering railings and making kindling of chairs. The press stand was stormed and went down with a crash and every telegraph instrument at the ringside was trampled out of commission. Leonard's admirers fought for a chance to shake his hand and almost yanked his arms from his body. It was pandemonium pure and simple and it marked the ascendancy of the first New Yorker to the lightweight throne.'[49]

'The old guy went down like a real champion,' said Leonard after the fight. 'That's the way I want to go when it comes my turn. However, let me say this. If I find myself slipping, I won't stay in the ring to take any shellackings. As for the holler that Welsh was not knocked out, my first right in the ninth knocked him silly. I was surprised when Welsh failed to stay down for nine. But veteran though he was, he lost his head. After that, he kept fighting by instinct. I doubt if he knew what he was doing.'[50]

A few days after the fight, Arthur Duffy was writing in his 'Comment on Sports' column in *The Boston Post*, 'Harry Pollok is still putting up an awful howl over Freddie Welsh losing the lightweight title to Benny Leonard on account of referee Kid McPartland not counting Freddie out, but Pollok does not appear to have a leg to stand on. When Billy Gibson's champ put over that all powerful wallop to the chin, putting Welsh out of business, counting was not necessary.'[51]

'When I got home from the fight,' said Benny, 'there were hundreds of people in front of the house. They yelled and yelled until I stuck my head from the window. They wanted me to make a speech, but I couldn't say anything. I just held up my hands, yelled, "I love you all," and ran back. When I awakened in the morning,

49   *Syracuse Herald* 29 May 1917
50   *Ring* March 1960
51   Arthur Duffy *The Boston Post* 31 May 1917

I yelled to mother to give me some dope or something because I didn't feel a bit different. But it isn't that way at all. I'm just plain Benny Leonard, and glad of it.'[52]

---

52   *Racine Journal News* Wisconsin 6 June 1917

CHAPTER FIVE

'IN AN unpretentious Harlem apartment,' wrote John Reed for the *Philadelphia Evening Public Ledger,* 'furnished largely with very new and shiny things, and full of the atmosphere of a real human home, there is so much pride and happiness today that it seems as if the walls would burst with it. There are Mr and Mrs Leiner, who came to America as immigrants in their childhood, fleeing from the Jew-baiting persecution of old Galicia, and went through the dreadful mill of work and poverty on New York's East Side, and their sons, Willie and Charley, and the two younger boys, their baby girl, and their two married daughters with their children. The love, worship and admiration of all these human beings are concentrated on their son and brother, 21-year-old Benny Leonard, lightweight champion of the world.

'The mutual affection of the family reaches its culmination, however, in Benny Leonard's feeling for his mother, which is a real case of filial love carried to the point where it supplants all desire for a sweetheart. "My mother is my sweetheart," said Benny to me. "She's always taken care of me. I'm lost when she isn't around." I thought all that stuff about Benny's mother was simply press agent stuff until I saw them together. "The only fight I ever really lost badly was my second bout with Freddie Welsh. And that was because I didn't have my mother with me. You see I trained up at

Mount Kisco, and every night when I went to bed I used to miss my mother being in the next room and wish she was there. She wasn't there to see I ate the right stuff and got to bed and so forth. So when I got into the ring, I didn't know where I was at.'[53]

'Benny is a good boy,' said boxing writer Robert Edgren in May 1917. 'There's nothing of the old-time "pug" in his make-up. In all things, his mother is his pal. After every fight, no matter where the battleground, he immediately telephones his mother that his bout is over and that he is unhurt and will start home on the first convenient train. His mother is at home waiting near the telephone as the hour of the bout comes near. She is anxious. She always has a fear – like all mothers, I suppose – that her boy may be hurt in the rough game he has chosen for a profession. And Benny doesn't like to let her worry.

'They are calling Benny Leonard "another Joe Gans." Every lightweight who accomplishes anything in the ring is immediately heralded as "another Joe Gans" – at least by his manager. But Leonard comes nearer the Gans standard than any other lightweight I've seen in several years. He is unlike Gans in action, yet has something of the great Negro boxer's effectiveness and skill in self-defence. Like Gans, Benny is seldom hurt in a fight. Like Gans, he shows at his best when against the most skilful opponents. Like Gans, he has a first-class knockout punch, and like Gans, when he has his man "started" he wastes little time in bringing about the finish.'[54]

Nat Fleischer was a great admirer of Leonard. 'Sleek black hair plastered over a well shaped head. A pair of dark brown eyes that sparkled intelligence. A kindly face in which was traced all the lines of friendliness. Soft-spoken, alert, glowing cheeks, an upright, slim body in perfect condition. A lightweight more brilliant than any

53   John Reed *Philadelphia Evening Public Ledger* 6 June 1917
54   Robert Edgren *Syracuse Herald* 29 April 1917

other than the greatest of them all – the immortal Joe Gans? That's what this youth was!

'His name was Benny Leonard. He combined the boxing ingenuity of Young Griffo; the masterful technique of James J. Corbett; the clout of Jack Dempsey; the alertness of Gene Tunney; the speed of Mike Gibbons. A combination that brought to him that which comes only to an all-around master of the pugilistic art – world renown, a title, wealth …

'For years the fistic authorities have argued pro and con whether Gans or Leonard was the greater, which means the best of all time, but merely to be compared to the Baltimore Negro, was the highest compliment that could be paid to Leonard for Gans truly was what they called him – The Master.'[55]

In the January 1967 issue of *Ring* magazine, reporter Jersey Jones wrote, 'We recall, shortly after the close of World War I, when we were an aspiring "cub" in the sports department of the old New York *Globe,* and the Gans–Leonard controversy was at its peak, Benny was matched with a veteran but still formidable welterweight, KO Willie Loughlin, in Camden, New Jersey. The Gans–Leonard argument was getting a big play in the sports columns of the nation's press at the time, and was being used to excellent advantage in the advance publicity on the Camden bout. As a good angle to help the ballyhoo, and also as a timely feature for the press, the promoters invited Al Herford up from Baltimore.

'Herford had been Gans' manager, but had never seen Leonard in action, and after getting an eyeful or two of Benny, he figured to be in a position to speak authoritatively on the subject.

'With one of his typical exhibitions of brilliant boxing and accurate punching, Leonard stopped Laughlin in the ninth round. The newspapermen cornered Herford after the bout. What did he

---

55   Nat Fleischer *Leonard the Magnificent* 1947

think of Benny, and what would have been his prediction of the probable outcome of a match with Gans?

'"I wouldn't want to pick a winner," said Al. "Two marvellous fighters, but with entirely different styles; wonderful boxers, smart strategists and authentic punchers. Naturally, I'd be slightly biased in favour of Gans, but after watching Leonard tonight, I'd hesitate to hazard a prediction on the probable result of a bout between them. It would be a wonderful exhibition to see, but the only way I'd dare to pick a winner would be by tossing a coin."'[56]

'When Leonard won the world lightweight championship in 1917, boxing's old-timers would say that Benny couldn't have lived with Joe Gans of Baltimore, immortalised as "The Old Master" by the time he died in 1910. "Gans would have beaten Leonard," said George "Elbows" McFadden, who beat Gans in one of their three fights. "He was a better boxer than Leonard and a better puncher." When asked if he had seen Leonard in any of his greatest fights, against guys like Tendler, Mitchell, Rocky Kansas, McFadden replied, "No, none of them. I never saw Leonard."

'One of boxing's greatest trainers was Mannie Seamon, who was with Benny through his championship years. "He was the greatest lightweight the game has ever seen," Mannie said in a 1970 interview. When asked whether he thought Benny would have lost to Gans, Mannie said, "Not a chance. Gans seldom was in top physical condition. Had Joe taken care of himself the way Leonard did, well, the fact remains, Joe didn't. What made Leonard tick? Skill, dedication, attention to detail, diet, clean living, pride and determination." Leonard didn't concern himself particularly with the issue. "I don't know whether I could have licked Gans or not – and neither does anybody else. But if they have to dig up a dead one to lick me, I'm satisfied."'[57]

56   Jersey Jones *Ring* January 1967
57   John Jarrett *Champ in the Corner The Ray Arcel Story* 2007

Dave Anderson, Pulitzer Prize-winning sportswriter for the *New York Times,* interviewed top trainer Ray Arcel for his 1991 book *Ringmasters.* 'Having been around Benny Leonard, if anybody was ever close to Leonard, it was Sugar Ray Robinson. When people ask me who's the greatest boxer, pound for pound, I ever saw, I hesitate to say either one, but Leonard's mental energy surpassed anybody else's. Benny Leonard was a picture. He could make you do the things you didn't want to do. If you were a counterpuncher, he made you lead. If you were aggressive, he made you back up. He knew where to hit you. The solar plexus. The liver. He knew all the spots. He'd aim for those spots. If you look up his record, you will see that he always fought good fighters. If you didn't know how to fight, nobody would match you with Benny Leonard.'[58]

'While he reigned over the lightweight division, he was known as the fighting champion. He actually defended his title within one week after winning it, thereby setting a world record in fisticuffs. On that occasion he fought Joe Welsh in Philadelphia in a no-decision bout in which, had he been stopped, he would have lost his crown. He became champion on 28 May 1917 and fought Welsh on 4 June. The Philly promoter thought, naturally, that Leonard, having acquired the crown only a few days previously, would call off the contest but nothing of the sort happened.

'"Certainly I'll go through with it," Benny told the promoter. "Why not? You laid out your money to promote the show and I'm not going to see you lose just because I'm now the champion."'[59]

Benny had fought Welsh 18 months before while he was still hungry and he had knocked Joe out in five rounds. Now he was the world's champion, just a week after crushing another Welsh, Freddie, in nine rounds. Joe Welsh was taller than Benny and had

---

58   Dave Anderson *Ringmasters* 1991

59   Nat Fleischer *Leonard the Magnificent* 1947

a longer reach, and this time he came into the ring with a 33–16–11 record and stayed the six-round distance with Benny at the Olympia A.C. in Philadelphia. The local press report indicates that Benny was happy to take Joe along for the six rounds.

'There was ample evidence in each session that the champion did not want to inflict punishment on his opponent, as there were many times when he refused to take advantage of the tight places he would have Welsh in. Joe seemed timid from the start and did not box with his usual speed. Leonard forced the fighting and had Welsh on the defensive from the first round to the end of the contest.'[60]

Billy Gibson was negotiating for a title defence against Johnny Kilbane, the featherweight champion from Cleveland. It looked a box-office winner, a battle of champions, and the top bid came from Philadelphia, where both boys were popular. In the meantime, Benny took a ten-round match with Johnny Nelson at the Harlem Sporting Club, his New York debut as world champion.

'Nelson took a terrific beating, being floored six times in all, once in the second and five times in round three. When the bell rang to end the first round, Nelson had a few private ideas as to the general direction of his corner. He made it finally, but not on a bee line. Nelson will remember the third round the longest day he lives. A right-hand smash knocked him into arbitration and referee Kid McPartland grasped him to save both going to the floor. After going down for the last count, he arose very groggy and McPartland led him to his corner. It was the first time Nelson had been stopped.'[61]

'The contest between Benny Leonard, lightweight champion of the world, and Johnny Kilbane, featherweight champion of America, which is set for Shibe Park, Philadelphia, next Wednesday

---

60 *Harrisburg Telegraph* Pennsylvania 5 June 1917
61 *Hammond Lake County Times* Indiana 19 June 1917

night is attracting more attention than any other match of recent months. Leonard is at present in the best form of his career and is fast as a flash. Kilbane is generally regarded as a harder hitter than Leonard, though he has not had much success with lightweight contestants. Either of the boxers is able to score a knockout if he reaches the jaw, but if the bout goes the limit Leonard should win on points.'[62]

The *Philadelphia Inquirer* set the scene, 'It promises to be a big afternoon on Wednesday at Shibe Park. The Athletics returning from their Western trip will battle the Detroit gangsters in the afternoon and in the evening under the electric lights the champion fighters, Johnny Kilbane and Benny Leonard, will meet in the ring. This bout is attracting attention from all over the country, for it brings together two fighters, one who could not win the championship from Freddie Welsh, and the other who did. Kilbane has met and defeated some of the best men in and out of his class. Leonard was not accepted as a championship possibility until a comparatively short time before he won the title.

'He has gone down the line like a race horse. Youth, ambition and a stiff punch are his. Kilbane has profited from many more years of experience in the ring, and in gaining that he is passing along to Leonard seven years in age and probably as many pounds in weight. It looks like a pretty even proposition. You pay your money and bet on the man you like best.'[63]

There was disturbing news as the fight approached with superintendent of police Robinson taking steps to prevent any deception of the public by Kilbane and Leonard or the promoters in their scheduled meeting on Wednesday night. Some information had reached him, said the superintendent, that led him to think there was a possibility the men intended to give a fancy exhibition

---

62   *New Britain Herald* Connecticut 23 July 1917
63   *Philadelphia Inquirer* 23 July 1917

of boxing and not go at each other in earnest. 'I have instructed captain of detectives Tate to be at the ringside with a squad of his men and if it appears the men are not fighting in earnest, the bout will be stopped. Also, I shall make every effort to ensure the return of the admission money to ticket holders.'[64]

That would be $35,078 paid by 12,753 cash customers, but when the passes were counted, the crowd had swelled to more than 15,000, making it the largest gathering that ever attended a boxing bout in Philadelphia. The receipts were a record for a six-round bout.

The fighters did their job and nobody asked for their money back. It seems ridiculous now that a contest of this importance should be scheduled for six rounds, but it was the era of no-decision bouts throughout most of America and Kilbane could only win Leonard's title by stopping him by some means, within the rules, of course.

With that in mind, Benny Leonard entered the ring knowing he had to stop his man inside the six-round distance, not leaving any doubt as to his superiority.

Former heavyweight legend James J. Corbett wrote in his newspaper column, 'It was the old story – a good big man can lick a good little man any day. Kilbane was no match for Leonard. He was outweighed, outfought and outclassed and his seconds acted wisely in throwing in the towel when he dropped to the floor just as the bell rang at the close of the third round. From the beginning of the fight, it was evident that neither Kilbane nor Leonard had the remotest idea but that he would not be the victor ...

'I never saw two men in a championship fight who exhibited such remarkable coolness before the battle. Both were in excellent condition – trained absolutely to the minute. Kilbane was the picture

---

64 *Hamilton Evening Journal* Ohio 24 July 1917

of self-confidence. Leonard appeared the more determined. If there was any shade of favour of either as to the reception by the great crowd, it was in favour of the boy from New York. As they posed for the camera before hostilities, Kilbane was distinguished by his superior height which was more than offset by Leonard's superior weight and ruggedness.'[65]

'Round 1 – Leonard was the first to lead and landed a left jab to the face. Kilbane rushed Leonard to the ropes and they exchanged lefts. Leonard hooked a left to the head, but Kilbane ducked a right swing. Leonard was short with left and right. Leonard jabbed with a left and blocked a left hook. Leonard hooked a right to the heart. Leonard stuck a left to the body and they went to a clinch. Leonard hooked a right to the head. At the bell, Leonard ducked a wicked right swing. Leonard's round.

'In the second round, Kilbane was at the mercy of the lightweight king. His ring generalship might as well have been left at home; his defence might just as well have been in Honolulu; his fists were treated as if they had been a baby's blows. It was a tragedy for Kilbane, for he had beaten Welsh, the former lightweight king, and had reached the point where his friends and, doubtless himself, believed he was unbeatable in a no-decision bout …

'The boys sparred cleverly to open the third and while there was a lot of pretty work there were no blows landed. Leonard finally tore loose with a wicked right hand that caught Kilbane flush on the chin. It sent Kilbane reeling against the ropes and another right hand to the head dropped Kilbane to his knees. Leonard forced Kilbane all over the ring, whipping right and left to the head. Kilbane, however, managed to hold his feet under the bombardment. Leonard dropped Kilbane to the floor and at the count of five, the bell rang. Kilbane climbed to his feet and reeled

---

65   James J. Corbett *Syracuse Herald* 26 July 1917

like a drunken man. Just as he started to fall again, his seconds grabbed him and led him to his corner.'[66]

'He had never been knocked out before. Jimmy Dunn, Kilbane's manager and pal, evidently didn't believe in having his protégé counted out last night. Just as timekeeper Billy Rocap said to Joe Savino, "Pull the bell," Dunn flung a wet towel into the air, and before the moistened linen hit the floor, the bell rang.'[67] Time 2.59 of round three.

James J. Corbett told readers of the *Chicago Examiner* on 26 July 1917, 'For years I have been looking for a little man who compared in cleverness and all-round fighting ability with the great ringmasters of the old days. Tonight I saw not only the greatest living lightweight, but I saw a lightweight who could hold his own with any man of his pounds who has stepped into a ring in the last 30 years. It is not the fact that Benny Leonard defeated Johnny Kilbane which impressed most about the boy from the Bronx. It was the way he accomplished that feat.'

---

66   *Syracuse Herald* 26 July 1917
67   *Philadelphia Evening Public Ledger* 26 July 1917

CHAPTER SIX

'DAN MORGAN says that horse players, bar accidents, can live forever,' wrote Frank Graham, columnist for the *New York Journal American*. 'They have no money,' he says, 'so they have no worries. They can't afford to over-eat or indulge in strong drink too often and I have never seen one of them with the gout. They are out in the open every day, hot or cold, rain or shine, and they get their exercise running the length of the homestretch, rooting their horses in and yelling instructions to the jockeys.

'Dan is one of the last of the old-time fight managers. They were a great and colourful crew. They played hard. They played for keeps. They carried on feuds. But they knew a fighter when they saw one and knew what to do with him when they got their hands on him. Dan's greatest fighter was Jack Britton.'[68]

'Jack Britton rewrote the *Guinness Book* for boxing, at least in terms of active ring service. For although the *Ring Record Book* lists "just" 325 times this great lightweight and welterweight climbed through the ring ropes to do battle, 1930s ring historian George Pardy insists that Britton had been fighting for over seven years before his name appeared in any of the tabulated chronicle of fights. And Britton himself insisted he had fought over 400 times, a fact

---

68   Frank Graham *Dumb Dan* 1953

you could almost attest to by looking at his cauliflower ears. But is wasn't merely his remarkable record of more than 400 fights that entitles Jack Britton to join the pantheon of greats; it was his marvellous ring generalship, and a left hand that speculated like a doctor in search of a vein.'[69]

Jack Britton was still pretty good when 'Dumb' Dan Morgan brought him to New York to fight Benny Leonard that October night in 1917 at the Harlem Sporting Club. Jack brought a record of 130–32–25 and he was between spells as welterweight champion. In fact, he and Ted 'Kid' Lewis bounced the welter title between them in a 20-fight marathon over the period of 1915–20. Britton was 32, Leonard was a 21-year-old veteran of 120 fights and was a brand new lightweight champion. The club was packed when referee Billy 'Kid' McPartland got them away on their ten-round journey. Britton weighed in at 139 pounds while Leonard proved he was a genuine lightweight at 133 pounds. Manager Billy Gibson had figured the weight would trouble Britton, who had been fighting at around 142 pounds, but the veteran seemed as strong as ever.

'Leonard started out with a rush, taking up the aggressiveness right off the reel. It was evident that the lightweight was out to win by a knockout. He had the better of the first, third and fourth rounds because of harder punching. Britton led in the second, fifth and sixth, mainly by the use of a left jab and a hook with the same hand. With six rounds over, Leonard began to show real speed and he bewildered Britton with his footwork and fast action with both gloves. Benny took the seventh while Britton came back and won the eighth. Then the lighter man finished up in flashes, coming out on top in the ninth and tenth rounds.

'When Leonard sparred for an opening with the intention of trying for a knockout, Britton's left hand was much in evidence and

---

69 Bert Randolph Sugar *Boxing's Greatest Fighters* 2006

in Benny's face. On the contrary, when Leonard boxed he had little trouble outpointing Britton and Jack's wide misses made him look bad and Leonard good. The bout was one of the hardest-fought matches seen by the writer in a long while. In the seventh round, Britton made a lunge with a wild right hand at Kid McPartland, accusing the referee of giving him the worst of it in breaking the boxers when clinched.'[70]

'Britton's manner was unusually stormy all during the bout. He complained that he was being hit low but the referee simply waved him back to the firing line. In the seventh Britton threw up both hands and cried, "O, ho, so I have got to fight two men, well, so be it. I'll do my best to whip the two of you."'[71] As it was, Britton couldn't whip one of them as Leonard was adjudged the better man by the newspapermen covering the bout. They would meet again.

'The United States entered World War I by declaring war on Germany on 6 April 1917. That was the easy part. America lacked an army capable of fighting a major conflict and since voluntary enlistment moved slowly, Congress passed the Selective Service Act on 28 April. The national draft came into effect a few weeks later. Millions of young men would be inducted into the army over the months that followed. Many of those from Greater New York City were sent to train at a mosquito-infested Long Island swamp called Camp Upton, where the 77th Division was being formed. These men came from all walks of life. Many were immigrants or the children of immigrants, who had known nothing but poverty. A quarter of them were Jewish.

'Benny Leonard came from the same background. On 28 May 1917, Leonard claimed the world lightweight title. He didn't get much time to celebrate. That summer, Leonard was commissioned a boxing instructor for the U.S. Army with the rank of second

---

70   Louis H. Jaffe *Philadelphia Evening Public Ledger* 20 October 1917
71   *Boston Daily Globe* 20 October 1917

lieutenant, and in October he was sent to Camp Upton, also known as Yaphank. Leonard had to cancel most of his professional bouts, potentially losing thousands of dollars. But he loved his work with the soldiers. "You never saw a scrappier bunch than the boys at Yaphank," he told reporters. "They are crazy to box and they plead for chances to put on the gloves. By the time I get through with some of them, they'll make their mark in the ring if they come home safe from the other side." Benny didn't get to go to France. He had to stay stateside and keep training men. Leonard worked with the men of the 77th Division and carried them through regimental championships in six weight classes. By the time the division set off for Europe in March–April 1918, he had boxed personally with 3,500 men. Benny insisted on boxing individually with each of the officers. None of them could avoid a round in the ring and keep the respect of his men.'[72]

In June of 1918, 'Ringsider' was writing from Chicago, 'Now that the edict has gone forth from Washington for every able-bodied man between the ages of 21 and 50 to either fight or work, it begins to look like boxing, prize fighting and sparring will go into hock for the duration of the war. The edict of Provost Marshal General Crowder perhaps hit the boxing game about as hard, if not harder, than any other line of sport. Already most of the stars, like Benny Leonard, Mike and Tommy Gibbons, Johnny Kilbane, Eddie McGoorty and others are in Uncle Sam's service, either in active service or at the training cantonments showing the doughboys how to handle their fists for possible contingencies with the Hun in hand-to-hand battles.'[73]

'Leonard had extreme confidence in his ability to whip any lightweight or welterweight,' wrote Fleischer, 'and it was this feeling that eventually led to a second match with Jack Britton. Jack, one of

72 Edward Lengel *Never in Finer Company* 2018
73 'Ringsider' *Lincoln Sunday Star* Nebraska 9 June 1918

the great masters of scientific boxing, agreed to make 141 pounds for Benny and at this weight the match was set for Shibe Park over six rounds.

'Philadelphia never saw a more brilliant exhibition than it did on the night of 26 June 1918. Benny forced the milling from the start because he knew that the defensive skill of Britton would not enable him to fight otherwise. He realised that to gain the upper hand he would have to be the aggressor and would have to lead in the attack. Hence from the start of the opening gong, Benny tore in and made a fight of it.

'Britton was not dismayed. He never displayed more cleverness than against Leonard's attacks. There was little advantage for either in the opening rounds. Britton used straight jabs to check Leonard's rushes but Benny kept coming in. Britton swung a lot but Leonard kept under those punches and landed with left and right counter blows. The last two rounds were the hottest. The champs went at each other like wildcats. Leonard made Britton miss often in these sessions while his punishing right kept Jack off balance and landed with effectiveness. When the gong sounded ending the battle, the fans agreed that they had been treated to an excellent exhibition and also agreed that Leonard had had the better of the mill.'[74]

'Benny was very much peeved when he reached his dressing quarters,' recorded James S. Carolan. 'It was the first time since he became champion that there was the least chance to question his right to the decision. Britton refused to be intimidated and fought as courageous and aggressive a fight as any fan would care to witness. It was the first time that Benny ever was so disturbed. He had been the recipient of many unblocked punches and Benny very much disliked being on the receiving end. He was marked; there was no getting away from that. His mouth was cut and swollen, his left eye

---

74 Nat Fleischer *Leonard the Magnificent* 1947

slightly discoloured and the right side of his neck bruised. Those left hooks which missed the jaw had to land somewhere, so most of them found a resting place on Benny's neck.'[75]

After the fight, Jack Britton told the reporters, 'The greatest puncher I ever faced – Benny Leonard. You can take it from me and I've fought 'em all. I have battled him twice and I am an excellent judge of his hitting. If he ever had found me unguarded, it would have been curtains for me. To fight Leonard and do it with any degree of success, it is excellent advice to beginners and veterans, and this applies to me, never take the eye off him. He knows all the tricks and executes them perfectly. He is only a little fellow, but he can hit harder than any middleweight I ever fought. I have met the best of the small middleweights, but never tasted a harder punch than the one delivered by Leonard.'[76]

A couple of weeks later, Benny Leonard received an ovation lasting several minutes when he stepped into the ring at Madison Square Garden for a bout with Willie Jackson. It was one of the bouts on a charity card for the War Department's training camp activities to buy athletic equipment for American soldiers; over $20,000 was raised. 'Two boxing champions will appear in a big carnival to be staged at Madison Square Garden 20 June, the War Hospital Entertainment association announced today. Benny Leonard has volunteered his services and will box any opponent selected for him. Ted Lewis, the welterweight champion, will also appear.'[77]

There will be 10 six-round bouts.

'The big benefit boxing show was a great disappointment to the fans who crowded the building. The chief bout of the evening between Billy Miske and Jack Dempsey did not come off as Dempsey, a year away from becoming heavyweight champion, had

---

75   James S. Carolan *Philadelphia Evening Public Ledger* 26 June 1918

76   *Kokomo Daily Tribune* Indiana 27 June 1918

77   *New Castle News* Pennsylvania 14 June 1918

sprained his right ankle in a gym workout. Miske boxed George Ash of Philadelphia and won easily. Although there was little fireworks connected with the Leonard–Jackson fight, it was the first time the fans have had an opportunity to see the two men in action. It appeared that Leonard could have stopped Jackson at almost any time he wanted to do so. Benny was awarded the newspaper decision.'[78]

Ted 'Kid' Lewis was possibly the greatest British fighter to campaign in the United States, and in 1918 he was more than a little upset at Benny Leonard being referred to as the greatest of all the living world champions. At that time, Lewis was welterweight champion of the world, having reclaimed the title from arch rival Jack Britton.

'If he could trounce Leonard at catch-weights,' wrote Morton Lewis in a biography of his father, 'there would be pressure for a title contest and he was confident he could reduce to 135 pounds. If he succeeded, then the whole fistic world would accept Ted 'Kid' Lewis, the London cockney, as the boxing Colossus of his day, in skill if not in poundage.

'But there was a snag in such a contest. Leonard had extremely high principles. Benny stated openly that though he would be only too pleased to test his skill against Lewis, he would not do so as long as the Britisher was handled by Jimmy Johnston, known in the beak-busting business as "The Boy Bandit." Lewis began to think that Johnston, far from being his guide, was much more of a load on his back.'[79]

When he first arrived in the States in 1915, Lewis was handled by Charley Harvey and Jimmy Johnston, but a couple of years later Lewis figured he would be better off without Jams J. Johnston. He went to see Charley Harvey.

---

78 *Boston Daily Globe* 17 July 1918
79 Morton Lewis *Ted Kid Lewis His Life & Times* 1990

'I've had enough of Johnston,' he told Harvey. 'He's done me forwards, sideways and backwards. I'm going to tell him to jump in the lake.'

Harvey was more than happy to take over the reins. 'Now Ted, put yourself in my hands and we'll make a real killing.'

'I don't want a killing,' Lewis said to Harvey. 'But I'll tell you what I do want. I want one contest – against Benny Leonard. I want Leonard. Get him and you can handle me.'

Two weeks later, Harvey phoned Lewis and told him to start training. Leonard raised no objection when he learned that Lewis had split with Johnston but he imposed certain conditions. 'Firstly,' said Harvey, 'he wants his chief second, George Engle, to be in your corner throughout the contest. Secondly, we must accept Leonard's nomination as referee.'

Lewis waived the conditions; he just wanted the fight with Benny Leonard. Harvey signed for the fight to take place on 23 September 1918 at Weidenmeyer's Park in Newark, New Jersey. It would be over eight rounds at 142 pounds. No-decision. Referee Patsy Cline.

The fight was a box office winner, with a reported 10,000 paying a gate of $32,000, but there were a few thousand more who got into the ground one way or another without paying. There was a problem when the referee announced that both men were within the prescribed limit. Leonard's manager Gibson demanded that the correct weights be announced or there would be no fight. Leonard had weighed in at 135¼ pounds to 140 pounds for Lewis.

The story of the fight was in the headlines next day.

LEWIS HAS BETTER OF LEONARD IN FAST BOUT – LIGHTWEIGHT KING LEONARD IS TOO MUCH FOR LEWIS AT NEWARK

'Benny Leonard, world's lightweight champion, barely managed to win from Ted Lewis, the welterweight titleholder, in their eight-round bout at Newark last night. Leonard started rather poorly, but once he fathomed Lewis' long left arm the lightweight scored enough points to give him the decision by a shade. The superior reach of the Briton was used effectively in the early rounds and it looked as if the lightweight king was in for certain defeat. Slowly Leonard solved Lewis' left hand. Once the tide turned, Leonard outboxed the welterweight.

'There was no doubt, however, but that Leonard's supporters were greatly worried in the early rounds. Lewis used his long left like a sabre and cut and slashed at Benny till the lightweight champion backed around the ring. Leonard's cool, crafty head carried him through the storm, however, and after two rounds, he solved his opponent's attack and began to turn the tide.' (*Middletown Times Press*, New York, 24 September)

'When Benny Leonard and Ted 'Kid' Lewis finished their eight-round bout in Newark Monday night, the honours were about even, although Lewis gave Leonard the toughest scrap of his career. The cleverness and aggressiveness of Ted were always evident to make a barrier for Benny's clever glove work. Leonard executed the only damage that was done in the fight when he opened a cut over Ted's eye in the middle of the scrap. It was a case of two ring masters both handling themselves so cautiously and cleverly that most of the boxing was of a defensive sort. The eight rounds failed to show which of the boxers was master and it would require a much longer route before either one could be proclaimed the winner.' (*Racine Journal News*, Wisconsin 24 September.)

'Ted Lewis, welterweight champion, had the better of Benny Leonard, lightweight champion, in a fast eight-round bout here tonight. Lewis was the aggressor the most of the time and carried the battle hard to Benny. Neither boxer, however, was in any great danger, and the margin on points at the end was very slight. Leonard's boxing was very pretty, but it was not as fast as he has shown on previous occasions. There was a great difference of opinion in the crowd, almost as many figuring Leonard the winner as favoured Lewis. It was a good boxing exhibition and one that will have the fans arguing for a long time to come. More than 10,000 persons saw the bout.' (*Washington Post* 24 September). Leonard and Charley Harvey wanted a return bout with Lewis but the Kid had other plans and they never met again.

'One angle of the Leonard–Lewis contest that appears to have been overlooked is the weight handicap that the lightweight champion overcame, as highlighted in the *Wilmington Evening Journal*. When it is considered that Leonard conceded at least six pounds to the craftiest boxer and hardest hitter in the welter division, the performance of the lightweight champion in making so remarkable a fight against odds looms up as one of his greatest battles.'[80]

Syndicated columnist Frank G. Menke didn't see the fight that way. Beneath a headline that read 'YOU'VE HEARD OF ROQUEFORT CHEESE; EAT IT AND YOU WILL HAVE A TASTE LIKE THAT OF THE LEONARD–LEWIS GO' the esteemed Mr. Menke wrote, 'Roquefort – that's the word that adequately describes the Benny Leonard–Ted 'Kid' Lewis affair a brace of weeks ago. The alleged contest was nothing more than a joke exhibition – a "fraud" as one writer put it – and the farcical nature has dealt pugilism another terrific body blow. The bout went eight rounds and during the entire eight only about two solid blows were hit and it looked as if these were accidental. Of the 24 minutes of action, about 24 were devoted to clinching. The boys exhibited amazing fondness for each other and never seemed happy unless they were clasped in each other's arms. Clinching is not cleverness – and that's about all these fellows did.'[81]

---

80 *Wilmington Evening Journal* Delaware 1 October 1918
81 Frank G. Menke *Salt Lake City Deseret Evening News* 9 October 1918

Old-time fighter Jack Skelly was nearer the mark when he wrote in his column, 'The great majority of those who paid high prices for near-ring seats were not only dissatisfied with the result, but were very much confused in their opinions as to who won the much-disputed bout. In my honest judgement, I don't think there was any winner. In fact, the two champions were so evenly matched in science and ringcraft that it would take at least a 20-round combat to a referee's decision to test the pair out properly in many ways, especially in gameness and endurance.

'There is no question about Leonard's and Lewis' artistic skill, but there is a question about their endurance and grit. Not that I doubt their courage in the least. Lewis has fought several stiff 20-round battles. Leonard has so far failed to fight an extended bout so we cannot tell how he would figure in a 20-round mill to a decision. I predicted weeks before the contest that there would be no knockout, as the bout was short in the first place and secondly the young champions were both too careful and courteous to cut loose and become aggressive or take a chance.'[82]

Bat Masterson built a reputation as a gambler, saloon keeper and lawman in the Old American West before moving to New York, ending his days there as sports editor of the *New York Morning Telegraph*. Doc Almy, veteran boxing writer for the *Boston Post*, had this in his column. 'Bat Masterson, who in his day saw a lot of real ring contests, continues to pan the modern counterfeits. In discussing the recent Lewis–Leonard affair, he says, "Comparing Benny Leonard and Ted Lewis with men of their weight 25 years ago is about as asinine a proposition as could well be imagined. We had some fighters in those days, not a lot of commercialised stallers and weight fakers as is now the case. "When such men as Jack McAuliffe, Tommy Ryan, Joe Walcott, Mysterious Billy Smith

---

82   Jack Skelly *Salt Lake City Herald* 13 October 1918

and Andy Bowen were fighting as lightweights, they scaled 133 pounds ringside as the rules required, and a decade later, with Frank Erne, Joe Gans, Battling Nelson and Ad Wolgast, it's a shame to think what these men could have done to the lightweights of today, including Benny Leonard at 135 pounds ringside. Any one of the men named above would have made Benny Leonard take the count or jump through the ropes in a battle of 20 rounds or to a finish, such as they always fought when the championship was at stake.'[83]

It was the old argument. Were the old days the best days? Were the old champions better than the present crop? It is an argument that can never be won.

---

83   Doc Almy *The Boston Post* 2 October 1918

CHAPTER SEVEN

'CLASSIFYING BENNY Leonard seems to be a popular sport these days,' wrote the *Bridgeport Times and Farmer,* as January 1919 came into view. 'Some persons hold that he is the greatest fighter who ever wore the lightweight crown. Others believe that he would have been an easy victim for more than one of the former champions. Leonard is the ninth lightweight champion since glove fighting came into fashion, the others being Welsh, Ritchie, Wolgast, Nelson, Gans, Erne, Lavigne and McAuliffe.

'Leonard's footwork is his long suit. He has the greatest pair of legs of any lightweight champion. Leonard's one great weakness is his temperament. He goes up in the air when his opponent rushes him, as has been shown on every occasion when the opponent has carried the battle his way. Little Johnny Dundee has held Leonard even or better on no less than five occasions, simply because he forced the fighting too hard for Leonard's liking. With no hitting ability and wide open at all times, Dundee has offset all Leonard's innumerable advantages by following a line of attack that really should have made him the easiest kind of victim for Benny if the latter possessed a fighting temperament that matched his ability in other directions.'[84]

---

84 *Bridgeport Times and Evening Farmer* 25 January 1919

'Kid North, the coloured gentleman of light hue who was Joe Gans' confidant in the old days, was in San Francisco the other day. The Kid is selling shirts for a Los Angeles firm and strayed this far north. Told us he had seen Benny Leonard in action in Los Angeles and was promptly asked whether he thought Benny could beat Joe with both boys in the best of shape. "Not a chance in the world," he said. "Of course I have to base this statement on what I saw of Leonard and I realise that it was not a fair test. But here's the way I figure it out. When Joe Gans was at the top of his form, there was talk right here in your own city of matching the lightweight champion with Stanley Ketchel, who was a middleweight. Have you ever heard any talk of matching Leonard with the present-day middles, most of whom don't come close to Ketchel? I should pause to remark that you don't. There's my answer to the talk of matching the two lads."[85]

Fight night, 20 January 1919, First Regiment Armoury, Newark, New Jersey, eight rounds; Benny Leonard, world's lightweight champion, versus Johnny Dundee, no-decision bout.

William (Scotty) Montieth, fight manager, remembers when he first saw this Sicilian kid. 'It was early 1910, my wife had just been operated on for appendicitis, and the doctor told me clam broth would be good for her. So I went hunting for clams and found a fish store, operated by an Italian named Carrora, on 41st Street, between Eighth and Ninth Avenues. As I left the store, the first thing that caught my eye was a street fight between a couple of kids. One was a skinny little toddler, who must have been at least ten pounds lighter and several inches shorter than the other guy, but I liked the way he tore into the bigger fellow.

'At the time I was managing a couple of pretty good fighters, Tommy Houck and Kid Alberts, and, naturally, I was always on the

---

85 Kid North *Portland Sunday Oregonian* 23 June 1918

73

lookout for promising ring material. I got to talking with this kid and learned he was a son of the chap who ran the fish store where I had just bought the clams. Well, one thing led to another, as things have a habit of doing, and I had another boxer in tow.

'I don't think Dundee weighed more than a hundred pounds at the time. He was 17, but a frail, undeveloped kid. He loved fighting, however, and I made an appointment with him for the next day at a west side gymnasium. The punching bags there were too high for him and he had to jump in the air to get a swat at them. I often think that jumping had a lot to do with developing the cat-like spring that became one of the features of his remarkable boxing style.'[86]

Scotty Montieth changed Giuseppe Carrora to Johnny Dundee, after his old hometown in Scotland, and Johnny was tabbed the 'Scotch Wop' by Danny Lyons, then boxing writer for the old New York *Globe*.

He had a remarkable boxing career. When he hung his gloves up in 1932, Johnny Dundee was in the record book 341 times, world featherweight and junior lightweight champion. He fought Benny Leonard eight times; four prior to Benny winning the lightweight title and four times after, and every battle was just that. It was the no-decision era and Dundee would have had to stop the champion inside the distance to get the title. He never could. But he did give Benny a terrific scrap one night in 1919.

'And so we have the story of the toughest fight Dundee ever fought,' wrote Nat Fleischer, 'one of the eight with Benny Leonard. It was in the Fourth Regiment Armoury of Newark that Leonard, for the first time since he became the lightweight champion, was adjudged the loser in a no-decision bout. Dundee amazed a capacity gathering by carrying the battle to the champion from start to finish

---

and winning easily. He took everything Leonard had to offer and in the eighth and final round, Dundee fought the title holder off his feet.

'Dundee was a Queensberry tiger throughout and while Leonard landed many apparently solid blows to the Italian's chin, especially right uppercuts that seemed powerful enough to stop any opponent, Dundee shook them off and waded in more viciously than ever. Leonard was clearly outpointed.

'Dundee sprang out for the seventh round like a maddened panther and mauled the champion all around the ring. Leonard was unable to check the furious attack of Dundee, who was hammering away merrily at the gong. The eighth and last session was a repetition of the seventh. The Italian rained smashing blows on the face and body of the champion and got little punishment in return ... Dundee's fighting amazed the crowd and he was wildly cheered by his supporters.'[87]

Johnny Dundee was just 25 years old at the time and already a veteran of 194 fights against the best in the business, names like Johnny Kilbane, Freddie Welsh, Willie Ritchie and Leonard. A master of ring trickery and dazzling footwork, he was especially adept at launching punches while bouncing off the ropes. Dundee presented a variety of styles which opponents found very difficult to decipher.

'Benny Leonard was one of those. "Dundee came at me in a different manner than any other fighter ever had done," he recalled. "He was like a small edition of a Harry Greb, only Greb copied Dundee rather than the other way around. I couldn't get a clean crack at Dundee's jaw, for he had the most peculiar way of letting a hard blow glance off his face so that the force of it was pretty well spent."'[88]

---

87   Nat Fleischer *Leonard the Magnificent* 1947
88   *Ring* October 1947

Billy Gibson figured a change of scenery might do them both good so he took Benny off to California, where he arranged a series of fights.

'The 1914 anti-professional boxing amendment ushered in the four-round era in the state. Boxing cards with exclusively four-round bouts were nothing new in California. Such cards had been staged in San Francisco with much success and were popular with the fans for a number of years. Despite the fact that the anti-professional boxing amendment stated that a boxer could not get a prize worth more than $25 for a bout, it was no secret that many boxers received purses (often referred to as "medals") of hundreds or even thousands of dollars.'[89]

Ten days after fighting Dundee, Benny was in San Francisco to box local favourite Joe Benjamin in a four-round bout at the Civic Auditorium. Joe had mixed with some good boys but he was mindful of trying anything with the world's champion and Benny eased to a comfortable points win, after having Benjamin on the verge of a knockout in rounds two and three, and seemed reluctant to end it.

Five days later, he moved across the bay to Oakland for a date with Spider Roach at the local Municipal Auditorium. The Spider was due out of the navy soon and he realised if he made a good fight with the champion, there would be plenty of work for him. Benny appeared to be trying to sink the sailor in each of the four rounds, but at the final bell Roach was still on his feet and was cheered to the echo by his local fans. Had a decision been rendered, Leonard would have won it.

Sacramento was the next stop for the champion, with namesake 'Wildcat' Leonard coming out of the other corner. Benny quickly found the range and skinned the wildcat in the fourth and final

---

89   *Boxing in Los Angeles 1880-2005* Tracy Callis, Chuck Johnston 2009

round. Happy with the knockout, manager Gibson had bad news. He had hoped to stage a big show with promoter Jimmy Coffroth in Frisco's Civic Auditorium, with Benny fighting former world lightweight champ Willie Ritchie, still a big name in California. But the *Associated Press* reported on 6 February, 'Former lightweight champion Willie Ritchie has announced in San Francisco that he is through with the boxing game for all time. He also stated that he has mailed in his resignation as boxing instructor of the Western department of the United States army.'[90]

Then Willie changed his mind. His last fight had been on 10 May 1918. When he was discharged from the army in February 1919, the ex-champ of the lightweights decided to meet the current lightweight kingpin, Benny Leonard, in a four-round bout in Frisco's Civic Auditorium. 'I hemmed and hawed and I hesitated,' said Ritchie. 'Then the thought struck me that I had been pretty well advertised as a champion, and this bout is going to show whether I'm a real fighter or not. I would not re-enter the ring except against a real champion, and that's what Benny Leonard is. The only thing about this battle that will give the people a chance to shake their heads is the weight. Maybe when we get in the ring, I'll have a few pounds of advantage. Gibson and Leonard believe that Benny has no reason to worry about a few pounds. It's up to me to show to the sporting world that Willie Ritchie comes pretty close to being 100 per cent guy.'[91]

Ritchie not only surprised Benny, but all of the fans in the 10,000-strong crowd by his grand condition. He only weighed 140½ pounds at 5pm, some five or six pounds more than Leonard, and was as lean and active as he was in his salad days.

'That's where the crafty native son fooled them all,' wrote Jack Skelly in his column. 'He had been secretly training for months for

---

90   *Salt Lake City Telegram* 17 February 1919
91   *Salt Lake City Telegram* 17 February 1919

Leonard and certainly made a most remarkable comeback. Billy Gibson had the shock of his life when he saw Ritchie slugging his clever champion for a knockout. Gibson then realised how he had been outwitted and lured into a supposed easy match for Benny against a fat, stale has-been, as he supposed. The Bronx impresario got a fine lesson in the art of matchmaking which he won't forget for many moons to come.'[92]

'Willie Ritchie, former lightweight champion of the world, tonight showed fight fans of San Francisco that he is just as good as he was at the time he lost the title. He fought champion Benny Leonard four rounds and Ritchie had the best of the argument in every round except the fourth. Leonard shaded his opponent in this round. It was one of the best boxing exhibitions seen here in many days. Ritchie's showing was a surprise to his most ardent admirers and he displayed all his old-time form. Referee Jim Griffin gave the decision to Ritchie and his judgment was approved by the majority of those present. Both Leonard and Ritchie entered the ring full of confidence and they gave the fans the best they had for the full four rounds. They stood toe to toe and slammed each other often but neither suffered any serious damage.'[93]

Top boxing writer Robert Edgren recorded from ringside, 'Only a desperate last-minute rally saved Benny Leonard from being soundly thrashed by Willie Ritchie. The fourth round came near seeing Benny's finish. Ritchie was plunging furiously and driving crashing rights to the champion's head, beating him back until his shoulder blades were bent over the ropes. Leonard's left eye had been closed tight in the third round, apparently by a succession of Ritchie's rights that he had been unable to avoid.'[94]

92 Jack Skelly *Salt Lake City Herald* 9 March 1919
93 *Warren Morning Chronicle* 22 February 1919
94 Robert Edgren *Salt Lake City Herald* 9 March 1919.

'Nothing has surprised pugilistic followers so much in recent months as the beating handed Benny Leonard in a San Francisco ring the other night by Willie Ritchie. Since that time, many have been trying to find out an excuse for the upset, while others contend that the champion is slipping. One of these is Willam H. Rocap, sports editor of the *Philadelphia Public Ledger,* who has the following interesting story on the question: "Is Benny Leonard slipping? The writer believes he is, so far as his hands are concerned. They have become tender and the champion has to hit carefully to safeguard his tools. That has been evident in all his bouts this year.

'"When boxing a rough, tough opponent, one who could stand a good crack on the jaw and who would invariably come back for more, Leonard has studiously picked out the soft spots to hit. He has directed most of his attacks to the body until his opponent's guard drops and then tried for a swing or hook to the jaw. Leonard has to nurse his hands, and in the writer's judgement, the first strong welterweight who is able to take what the champion can hand out and sail into Leonard, the latter will be due for a beating."'[95]

Four weeks later, Leonard arrived in Kansas City to train for a fight with Harvey Thorpe in Joplin. 'Willie Ritchie made a great show against Leonard,' Billy Gibson told reporters, 'but I don't believe he could have lasted if the bout had been a round or two longer. Leonard was just beginning to get warmed up in the final session while Ritchie was tiring fast. There has been some talk of a return match but I don't believe it will be staged. While on the coast, I offered to wager $10,000 that Leonard could defeat Ritchie in a second bout allowing Willie to weigh in at 138 pounds, but I received no reply.'

'Leonard expects a hard bout when he crosses gloves with Harvey Thorpe, Kansas City's lightweight contender, in a Joplin ring 26

---

95   Harold C. Place *Des Moines Daily News* 3 March 1919

March and will begin a week of hard training here today. The champion has engaged Joe McGowan, Harry Brewer's promising lightweight, to help him train for his bout with Thorpe. The pair will do roadwork today in Penn Valley Park and starting tomorrow will work out in the Kansas City Athletic Club gymnasium.'[96]

'Benny Leonard, greatest of all lightweight champions, gave Harvey Thorpe a boxing lesson last night at the Joplin Theatre, gave him a lesson that will be remembered by the Missourian for many moons. At no stage of the ten rounds contest did Thorpe look to have a chance to even tilt the crown worn by the Easterner. Leonard said in the *News Herald* yesterday that the aforesaid crown was glued on. IT WAS. From the opening 60 seconds of the first round, it was seen that Leonard was to have easy sailing. Ringside critics speedily saw the difference, the vast difference, between the two men, but as Leonard was good enough to say this morning at an early hour, Thorpe was a mighty tough nut, one of the hardest men he had ever met.

'Benny knew what he was up against; on a November night in 1916 Thorpe stuck with Benny the best part of 12 rounds, suffering a knockout ten seconds from the closing bell in the final round. There would be no knockout this night in Joplin but "Harvey was in there at the finish, bellowing in the champion's ears that he wasn't hurting him."'[97]

The world champion's victory was given a scant few lines in the morning sports pages, while a female boxer named Vera Roehm was given half columns in quite a few of the daily press. In the *Chester Times*, she was called champion woman lightweight boxer of the world, and was noted as having sparred with two leading contenders for Leonard's title, Charley White and Johnny Dundee, the latter telling reporters, 'She sure slings a wicked left.' Also among the

---

96   *Kansas City Times* 19 March 1919
97   *Kansas City Times* 27 March 1919

lady's admirers was no less a person than 'Gentleman' Jim Corbett, the former heavyweight champion, 'who taught her from his store of ring lore'. 'A man wouldn't have a chance in the world in the ring with a woman,' Miss Roehm said. 'You see, all she would have to do was use her eyes, and other feminine wiles, and the poor man would be helpless.'[98]

Alongside the story was a box comparing the vital statistics of Miss Roehm and Master Leonard. They were a good match. But Benny would never fight Miss Roehm, or any other woman for that matter. His mother would not like that at all.

---

98   *Chester Times* Pennsylvania 27 March 1919

CHAPTER EIGHT

'BENNY LEONARD, the lightweight champion, is a mama's boy,' Vincent Treanor was writing from New York. 'On his way back East from California, he has caused his manager, Billy Gibson, to refuse matches at Salt Lake, Tampa, Idaho, Kansas City, Denver and Toledo. Why? Because he wants to be home 7 April for his birthday party which his mother has arranged … Benny was born 7 April and his brother Charlie on [the] sixth, so the party is a sort of a double event. The dates passed up might have added considerably to Benny's bank account, but it seems he'd rather be home with mother.

'Newark has been in touch with me,' writes Gibson, 'regarding a return Leonard–Ritchie affair. Up to this writing, I have not settled on anything regarding this match. One thing is sure, Ritchie will not come in a heavy welterweight, should they ever box again. He will have to travel longer than the four-round route, too. I showed Jim Coffroth and referee Jim Griffen copies of some of the New York papers after the Ritchie contest in Frisco, and they both had a hearty laugh. Cannot understand how the Eastern papers had the affair so one-sided when in some of the San Francisco papers Leonard received the decision.

'Harry Smith, sporting editor of *The Chronicle*, declared the contest a draw. No San Francisco paper printed anything like the stories published in New York. On top of all this, Ritchie was entitled to a wonderful lot of credit. From the time the bell rang for the first round, the tremendous crowd of fans were standing on their feet cheering. The men fought harder in four rounds than some boxers have to in 20.'[99]

The Newark Sporting Club in New Jersey was a fight club run by Babe Culnan, Nick Kline, Harry Blaufuss and Frank Black. Known as the 'Four Horsemen', whatever their business venture they split the profits four ways. They knew boxing from A to Z and their promotions were a huge success. In the spring of 1919, the boys had a visit from former lightweight champion Willie Ritchie. Willie had recently married and announced his retirement from boxing. He had brought his new bride east on a honeymoon trip, and this prompted a question from Culnan. 'How's the dough holding out, Willie? Don't you think you could use a little of the thousands that are flowing around here now? You and Benny Leonard would do a big business. Why don't you reconsider your retirement and take just this one more fight?' Ritchie explained that he had come on a honeymoon trip, not a fighting trip, but added that he could use some extra dough. 'Well, let's put on the fight,' added Culnan, whereupon he went to the telephone, got Billy Gibson on the wire, and in a few minutes Ritchie and Leonard were matched for 28 April 1919 at the First Regiment Armoury of Newark, with Culnan giving Willie a guarantee of $10,000.[100]

Willie pocketed the ten grand and headed back to the honeymoon hotel. Telling his bride about the Leonard fight, he maybe told her of the money or he maybe just promised her a new outfit before heading off to the gym. He had work to do.

A crowd of 15,000 jammed every inch of the Armoury and they loved every minute. Ritchie, like the champion, had fought from

---

99 Vincent Treanor *Syracuse Herald* 19 March 1919
100 Nat Fleischer *Leonard the Magnificent* 1947

being a teenager against Ad Wolgast, Harlem Tommy Murphy, Jack Britton, Freddie Welsh, Mexican Joe Rivers and Charley White, in the days when they were great fighters. He was still only 28 going in with Leonard and he gave the champion a stubborn argument. They were scheduled for eight rounds, according to New Jersey law, and Willie almost made it. 'A fighter just married is never any good,' said bachelor boy Benny, 'not because of the condition of his body, but because of the condition of his heart. He is romantically inclined just after marriage and not for breaking another guy's nose. He loves everybody.'

But Billy Gibson and his champion were still smarting from the headline on Jack Skelly's column after their San Francisco meeting. 'Ritchie Outwitted Leonard and Gibson in Recent Bout on Coast.' It was time to put the record straight.

'Ritchie fought gamely throughout the contest, which was fast all the way. Leonard floored him in the second round and punished him severely in the seventh. Leonard had the better of every round with the exception of the third, in which Ritchie sent effective right-hand blows to the body but went to his corner himself with nose bleeding from a hard right. Ritchie tried to carry the fighting to his opponent, but when he let up Leonard kept right after him, giving him no rest.

'Leonard sent Ritchie down for the count of nine in the second with a right uppercut. In the fourth Leonard landed several hard lefts and Ritchie appeared all in, but came back in the fifth, trying to force the pace. Leonard took the aggressive in the sixth and staggered his opponent in the seventh when he landed a right to the stomach followed by a right cross to the jaw. Leonard sent across another right and left but Ritchie came back for more. In the eighth, Leonard hooked his left to the head frequently. A left to the jaw sent Ritchie down for a count of nine for the second time in the contest. As he rose, Leonard jumped at him with right and left, anxious to send a decisive blow across before the final bell rang, but the referee intervened as Ritchie was hanging on the ropes. There were just 40 seconds left in the fight as Benny took his revenge.'[101]

'Thousands of dollars changed hands last night when Benny Leonard was credited with a knockout over Willie Ritchie in New Jersey. The betting was 4 to 1 that Willie would last the limit and local and San Francisco people took the Ritchie as fast as it was offered. At least $2,000 was bet locally last night and when the word arrived that the fight had ended in a KO, the little glooms took possession of Broadway. The Leonard money was wired here (Oakland, California) from New York and commissioners had no difficulty in placing it.'[102]

The gross gate was $58,500, with the fighters receiving $21,060 to Leonard and $13,162 to Ritchie. Before leaving the stadium, Willie Ritchie announced to the press, 'There is the greatest fighter who ever walked into a ring,' referring to Benny Leonard. 'You can talk about your old-timers and their all-week battles, but when it comes to real championship timber Leonard has that and everything that should go with it. I have been defeated fairly and squarely and will now retire permanently from the ring.'[103]

Willie actually had a further five bouts, winning four and retiring finally in August 1927 with a record of 79 bouts. And he was once lightweight champion of the world ...

Benny took a trip to Montreal to appear at the Theatre Francais. He was meeting Charlie Pitts, an Australian living in New York, and he gave a good performance. At times Leonard burlesqued the bout, dancing around his opponent, tapping him and breaking away, giving Charlie every opportunity to land a punch, but Charlie didn't take the gamble. He did gamble at the box office and came

101 *Bridgeport Standard Telegram* 24 September 1919
102 *Oakland Tribune* 29 April 1919
103 *Bridgeport Times Farmer* Connecticut 29 April 1919

out a winner, guaranteed $250 with an option of 17½ per cent of the gate. Charlie took the option and went home with $1,375, his largest ever purse in 42 bouts. Benny took a percentage against his guarantee of $2,500 and came out with $3,008.

The crowd enjoyed the bout so everyone was a winner.

A week later, Benny was in Philly with his old dance partner Johnny Dundee. Leonard made a show of Dundee in the fifth round, landing ten straight left jabs to the face without return before Johnny missed another of his 'bring home the bacon' wallops and went hurtling halfway through the ropes. At the final bell, Dundee was still trying to take Benny's head off!

It was big fight time in Toledo, Ohio, where Tex Rickard had built a wooden arena on the shores of Maumee Bay and pulled in a crowd of 19,650 fans to the sweltering arena. They paid $452,224 to see Jack Dempsey annihilate giant Jess Willard in three vicious rounds, taking the world heavyweight championship from the big fellow. Benny Leonard was there to see it.

A couple of weeks before the fight, Billy Gibson was notified by the New York Central Railroad authorities that the government ban on special trains would have no effect on the special train he would run to Toledo for the Willard–Dempsey fight. 'Your train will leave the Grand Central, as contracted for, on 3 July, as second section of the Twentieth Century Limited.'

'When Dempsey and Willard were matched to battle for the heavyweight championship of the world, The *Philadelphia Inquirer* realised that the fight would touch the high water mark in the world of athletics. Thus convinced, the *Inquirer* straightway arranged to cover the bout as no other sporting event has ever been before. The best sporting and specialised reporting talent was signed up to give to the *Inquirer* readers the real dope on the ring classic.

'William Muldoon, the world's greatest conditioner of athletes, was secured to look the men over in the camps and tell of their condition; Benny Leonard, lightweight champion of the world, was signed up to make a study of the fistic ability of the big fellows; Rube Goldberg, famous cartoonist and sporting writer, was the third big figure in the sporting world to be sent to Toledo by the *Inquirer*.

'Leonard's first dispatch from Ohio was dated 1 July 1919. "Bronzed and big with a broad happy, contented smile festooning his boyish face, Jack Dempsey lolled in an easy chair at his training camp on the shores of Maumee Bay today. Not a care in the world did he seem to have. So he impressed me as I invaded the more or less sacred precincts of his clubhouse to lunch with him at noon today. His greeting was extremely cordial and after the usual formalities, I opened the attack by asking, 'How do you intend to fight Willard?'"[104]

'Benny listened to the challenger, and two days before the fight headed his column "DEMPSEY WILL WIN". Furthermore, this super-expert on boxing told his followers just how Dempsey would fight the champion – the challenger having conferred with the lightweight monarch several times in the early part of the week. On Wednesday and Thursday, when the sentiment appeared to be swinging from Dempsey to the titleholder, Leonard did not back water on his statement that the title would change hands. On the contrary he followed his Thursday story up with another on Friday, re-asserting his conviction that Dempsey would win.'[105]

Back home in New York there was a nice bonus for Benny, the boy reporter. Then Billy Gibson figured it was time his champion lightweight got back to what he did best – fighting – and lined up a few bouts to get Benny match-fit again.

Jakob Bartfeldt was born in Budapest, Hungary in 1892 and when he moved to the United States he made his home in Brooklyn,

---

104 Benny Leonard *The Philadelphia Inquirer* 2 July 1919
105 *The Philadelphia Inquirer* 3 July 1919

New York. Growing up, he spent so long in the army he was given the name of Soldier Bartfield. During five years' service in the infantry, he credited Uncle Sam with teaching him to fight with his fists and with a rifle at the same time. In 1913, he was with the Eleventh Infantry in Wyoming and did five months on the border, fighting, or ready to fight, Mexicans. Five months in the tropics gave him a fever from which he recovered. Boxing made him strong. The soldier would have a remarkable career with the gloves on, with over 220 recorded fights, 55 of those against recognised world champions or title claimants. Four of those contests were with Benny Leonard.

'The lightweight champion spent many hours training at the famous old Grupp's gym in New York. Ending his daily session with trainer Mannie Seamon, they watched Soldier Bartfield working out. Benny commented to Seamon, "He's dropping his left hand every time he jabs. Anybody could drop him with one shot."

'Bartfield didn't appreciate this observation. "What are you trying to make a clown out of me for?" he yelled at Leonard. Benny's response only stoked things up: "That's not hard." The two men had it out in the ring and what followed was a painful experience for Bartfield. Moving into Leonard with bad intent, Soldier sent out a range-finding jab and Leonard countered with a hard and fast right. Bartfield's legs turned to jelly, but the message was still lost on him. He jabbed again and another snapping right bowled him over. Leonard looked at Mannie Seamon and said, "The lesson's wasted. Wait for me, we'll be leaving for downtown in a few moments."'[106]

The first fight for the record book took place on 5 September 1919 at Philadelphia. 'In a wild and amusing if not scientific bout, there was no chance for science, Bartfield raving around like a madman. Leonard was kept busy tossing off his burly opponent

---

106 *The Mike Casey Archives* 2008

and several times completely turned the soldier around, smashing him in the face as he did so. Bartfield's peculiar style of fighting sideways, with his left shoulder high up and his head low down in the opposite direction, prevented Leonard from getting over his famous right. He, however, hit Bartfield hard at times, and the soldier took it gamely. Everybody seemed to enjoy it.'[107]

Three months later the boys were at it again, at the Fourth Regiment Armoury in Jersey City, the lightweight champion giving away ten pounds to the soldier boy. Leonard rained punches upon his heavier opponent throughout the bout and took the honours in every one of the eight rounds. Two weeks later, they were back in Philadelphia and the crowd didn't like it one bit, booing and throwing paper balls and cigar stumps into the ring before Benny went into top gear in the sixth and final round to grab the decision.

It was not until May 1922 that Benny figured he had had enough of Bartfield, in one of ten four-round bouts at Madison Square Garden. In the final round, the soldier cut Benny's nose with a left hook and was smashed to the deck three times as Leonard went for the finish. The soldier was on the verge of a knockout when the bout ended.

To take Benny's mind off the soldier, Gibson matched him with Irish Patsy Cline and he outfought Patsy all the way for the newspaper decision. The same newspaper reported, 'Champion Benny Leonard has no intention now of retiring from the ring. He changed his mind on Monday night in Philadelphia after he drew down $11,355.75 for outboxing Irish Patsy Cline all the way for six rounds. In the fifth, Cline seemed to get some ginger and cut loose. He had caught the champion with a left hook which landed too high to do much damage. It did, however, cause Leonard to open up with the best he had in shop. A series of left jabs kept

---

107 *Racine Journal News* Wisconsin 5 September 1919

sending Cline's head back, and the latter seemed unable either to block, parry or avoid the straight blows which were sent across with unerring judgement. Cline took these blows without wincing and came back for more, and he got it.'[108]

The *Syracuse Herald* reported on 9 September, 'Johnny Clinton, New York lightweight, took two million punches on the jaw at the Arena last night. He is not in the hospital because in critical moments lightweight champion Benny Leonard decided against having the brand of Cain on his soul. Clinton had nothing, not even a vague hope, and Leonard could have knocked him out from the sixth round on. It was a pretty fight to watch, as Clinton's inferiority served to show the champion's brilliancy, speed and cleverness in the best possible light.'

On another night, Leonard took a train to Detroit and Charlie Metrie of Milwaukee wished Benny had stayed at home. The aspirations of Charlie for the lightweight crown went glimmering in the seventh round when the bout was stopped with Metrie helpless on the floor from two terrific right-hand punches on the jaw.

A trip to Tulsa, Oklahoma, saw Benny matched with Lockport Jimmy Duffy. 'Just before the first round was over,' Benny recalled some time later, 'I crossed a short right hook to Duffy's temple. It was not a hard punch, but one that hit a vital spot. Duffy went down. He got up at nine. I noticed that he was badly hurt. His legs were gone. He tried to swing but his legs rocked his body from side to side. He lasted the round because I did not try to hit him. He came out for the second. He was absolutely helpless. He had no defence. I jabbed him a couple of times, then the referee noticed what was wrong and stopped the bout.

'Duffy was examined after the battle by a physician. Over his temple there was a black and blue mark as big as a half dollar.

---

108 *New Castle News* Pennsylvania 15 August 1919

The doctor said that punch had injured a nerve and caused a slight paralysis of the legs.' 'It was real funny,' said trainer Mannie Seamon. 'Duffy was scared stiff of Leonard, who was at his peak. Billy Gibson didn't have to bring Kid McPartland as referee. Benny could have refereed himself. It was all over in the second round.'[109]

Somehow, Johnny Dundee managed to squeeze into Benny's busy programme for what was their seventh bout, this time at Newark, New Jersey. And this time again, the boys gave the fans eight rounds of entertainment and nobody got hurt. At the final bell, Johnny walked to his corner, shaking his head. One of these days ...

One of these days could have come at the end of October 1919. But a news report on 16 October stated, 'Just when the boxing fans of Connecticut were all set for the championship battle arranged by Joe Mulvihill between Benny Leonard and Johnny Dundee, the whole show is stumped – backed right off the boards, in fact. The battle was to have been staged in Hartford within three weeks and was to have been a 15-round affair to a decision.

'The length of the bout and the fact that the referee was to give a decision strongly appealed to the public, and undoubtedly they would have taken kindly to it. That it would be well supported goes without saying and even though Mulvihill was forced to guarantee fabulous sums to the fighters, he would have made a clean-up on the show.

'The armoury in Hartford is the only suitable place in which to stage the show, but it won't be held there. At least Colonel Charles W. Burpee, the commanding officer of the First Military District, says so, and he ought to know. He said yesterday, "I noticed a story in the morning paper that there was to be a boxing match between Benny Leonard and Johnny Dundee in the state armoury on the night of 27 October. In reply to this, I want to state that no permit

---

109 Benny Leonard *The Philadelphia Inquirer* 7 August 1921

for the use of the armoury has been given and that none will be given.'"[110]

The boys were still trying. The *Bridgeport Telegram* reported on 10 December 1919, 'In order to make sure that Vincent Reina, the fight promoter of New Haven, Connecticut, will be able to bring off the 20-round bout between Benny Leonard and Johnny Dundee, the Italian lightweight, at the Arena in the above city on 16 January 1920, Billy Gibson, manager of Leonard, has demanded that Reina post a forfeit of $5,000 that the bout will be fought. Each fighter, according to the articles of agreement, will have to post a forfeit of $3,500 that he will go through with the match.'

That fight never happened. The boys did meet for the eighth and final time on 9 February 1920, at Jersey City, eight rounds, no decision. The newspaper vote went clearly to champion Benny Leonard.

---

110 *Bridgeport Times and Evening Farmer* Connecticut 16 October 1919

CHAPTER NINE

'THERE IS a battle in the making to be staged in the Jersey City Armoury that has all the earmarks of being highly entertaining. It is the intention of pitting Benny Leonard, the lightweight champion, against Mel Coogan, who outjumped Johnny Dundee in Jersey a few weeks ago. Coogan won so impressively against Dundee that spectators began figuring his chances against Leonard, and Coogan did not want for friends. Dundee did not know just what to do against Coogan because Coogan used Dundee's thunder and sprinkled it around more persistently than did Dundee.'[111]

A week before the fight was due, promoter Dave Driscoll was forced to postpone the show when Leonard reported still feeling unwell after his bouts with Bartfield and Duffy. Friday, 10 December was the new date and the boys reported for duty accordingly. Coogan, a Chicago lad, was now settled in Brooklyn and was having a new lease of life, courtesy of Fred Walker, one of the leading football, baseball and basketball coaches in the east. Walker was director of athletics at the Newport Naval Training station when he became associated with Coogan, who served as a boxing instructor there. He saw that Coogan had qualities not fully used in the ring and advised him to put more steam into his work ...

---

111 *Bridgeport Times and Evening Farmer* Connecticut 22 November 1919

'You ought to be a top-notcher, Coogan,' said Fred one day. 'You box as though you're afraid of hurting your opponent. Why don't you change your style? Go in there and trade punches with all of them. Treat 'em rough – that's it. Boxing's a pretty rough game and it calls for just that very thing. Try it, Mel. I think you'll surprise yourself.' He soon found that his change of tactics brought him popularity and it was due to his determination to take Walker's advice that led to arrangements for a match with Benny Leonard.'[112]

In his last fight, Coogan was badly hurt in the first round when he was floored twice by local favourite Pinky Mitchell in Milwaukee, but he stayed the course to lose the newspaper decision. Manager Scotty Montieth said Mel was 'a sick boy' that night. Now he was fit and ready for Leonard. Unfortunately for Mel, Benny had recovered from his illness and was raring to go.

'According to Benny, "Montieth was hard up and needed ready cash. I accepted the fight and was asked not to be too hard on Coogan, to carry him along so that he could be used again in a lucrative bout because he went the limit with me. I agreed and told Gibson not to worry, but at weighing in, a heated argument developed between Gibson and Montieth and something Scotty said about me ruffled my feelings. 'Just for that,' I shot back, 'I'll take care of your Mel tonight. I'll knock him flat.'

'"The fight that evening found Coogan in fine condition. He came out fighting and in a mix-up, he hit me one good shot in the body. I felt it. I began wondering whether I could make good my threat, but didn't give up so quickly. I noticed that when I feinted, Mel got scared and dropped his guard. That was all I wanted to know. The second round had hardly gotten under way when I feinted Coogan into a lead and whipped over a left hook to the jaw. He went down like a log. It was a custom in those days for the seconds of a

112 Jack Velock *Logansport Pharos-Reporter* Indiana 11 December 1919

beaten fighter to grab the water pail and dump its contents over the head of the fallen fighter. I saw Scotty do this on more than one occasion and I quickly sensed that he would do it here.

'"In the split second after I dropped Mel, I scooted across the ring to Coogan's corner and as Montieth stretched his hand into the corner to grab the bucket, I kicked it and the water spilled all over him. Coogan was out and so was Scotty Montieth. I had called my shot but made it a double header."'[113]

That was one of Benny's favourite stories when he used to visit the war veterans' hospitals and sometimes he missed a bit. One news story reported, 'Coogan was floored three times in the second round. The referee was counting him out, his seconds were heaving water in his direction. Leonard was halfway through the ropes trying to kick the water throwers when the referee stopped counting and dragged Coogan to his corner.'[114]

On his trip to California Benny boxed a local kid, Joe Benjamin. He was so impressed with his form he prevailed upon him to sign up with Gibson and come east. Taking a keen personal interest in Benjamin, Leonard worked with him in the gym and made a point to see that Benjamin appeared in supporting bouts on cards headlined by him. When Benny fought Coogan, Joe boxed the semi-final bout against veteran Tommy Touhy.

'Leonard stood outside his dressing room watching his protégé in action, Benjamin knocked Touhy out in the fifth round, but Leonard was disappointed with his performance. "You made a tough fight for yourself when you didn't have to," he said to Benjamin in the dressing room. "You were throwing punches like a raw amateur. Now, you watch me against Coogan. I'm going out in the first round and I'll fight just the way you did, and you'll see what a bum I look."

---

113 Nat Fleischer *Leonard the Magnificent* 1947
114 *Santa Ana Register* 11 December 1919

'"What about the second round, Benny?" someone said. "Oh," said Leonard casually, "it'll all be over in the second round." And it was.'[115]

The day Benny fought Coogan, Jack Keene reported in his column, 'Within a few days, the champion will be performing before a motion picture camera. Leonard will be featured in a 15-episode serial and the work on the picture will start soon in the studio of the Hallmark Pictures Corporation.'[116]

Benny would recall a night in December 1919. 'Atlanta had developed what they believed was a promising boy. It was Jake Abel. He was a 145-pounder and had given Jack Britton a good fight. Then they thought he was good enough to rock me to sleep. Abel was giving me a good fight for five rounds. Near the end of the seventh round, I stepped inside his guard and planted a right to the jaw. Abel crumpled and looked to be out.

'Suddenly the crowd began to yell, "Benny, don't knock him! Don't knock him out! Let him stay. Benny, don't knock him out." I never heard such noise before. The round had only 20 seconds to go and the crowd howled its head off as Abel got to his feet at the count of nine. Then I admit that I clinched with him and pushed him around until the end of the round.

'When I went to my corner, I looked at Billy Gibson and my brother Charley. "What'll I do, Gib?" I asked. "I got him where I can put him away with one shot. What'll I do?"

'Well, I let down for the last two rounds. But I did not damage Abel. When the fight was over, I never heard so much applause. I gave the crowd what it wanted. Here was an audience that wanted their home boy to stay, and stay he did. The next day, the newspapers in Atlanta gave me some of the greatest write-ups that I ever received. A fighter likes nothing better than to see KO after

115 Nat Fleischer *Leonard the Magnificent* 1947
116 Jack Keene *Hattiesburg American* Mississippi 10 December 1919

his name. Here, I lost a chance to add one. But I feel that I did the right thing.'[117]

From the first week in February 1920 through to the first week in July, you could see Benny Leonard on the silver screen, as advertised in your local newspaper. 'Benny Leonard the new and successful star will provide sensational thrills in the 15 episodes of "The Evil Eye."' You rarely saw the world lightweight champion working out in a gymnasium, which was a pity, for Benny had a serious challenger waiting for him out there in Michigan.

Charley White was born Charles Anchowitz on 25 March 1891 in Liverpool, England to Jewish parents, who emigrated to America when the boy was just seven. His father, a struggling tailor from Russia, settled the family in the Jewish Ghetto on Chicago's West Side. Young Charles was only 13 when he contracted tuberculosis and sustained damage to one of his lungs. His father sent him to Chicago's O'Connell's Sports Club to build up his strength, and after gaining weight and working out, Charles took up boxing in the club and within 18 months was diagnosed free from tuberculosis. At 15, Anchowitz changed his name to White and started his professional boxing career. He fought world champions ten times, losing to men like Abe Attell, Johnny Kilbane, Johnny Dundee, Freddie Welsh, Willie Ritchie, Ad Wolgast, Rocky Kansas, Ted 'Kid' Lewis and Jack Britton. And Benny Leonard.

'That was one of the times when I was grossly overweight and out of shape,' Benny would recall. 'I had just finished making a serial picture in California which took six months to make. I fell off a bridge and tore a tendon and broke a blood vessel in my leg. Billy Gibson, my manager, made the match two days prior to my accident, but I told Gibson that White was a cinch and I would box him with one leg. I was so fat from rest and inactivity, I practically waddled.

---

117 Benny Leonard *The Philadelphia Inquirer* 7 August 1921

'So you can readily see I wasn't in shape for my fight with Charley White. When the bell rang in the first round, I moved around and was outboxing Charley for the first three rounds. Then he hit me with a left hook on the arm which paralysed it, then my leg went back on me. I felt a muscle pull and I could hardly navigate on it. Now I really was in bad shape, for White could hit with that left hook. I found that out in the next round. He hit me on the chin and out of the ring I went. The referee started to count – he was up to three when my brother Charley came to my assistance and pushed me back into the ring.

'I fell into a clinch and started talking to him. I said, "So, that's it, eh? Well, Charley, it's a fight from now on," and with both hands I pushed him as hard as I could, out of the clinch. I could see White was scared – my bluff worked – he laid back and allowed me to stall for time. Boy, I needed that time.

'Finally, in the ninth round I went out to take a chance and win the fight, as I was being licked up to now. I hit White on the chin with a short right-hand punch, and as I did he stiffened up, his eyes were glassy and I knew I had him. I hit him again on the chin and down he went. He was in good shape for I had to knock him down three times to keep him there. I sure was lucky that night, and I made myself a promise that I would never go into the ring again without being in first class condition.'[118]

The fight took place at Floyd Fitzsimmons's open-air arena at Benton Harbour, Michigan on Monday, 5 July 1920. Benny Leonard, lightweight champion of the world, 24 years old, 139 wins in a total of 167 fights. Charley White of Chicago, 29 years old, the perennial contender, 104 wins in 139 fights, possessed of a killer left hook. Seconds out!

---

118 Benny Leonard *Hobbs Daily News* New Mexico 31 January 1939

CHAPTER NINE

The first round went to Leonard by a slight shade. He kept dancing throughout and when he resumed the fancy stuff in the second, the crowd booed him. The third round was even, but White started on the lightweight king's trail in the fourth and his great attack earned him the edge in this session. His best round was the fifth.

'For a moment, the Chicago bugs had visions of having a world's champion as a resident of their city. White cut loose with one of his left hooks, caught Leonard flush on the jaw, and knocked him clear through the ropes in his own corner. The huge throng gazed on the champion, his legs dangling over the lower ropes while his shoulders reclined outside the hemp. His seconds had to assist him, and they did so, although it is considered a violation of the ethics of the game.

'But the champion gathered himself to a semblance of defence simply by dependence on his wonderful thinking apparatus. In the eighth, Leonard started to recover in cleverness and punching power and his brain returned to its ordinary functioning. He played the game as a master plays it, then came the ninth and he led White into position for a right cross that carried all the power that he possessed. White sagged to the canvas.

'It was a heart-breaking blow and it sickened White, but he gamely struggled to his feet without a count, only to be knocked down again. He got up again and he went down again, but there was no getting up again after that. White was a limp, helpless creature on the canvas. After he had been counted out he got to his feet unassisted, but his legs wouldn't hold him and he fell over on his back.

'This had been a battle in which brainwork counted more heavily than anything else. That Benny Leonard is champion instead of ex-champion today can be attributed to his wonderful use of the grey matter, with which he fortunately is endowed. The comparison,

99

as far as alert thinking is concerned, shows White at a decided disadvantage.'[119]

Several boxing writers of the day made a point of highlighting Charley White's mental ability in relation to his undoubted fighting ability. Hype Igoe wrote, 'White is like the artist who can't resist the temptation of stepping back and admiring his uncompleted work.'

Author Ken Blady wrote in his 1988 book, *The Jewish Boxers' Hall of Fame*, 'Had he been able to think and punch at the same time, he would certainly have been a world champion.'

Nat Fleischer, in his biography of Leonard, would write, 'Out of Chicago came the left hook artist Charley White, whose high, intellectual brow hid a slow-thinking mind. For four rounds, Benny had outpunched and outgeneralled Charley. The left hook artist didn't have a chance until the fifth round when Leonard, thinking he had White at his mercy, got careless.

'White suddenly launched his famous left hook. It struck like a flash of lightning, contacting Leonard's jaw. The power behind that wallop was so great, it sent Benny out of the ring.

'When Leonard got back in time, White dropped his hands to his side. He had a blank look on his face. At that moment, it seemed to me that Charley White's mind had ceased to function again and he became just another fighter.

'For the next few rounds, Leonard leaped around White, jabbing, hooking, uppercutting. He was the master once more. In the ninth round, a short right to the chin brought Charley to his hands and knees. Up at two, a right to the jaw again dropped White. Taking a count of eight, Charley was no sooner back in the fight than a powerful right sent him half out of the ring, hanging over the middle rope.

---

119 *Iowa City Press Citizen* 6 July 1920

'Back in action after another eight count, Benny threw a left to the body and a right to the jaw and Charley tumbled for a further count of seven. Leonard was on him in a flash and there was no coming back from the terrific right uppercut that ended Charley's title dreams.'[120]

In 1958, Nat Fleischer, publisher of *The Ring* magazine, rated Charley White the tenth greatest lightweight of all time.

'Criticism of Leonard has been heard for some time past and chiefly because of the fact that he has not been scoring knockouts as freely as he used to do some two years ago. During 1919, he only put seven opponents to sleep out of 18 contests and in 1918 he hung a dreamland wallop on the chin of only two victims, whereas in 1917 his private graveyard listed 15 kayoes out of 27 contests. Perhaps it is true that Leonard is slipping, but if he is then the sturdy little Jewish boy will go down to defeat happy in the knowledge that he firmly established himself as one of the hardest hitters that the lightweight class ever produced.

'Leonard has only been boxing in public eight years. In that period, he has made a marvellous record. No one ever flattened Freddie Welsh, the young lightweight champion, until Leonard stepped into the limelight. Who was ever able to make Johnny Kilbane throw up the sponge? Not a boxer in the world until Leonard with his punching power and skill began to measure arms with the king of all featherweights. Leonard has done more than that.

'As has been the case with nearly every champion of the class, the present titleholder generally is regarded as invincible. In fact, it has been so difficult to find worthy opponents for Leonard that for months past he has been compelled to box welters. Therefore, when Eddie Fitzsimmons, product of Harlem, began to exhibit a

---

120 Nat Fleischer, *Leonard the Magnificent*, 1947

knockout punch that scared off all the available lightweights, the opinion grew that a logical opponent for Leonard finally had been discovered.' [121]

Sadly, Eddie Fitzsimmons was not the guy. In 1920, this southpaw lightweight was 24 years old, sported a record of 36–13–7 with 14 KOs, and was matched with champion Benny Leonard over 15 rounds at Madison Square Garden for the world's championship on 17 September. A week before the fight, Eddie's manager, 'Dumb' Dan Morgan notified promoter Tex Rickard that Fitzsimmons 'seemed disinclined to meet the champion'. Morgan assured Rickard that he had done all in his power to keep the engagement, but that Fitzsimmons refused to go forward with the match.

'Truth be told, Benny Leonard himself wasn't so crazy to go through with the match as some of his supporters would have the fight fans believe. When Dan Morgan brought the news that his battler didn't feel himself capable of holding off the champion just yet, there was more joy than disappointment in the Leonard camp. When Leonard agreed to post a forfeit of $20,000 to insure his appearance eight hours before the bout, at 135 pounds, he honestly believed he could accomplish the poundage with the few weeks' time given him to get in condition, but when he started after the surplus weight he found it didn't come off as readily as he had anticipated. The result was that he began to grow concerned.

'There isn't any doubt now in the minds of most fight followers that the champion really can pare himself down to the legitimate weight at which he should be forced to fight, but he couldn't do it in the time he had to train. Fitzsimmons, ignoring the fact that he had the chance of a lifetime to catch this wonderful champion off form, began to hedge on the terms accepted for him by his manager,

121 *Joplin Globe* Missouri 10 February 1920

Dan Morgan. The result was that the bout was called off, and both fighters breathed a sigh of relief.'[122]

On Friday, 29 September, Eddie Fitzsimmons climbed into the ring at the Garden, not to fight champion Leonard for his world title but to contest 15 rounds with Willie Jackson, at 23 already a veteran of 114 fights. With the hope of landing a title match himself, Willie knocked the southpaw out in ten rounds. Carried to his stool, Fitzsimmons collapsed and almost rolled out of the ring. Manager Dan Morgan signalled that his man was through.

'Rickard still has Leonard signed to a contract calling for his appearance against some battler yet to be selected. Who that will be now remains a matter for great speculation for there are very few lightweights now doing business worthy of a chance at the title. Lew Tendler, the Philadelphian, obviously is afraid of Leonard, and so is Fitzsimmons. They do not care to risk their capacity for earning dollars in a bout with the champion. This leaves only a very few from whom an opponent for Leonard can be selected. There is Ritchie Mitchell, the Westerner, who already has once felt the crashing power of Leonard's knockout punch. Willie Jackson has stated the belief that he has a chance against Leonard. Joe Welling would like to have a crack at the title and Freddie Welsh has intimated that he might some day try to come back again. Aside from Mitchell, the boys are not worthy of real title matches. Jackson is a very ordinary scrapper, built on the reputation he acquired when he accidentally knocked out Dundee. Of the lot Mitchell is the best, with Welling probably second choice.'[123]

Men wanted! Apply Mr W. Gibson.

---

122 *Steubenville Herald Star* Ohio 11 September 1920

123 *Jacksonville Daily Journal* Illinois 11 September 1920

CHAPTER TEN

'PINCH-WAISTED, ONE-BUTTON suit, slenderest of cravats, a shirt from a collection of hundreds, pearl-gray spats buttoned around silk-hosed ankles, toes of the toothpick shoes peeking out from the spats polished to a gleam. Pixie smile, the "vivacity of a song and dance man," a charm that made him arrive in the Senate Chamber like a glad breeze. The Prince Charming of politics, slicing through the ponderous arguments of the ponderous men who sat around him with a wit that flashed like a rapier. Beau James.'

That description by author and journalist Robert Caro of James (Jimmy) Walker fitted him like one of his toothpick shoes and was quoted by writer Arne K. Lang in his tribute to Walker, the man who transformed boxing in New York in 1920.

'One hundred years ago, on 24 March 1920, a boxing reform bill sponsored by Senator James J. Walker passed the New York State Senate. The bill ultimately became law and its provisions came to be adopted by law-makers in other states, bringing some uniformity to the most anarchic of popular sports. Prize fighting was an outlaw sport in the Empire State until 1896 when the legislature passed the Horton Law, which allowed bouts up to 25 rounds with five-ounce gloves. A spate of fixed fights and ring fatalities sparked a cry for reform and the law was repealed in 1900.

'The Lewis Law reduced the maximum number of rounds from 25 to 10 and stipulated that no decision would be rendered. The Lewis Law also restricted patronage to members of the athletic club sponsoring the event. The Frawley Law of 1911 re-opened the fights to the general public but otherwise left the provisions of the Lewis Law pretty much intact. During the last years of the nineteen-teens [1913–19], several boxing reform bills were presented to the New York legislature. In fact, the Walker Bill was one of four that was taken under consideration. After passing the Senate, the Walker Law passed the Assembly, was signed into law by Governor Al Smith on 24 May 1920 and took effect on 1 September. The Walker Law became the template that lawmakers in other jurisdictions followed when they introduced their own boxing bills. By 1934, boxing was legal in every state in the union. A key feature of the Walker Law was that everyone involved in a boxing match had to be licensed. The licensees were accountable to the boxing commission, a panel appointed by the governor. The Law approved matches up to 15 rounds and allowed official decisions. Two judges would determine the winner and if they disagreed, the referee would act as the tie-breaker.'[124]

In 1925, Jimmy Walker was elected mayor of New York City. He was a popular leader even though he had come to symbolise the free-wheeling life of speakeasies and Tammany Hall improprieties. Shortly after his re-election in 1929, rumours of corruption surfaced and he resigned in 1932 after being called to Albany by Governor Franklin D. Roosevelt.

Walker was a great follower of boxing and was a regular ringsider at Madison Square Garden. He was a featured speaker at the Boxing Writers Association annual dinners and in 1940 received that organisation's award for long and meritorious service to boxing.

---

124 Arne K. Lang 27 March 2020

The award was renamed the James J. Walker Memorial Award after Walker's death in 1946. In 1992, he was enshrined in the International Boxing Hall of Fame.

'Professional boxing will be booming in New York by next fall,' wrote Jack Velock. 'With the game restored to good standing through the medium of the Walker Bill and the creation of the State Boxing Commission soon to be accomplished by Governor Smith, fisticuffs will be the rage here, along with Babe Ruth and Man o' War.'[125]

The first boxing show under the Walker Law was held on 17 September 1920 at Madison Square Garden, between veteran lightweights Joe Welling and Johnny Dundee. It was their eighth meeting, with Welling taking a unanimous decision and looking for a shot at Leonard's championship.

Writing from New York, *International News Service* correspondent H. C. Hamilton sounded a warning in his column, 'The Walker Bill, which legalised boxing in New York state, one of the best laws governing the ring ever spread on the pages of a statute book, already has received some heavy blows. Promoters, boxers and boxers' managers already have started wrangling and fussing with such effect that some fans are wondering if the Walker Bill can survive a full year. The Frawley Bill, which permitted ten-round no-decision bouts, was killed off quickly and effectively through a row between promoters and boxers. If wrangling continues, the Walker Bill will meet the same fate.

'The Walker Law got a famous start when Tex Rickard announced he had leased Madison Square Garden and would conduct bouts there. His resignation from the International Sporting Club, however, created a bad feeling in the camp of the International and caused some officials of that organisation to make

---

125 Jack Velock *Ogden Standard Examiner* Utah 6 July 1920

statements that attracted undue attention. Rickard was happy to let the contention fall flat and go on his way without making any remarks.

'That incident caused some wonderment, but it was forced into the background shortly afterward when Dan Morgan announced that Eddie Fitzsimmons would not carry out his agreement to fight Benny Leonard in Madison Square Garden. Morgan probably forgets that boxers cannot sign agreements and break them willy-nilly under the Walker Law. Later, it developed that another boxer had been offered a mill in New York with the champion, with the result that he declared he would not think of such a thing unless the champion would agree not to knock him out.

'It really would be a very black eye if the Walker Law should be throttled. If promoters, boxers and others connected with the game cannot take care of a law framed so well, they will have only themselves to blame for they well know what killed the Frawley Law.'[126]

With boxing in New York becoming legal from 1 September, Billy Gibson and his champion took their time before breaking back into the Big Town. They had dates to fill in New Jersey, Indiana, Connecticut, Ohio and New Jersey again. First on the bill was Willie 'KO' Loughlin for a date at the Armoury in Camden.

'Robert D. Maxwell was at the ringside for what he called, "one of the most exciting boxing bouts seen in these parts in many a day". It was a battle royal put on by a wild-swinging, hard hitting, game, rushing battler and a cool, scientific, finished boxer, with the result in doubt until the final sock nestled in Loughlin's whiskers. In the fourth, a lot of things happened out of the ordinary. In a toe-to-toe slugging match, Loughlin claimed he had been hit low and protested to the referee.

---

126 H. C. Hamilton *Omaha Daily Bee* 26 September 1920

'His seconds pushed a chair into the ring and the boxer staggered to his corner and sat down … When Leonard demanded that the bout continue, the referee walked over to Loughlin's corner and, while the boxer was sitting there, started to count him out. Willie got up at the count of six and the battle continued. When the ninth opened, the huge crowd felt that Leonard had met more than his match and would be very lucky if he lasted the 12 rounds. His punches did not seem to annoy Loughlin and he appeared to be arm-weary.

'However, Benny leaped out of his corner like Jack Dempsey pounced upon Miske. Two stiff jabs sent Willie against the ropes and he stood there, with his gloves covering his face. There was an opening for a punch to the body and Leonard saw it. Putting every ounce of strength behind the blow, Benny let it go. Loughlin's knees sagged. While he was slowly dropping to the floor, Leonard quickly shot his right to the jaw. It landed flush and Loughlin fell over the lower rope half out of the ring. Somebody then put out the lights. Referee Slim Brennan counted up to ten and the fallen gladiator was carried to his corner.'

Mannie Seamon, Leonard's trainer and chief second, recalled, 'Loughlin got hit in the belly about the sixth or seventh round. It was a beaut of a shot and these were the days when you could claim foul, so Loughlin grabbed his groin and started hollering. Al Lippe was his manager and Lippe jumped into the ring. The referee, Slim Brennan, should have ordered Lippe out and told Loughlin to resume fighting but he stood there like paralysed, saying nothing. In the meantime, the bell rang.

'The New Jersey commissioner had good sense and nerve. He jumped up and shouted to Brennan, "Count him out in the corner." Brennan listened and wouldn't you know it? At the count of six, Loughlin came running out, ready to fight again. Leonard belted him around after that and Brennan finally stopped it in the ninth round. But Slim didn't work too many fights for Gibson after that.'[127]

Next stop East Chicago, Indiana, 25 September 1920 – 'Benny Leonard, world's lightweight champion, easily outpointed Pal Moran of New Orleans in ten rounds today. Leonard apparently could not get started in the early rounds but in the last four he had the New Orleans lad at his mercy. Swift left jabs and his famous cross brought blood from Moran's mouth and opened a large cut under one eye. In the seventh, eighth, ninth and tenth, Leonard seemed continually on the verge of scoring a knockout, but Moran, battling gamely, hung on to the finish.'[128]

They called the guy Frankie (Young) Britt and they booked him to box Benny Leonard at Hartford, Connecticut, and they sold tickets because the people wanted to see the world's lightweight champion. Referee George Mulligan let the fans see Leonard through four rounds before stopping the set-up in round five. Britt sported a record of 83–25–21. How did he win 83 bouts and who did he beat? He should still have been driving his truck!

Leonard moved on to New Jersey, where he met Johnny Sheppard at the Paterson Armoury. The Englishman should have collected a gun at the door because that was the only way he was going to bother the world's champion. Referee Slim Brennan told him to go home halfway through round three.

Akron, Ohio, fans weren't too happy with what they paid for, either. The main bout, optimistically set for 12 rounds between Leonard and Johnny Tilman of Minneapolis, lasted the distance because Benny wanted it that way. He eased up when he had Tilman troubled, causing local commissioners to threaten to stop the bout. The boys threw a few punches in the last two rounds and the fans went home holding their noses.

---

127 Robert D. Maxwell *Philadelphia Evening Public Ledger* 11 September 1920
128 *Jacksonville Daily Journal* Illinois 26 September 1920

By the time he met former KO victim Willie Loughlin at Camden, New Jersey, Leonard was already matched to defend his title against Chicago lightweight Joe Welling in a 15-round title match at Madison Square Garden on 26 November. He knocked Willie bow-legged a few times but couldn't finish him. He saved the fireworks for Eddie Kelly a week later, a bout BoxRec reported as 'Leonard regarding as a trial for his title contest with Joe Welling nine days later'. The newly formed New York commission issued a statement prior to the bout saying it 'did not view with favour the proposed Leonard–Kelly bout scheduled for 17 November before the Commonwealth club and in the interest of boxing announced that if this bout appears to be a sham or a collusive contest, the commission will order the payments withheld and would take positive action against the boxers'. Benny must have read that statement because he let Kelly have both barrels and the referee stopped it in the fifth round. It was time for a real fight.

Harry Newman reported for the *Chicago Tribune*, 'The Leonard–Welling match is now a certainty. Nate Lewis, manager of Welling, wired Tex Rickard yesterday that the $5,000 offer for the Chicago lightweight to box the champion at Madison Square Garden on 26 November was accepted and at the same time authorised his New York agent Max Blumenthal to sign the necessary papers. This being accomplished, the two principals have started training in real earnest and the fans are in for a stirring contest when these two clever lads clash.'[129]

'When the Walker Law brought boxing back to New York in 1920,' wrote Jersey Jones in *The Ring*, 'the opening card staged by Tex Rickard in old Madison Square Garden featured Joe Welling and Johnny Dundee. It was announced that the winner would meet Benny Leonard in a lightweight title match. Welling won. Two

129 Harry Newman *San Antonio Evening News* 13 November 1920

months later he faced Leonard. Although Joe was a clever boxer, stiff puncher and ringwise campaigner, few of the so-called experts conceded him much of a chance against the great Leonard. Most of them picked Benny to score an early knockout.

'Benny didn't agree. We were labouring for the old *New York Globe* at the time, and one afternoon we hopped along to the Seaman Brothers gymnasium in the Bronx, where Benny was training. After the workout, we talked things over. "Welling isn't as soft as the sportswriters seem to think," said Leonard. "I'd rather fight any other lightweight in the world than Joe. He's not only a smart defensive boxer, and a hard guy to hit when he doesn't want to be hit, but he's loaded with annoying tricks that aren't obvious to the average spectator. When he jabs he moves in with his left foot and plunks the heel smack on your instep. Then in clinches, he has ways of twisting and wrenching your arms. Another of his tricks in close is to jab the thumb of his gloves into your biceps. A couple of rounds of that and your arms are heavy and sore. Believe me, this won't be a soft fight. I expect to win, but I'll have a tough time doing it."'[130]

At the 2pm weigh-in, Welling told reporters, 'I'm not a bit worried. I'm going in there to win, and I hope to become a champion. I feel great, better than I ever did in my career, and am fit and ready to put up my best battle.'

The champion promised a knockout, saying, 'I am not going to let any rival travel any further than I can help. Some guy is going to come along and slip one over some day, so you can't blame me for being on my guard. I hope Joe carries the fight to me. Then you will see fireworks exploded in large quantities.'[131]

The night of the Leonard–Welling fight, there was great excitement in the Schulberg home on Riverside Drive in Manhattan.

—

130 Jersey Jones *The Ring* September 1957
131 *Madison Capital Times* Wisconsin 26 November 1920

Writer Budd Schulberg was still a schoolboy and he remembered his father, movie producer B.P. Schulberg, as a passionate fight fan whose favourite was Benny Leonard. Now Benny was coming back to the Garden. It had been two and a half years since he boxed Willie Jackson in a four-round charity bout. There would be no empty seats this time. The fight drew a record gate for the lightweight division, $98,608.40. It was the first official championship staged in New York since Joe Gans quit against Frank Erne in the old Broadway A.C. in 1900. 'The Great Benny Leonard' was how he was always referred to in our household, wrote Budd Schulberg. B.P. knew Benny Leonard personally. All up-and-coming young Jews in New York knew Benny Leonard personally. They would take time off from their lunch hour to watch him train. They bet hundreds and often thousands of dollars on him in stirring contests against Rocky Kansas, Willie Ritchie, Ever Hammer, Johnny Dundee and Joe Welling. Young Budd pleaded with his father to take him to the Garden for the Welling fight, but he was too young. 'When my father gave me the blow-by-blow next evening, he admitted that our hero had underestimated Welling's appetite for punishment. B.P. and the rest of the young Jewish fancy had bet that Welling would fall in ten. B.P. was out 500 smackers. He and his pals had gone back to the dressing room to see the triumphant Benny, and the fistic star of David, still proud of his hair-comb, apologised for leading his rooters astray. Then the boys went out on the town to demonstrate Jewish power.'[132]

'Welling put forward a great battle, he was beaten but far from disgraced. With head bloody but unbowed, he went to his pugilistic Waterloo like the true fighter he was. Benny put everything he had in his punches from the sixth through the eighth in an effort to put an end to the fray. In the 13th, Leonard stepped in and drew

132 Budd Schulberg *Moving Pictures* 1993

Welling's guard down after bombarding Joe with lefts and rights to the body. Quick as a flash, he crashed a vicious right cross to the jaw that jarred Welling from head to heels and sent the blond-haired battler hurtling against the ropes in his own corner.

'Leonard's beady black eyes blazed like a rattler's, he flashed in close and lashed left and right to the head, followed with a short right drive to the body that made Joe gasp. Then came a vicious left hook to the jaw, sending the Chicagoan reeling across the ring. That was followed by a relentless attack that finally brought Welling down to the canvas. When Joe got to his feet, a right to the jaw sent him plunging through the ropes. He held the upper strand, then pulled himself back on his feet.

'The champion was fully on the scent, his prey was there for the killing. A left and right carrying the full force of Benny's body behind them sent Welling's body clear through the ropes and his head struck the ring platform with a thump that could be heard around the ringside. He got back into the ring, through bloody lips he breathed defiance, not sufficient to halt the titleholder; a terrible left to the jaw lifted Welling off the floor, landing him on his back. He was saved by the bell at the count of six. It was a round such as seldom seen in a championship match!

'Frantic work by Welling's seconds enabled him to come out for the 14th, but it was plainly seen that his number was up. Benny unleashed lefts and rights to the jaw, Welling was wobbly and a right-hander sent him to the deck; he struggled to his feet at nine. Leonard uppercut him twice, then came a right and left to the jaw and Welling [was] again down in a heap. Joe's sense of direction was now gone and as he staggered to his feet, referee Billy Haukop stopped the slaughter. Benny had come home in style!'[133]

---

133 Billy McCarney *The Ring* December 1948

CHAPTER ELEVEN

'MADISON SQUARE Garden is at once a building and a symbol,' wrote Bert Randolph Sugar. 'Originally a New York New Haven & Hartford Railroad freight yard and depot, the structure had been converted in 1874 by none other than P. T. Barnum into a magnificent hall that measured 425 feet by 200 feet, called Barnum's Monster Classical and Geological Hippodrome. In 1890, William Vanderbilt put together a syndicate of Ward McAllister's famed Four Hundred – including John Pierpoint Morgan, Hiram Hitchcock, and William F. Wharton – to raise $1.5 million to build a new "pleasure palace" on the spot at Madison Square. Opening in June 1890 with a concert and two ballets, it was described by the *New York Times* as "one of the great institutions of the town, to be mentioned along with Central Park and the bridge of Brooklyn".

'Now, some 31 years later, the famed old dowager hosted not only its first championship fight to a decision, but also many of New York's top debutantes and duennas. All were part of a sellout crowd, which included many of the celebrities who took part in a fundraising event for devastated France, a charity benefit run by J. P. Morgan's daughter, Anne, whose centrepiece was the Leonard–Mitchell fight.'[134]

---

134 Bert Randolph Sugar *Boxing Illustrated* May 1989

'When Miss Morgan and Otto Shuloff, a dress-goods merchant,' recorded Francis Albertanti, 'approached Tex Rickard and pleaded with him to put on a fight show for the worthy cause, Tex had no hesitancy lining up a stellar attraction. The best drawing card back in 1921 was undoubtedly little Benny Leonard. The lightweight champion had a terrific following and if he fought you or me, he'd pack 'em to the rafters. Rickard broached the charity angle to Billy Gibson, Leonard's manager. Then the dapper, shrewd Gibson said he was all for it.

'Opponent? Who'd be the best man? This was going to be a fight, not an exhibition. The writer suggested Richie Mitchell of Milwaukee. "That's okay with me," Gibson allowed. Rickard immediately wired Billy Mitchell, Richie's brother-manager. The reply was fast and furious. "Fight Benny Leonard?" the wire questioned, adding in the same written breath, "It'll be a pleasure. But it must be for the championship." Both Rickard and Gibson assured Billy Mitchell the 135-pound title would be at stake.

'The night of the fight was one long to be remembered. The old amphitheatre bulged on all four sides with the mass of humanity. You couldn't get another person in with a shoehorn. Leonard himself wagered $1,000 to $10,000 with the famous gambler, Arnold Rothstein, that he would flatten Mitchell in one round or less. In the contender's dressing room, there wasn't a soul to be seen. Richie walked in, mumbled something to himself and then shed his clothes. He looked as if he was going to the electric chair.'[135]

'When the doors to the great arena were thrown open, men in drab business suits swept like a wave into the Garden, filling the four galleries and much of the level stretches around the ring. Then in the big auditorium with its flag-bedecked balconies, its bright lights aloft and its dim haze of smoke, appeared a flying squadron

---

135 Francis Albertanti *The Ring* September 1948

of women in evening dresses of bright hues. They were programme venders, selling their wares for war-torn France.

'Shorty after Miss Anne Morgan had seated herself in her box, the Garden, filled to capacity, was plunged into darkness until the great cluster of lights over the ring was flashed on. When the first pair of boxers stepped into the ring, there was a stir and into the eyes of some women spectators came the light which must have shone in those of women of old Rome when gladiators met. As the bouts progressed, more evening dress was to be seen, and it was evident that women, although far outnumbered by men, had flocked to a boxing bout in numbers never before beheld in New York.

'Never before had two men battered each other in the presence of such a highly social gathering,' recorded Frank Graham in the *New York American*, 'and for the first time that night a Morgan or an Astor or a Vanderbilt could wear a top hat into the old arena without the gallery gods whistling at him and shouting, "Cab! Cab!"

'Also, the affair was notable because it was the only time that Al Smith ever was seen at a ringside. For one who grew up on the East Side and, at least in his youth, was on friendly terms with all the roughnecks in the neighbourhood, he had no use for prize fighting and actually had been hoodwinked by Jimmy Walker into signing the bill that legalised the sport in this state. Only the importance of Miss Morgan caused him, as Governor, to lend his presence. When he got there he was unhappy, and although the first round was one of the most thrilling ever fought in this town, Al went away shaking his head. He couldn't understand, he said, why everybody was so excited.'[136]

Even Miss Morgan was excited! 'When Tex Rickard asked her what she thought of the fighting, she replied: "It is all right, but this

---

136 Frank Graham *The New York American* 28 June 1921

is my first introduction to boxing and I'm crazy about it." Then the idols of the night, Leonard and Mitchell, stepped into the ring and the applause broke records. Mitchell entered the ring attended by his brothers, Willie and "Pinky", while Leonard was making his way down the centre aisle …

'Leonard, who was a prohibitive favourite in the betting, wore plain white trunks. Mitchell also wore the same, with a green band at the waist line. The men weighed in at 2pm at 134 pounds, one pound under the stipulated weight. The referee for the main bout was John Haukop of Brooklyn and the judges were Tommy Shortell of Brooklyn and Joe Ruddy of the New York A.C.'[137]

'Boxing probably has never known a more thorough student than Benny Leonard. Benny not only made a career of analysing, practising and perfecting every possible physical move in the ring, but he was a keen student of psychology as well. Many a fight Leonard won by out-thinking the opposition. Benny had a logical cause for feeling he had an excellent chance of registering a one-round knockout over Richie Mitchell, as he spoke with manager Billy Gibson and trainer Mannie Seamon in the dressing room. "Richie is a nervous, high-strung sort, and generally unsteady in the first round," Benny reasoned. "He'll be more nervous and unsteady than usual with me. He'll be remembering that I knocked him out in Milwaukee, the only time he's ever been stopped. If I step out fast, I may be able to take him in a hurry."[138]

'When famous racketeer and gambler Arnold Rothstein told Benny just before the opening bell that he had wagered $25,000 on the champion scoring a first-round knockout, Leonard agreed to oblige especially since Rothstein promised the brilliant pugilist a piece of the action.'[139]

—

137 *The Boston Daily Globe* 15 January 1921
138 Jersey Jones *The Ring* May 1951
139 Robert Portis *The Fight City* 14 January 2019

'Leonard was as full of fight as a badger,' wrote veteran ringsider Hype Igoe, 'and in Mitchell he had a playmate who was deadly as long as he could prop a stance. Benny promptly floored Mitchell three times in the first round and, looking towards Miss Morgan's place among the spectators, I saw all of them peeking at the drama through the fingers of both hands.

'Mitchell was down! He was up! He was down and up, flattened for the third time! He arose, staggering crazily. Leonard moved toward him with the sure tread of a catamount. Mitchell had been driven into a corner. Then Richie's torso fairly belched blows. Bang!!! That one to the button was a honey and under its impact Leonard went down, crashing like a tipped-over china cabinet. He turned from his squatting position on the canvas and tried to smile assurance to pop-eyed Billy Gibson. Slowly, he got up like a creaky old Civil War veteran paying his respects to the National Anthem!

'He faced Mitchell, a tiny trickle of blood oozing from each corner of his mouth. He was 20 feet distant. Then he did a wonderfully brazen thing. Grinning toward the far corner where the tormentor stood awaiting his arising, Leonard nonchalantly reached out with both gloved hands and beckoned for Mitchell to walk back into the glove duel! If Leonard at that second had attempted to stride toward Mitchell, he would have collapsed again!

'Gradually, Benny's super-fighting intellect reached absolute normalcy. He was seeing again and Mitchell sensed it. Leonard up with him in the sixth, as much pity in his heart now as you'd have found in the claws of a wounded grizzly. Mitchell came tumbling down as if from the top of the Palisades.

'Devastated France had been honoured in a manner which Miss Morgan could not have explained to her French committee. That white-haired lady, her companions, all of us, had seen one of the most glorious ring battles ever written into the pages of ring history.'[140]

'Benny Leonard is still number one among the world's lightweights,' wrote Henry L. Farrell, 'by the margin of a second, an inch or some other small measurement. Richie Mitchell is not number one by the same little difference. Fifth Avenue and First Avenue, Riverside Drive and the Ghetto saw the fine line of distinction drawn last night in Madison Square Garden. More than 15,000 spectators in evening clothes and sweaters, debutantes and shop girls, bank presidents and taxi drivers saw Leonard and Mitchell put up one of the greatest battles ever seen here.

'The sixth round was the winner but the first round was the thriller. At the tap of the gong, Leonard walked from his corner and went after the Milwaukee challenger. Before the crowd had its eyes focused on the bright ring, Mitchell went down under a left hook to the jaw. He came up after a count of nine and almost immediately went down again. Nine seconds were tolled and when he lifted his head his right eye was closed. Leonard, scenting victory, opened with another vicious attack and for the third time Mitchell went down. Coming up at nine, the Milwaukee boy was apparently gone. He was weaving around the ring and the pack was yelling for a finish. Leonard came in to give him the final application of the gloves, when all at once the left of the tall, groggy boy shot out and caught the champion flush on the jaw.

'Leonard went down flat on his back with a bump. He tried to get up and his knees sagged. In his corner, Billy Gibson, his manager, was pale with fixed eyes. He tried to shout instructions but he couldn't give voice to a word. He was dumbstruck. At the count of nine, Leonard rose to his feet. Summoning all his ring craft, the champion boxed with the boy who was too weak and too

---

140 Hype Igoe *New York Journal-American* 15 January 1921

far gone to follow up his advantage. The gong sounded and Mitchell walked slowly to his corner obviously aware of the fact that he had missed his best chance for fame and a fortune.

'Leonard was careful in the second and the following rounds. He boxed with Mitchell and waited his chance, getting stronger all the time, while Mitchell gradually grew weaker. The chance came in the sixth round. Leonard got an opening for a right cross. He put it over and Mitchell went down again. He came up with his gloves under his chin, desperately trying to stop the next blow. Leonard measured him and put over another smash to the jaw. Mitchell was hanging on the ropes helpless when the referee stopped the bout.'[141]

The American committee for Devastated France announced that it had received $90,000 from the fight. The gate receipts amounted to $162,746, the largest in the history of the lightweight division, of which $40,000 went to Leonard and $20,000 to Mitchell.

'Fans were still discussing the bout today, which all experts declared was one of the greatest in a decade. Discussing the blow Mitchell delivered in the first round which made the champion stagger down for a count of nine, Leonard said, "It was a dying lunge. It caught me fairly and it certainly bothered me. It came so unexpectedly. Oh, yes, Mitchell always was a dangerous man. When I dropped, I turned my head and winked to Billy Gibson to let him know I was all right."

'"I want to fight him again," declared Mitchell. "I almost had him licked, but I got careless. I was within one second of the lightweight championship of the world. I had Benny Leonard on the floor but he got up at the count of nine. Next time I will certainly do it."'[142]

The day after the fight, trainer Mannie Seamon told Leonard, 'Benny, I would have died if you hadn't got up.'

---

141 Henry L. Farrell *Sterling Daily Gazette* Illinois 15 January 1921
142 *Cedar Rapids Evening Gazette* Iowa 25 January 1921

It was about this time that Tex Rickard was struggling to get the money together for his Dempsey–Carpentier fight, after Brady and Cochran pulled out. Doc Kearns and Jack Curley joined Tex and they started a series of conferences. These lasted for hours and continued for weeks, with everyone talking in circles.

'The dickering was still going on when Rickard, to his delight, suddenly found himself tossed headfirst into the *crème de la crème* of New York society. This happened when Anne Morgan, daughter of one J. P. Morgan and sister of another, asked him to donate the Garden for a night to her favourite charity, The American Friends of France. On hearing that a championship fight would raise more money than any other sports attraction, Miss Morgan agreed to act as co-promoter.

'Rickard got her the most promising match in sight, Richie Mitchell versus Benny Leonard for the world lightweight title. For publicity purposes, the articles for this match were signed in the Morgan family's Madison Avenue mansion, which for the first and last time welcomed fight guys smoking ill-smelling cigars. The fight drew the sort of high-hat-and-ermine crowd Tex had dreamed about for years of luring to one of his fights. The scrap proved one of the great all-time thrillers in lightweight history. Leonard was dropped himself by a roundhouse wallop. He staggered to his feet just in time to save his championship, and went on to win with a sixth-round knockout.'[143]

Richie Mitchell didn't do too much after Benny knocked him out. They brought Joe Tiplitz to Milwaukee and Richie took the newspaper decision in ten rounds, then trekked over to Buffalo, where Rocky Kansas was the hometown favourite. Wrong move!

'Rocky Kansas knocked out Richie Mitchell in the first round of a 12-round bout here tonight. Mitchell was floored by a left to the

---

143 Charles Samuels *The Magnificent Rube* 1957

body and a right to the head. He gamely struggled over to his own corner and came to his feet at the count of nine. Kansas, rushing again, knocked Mitchell completely off his feet and sent him rolling through the ropes to the edge of the platform. He was struggling to his feet at the count of ten, but was helpless and the referee called it a knockout. Time 2.36 round one.'[144]

'That sure was a costly wallop for Richie Mitchell the other night in Buffalo, when Rocky Kansas dropped one over in the first round and knocked the Milwaukee boy cuckoo. That thump on the jaw just about reduced Mr Mitchell [by] 70 per cent as a box office attraction, and if you haven't got that attribute, you needn't come around. As a result of his splendid fight against the champion, Benny Leonard, several weeks ago, Richie was looked upon as the logical man to meet Leonard again, and preparations were on for matching the two all over. Now it looks as if this Kansas fellow will be called in to act the part originally assigned to Mitchell. It is just the mistake some boxers make of taking a chance to get some easy money in the sticks and bumping into the wrong spot.'[145]

Maybe Vincent Treanor got it right when he wrote in the *New York Evening World*, 'Last Defeat by Benny Leonard Broke the Fighting Heart of Game Richie Mitchell.'

It is possible that Richie is through, and if so his passing may be charged up to the two defeats he sustained at the hands of Benny Leonard. The last one broke his heart, and probably tightened him on a seat on the well-known toboggan hit by all of us in time. A quiet and retiring lad, with intelligence above the ordinary among boxers, he has for the past five years had his mind set on winning the lightweight championship. He didn't lose the ambition even after Leonard knocked him out in seven rounds in Milwaukee in 1917, because he knew he wasn't "right" that time.

—
144 *Cincinnati Commercial Tribune* Ohio 19 February 1921
145 *Appleton Post Crescent* Wisconsin 23 February 1921

'He came to New York to meet Benny again only recently with the firm belief that he would take the title back home with him. It will be remembered how he swung the right time and time again for Leonard's jaw at the Garden. Richie evidently had come to the conclusion that he could bring Benny down only in that way. He didn't stop to consider that Leonard is one of the hardest men in the ring today to reach with a clean right. He learned this, however, in defeat.'[146]

---

146 Vincent Treanor *The New York Evening World* 26 February 1921

CHAPTER TWELVE

IN THE 1920s, a popular topic for a good column saw the sportswriters dream up a match between a current headliner and a voice from the storied past of the fight game. You're talking Benny Leonard versus Battling Nelson, Jack Dempsey versus Jack Johnson, Mickey Walker versus Stanley Ketchel, and so on. You knew the readers would go for it, it would sell a few more papers and make the sports editor less grumpy. The boys with the pencils loved to theorise on the merits of Benny Leonard and the guy they called the greatest lightweight of all time, Joe Gans, The Old Master.

Leonard once said that Gans gave him his toughest fight. 'Gans?' questioned one of his listeners. 'Why, Benny, you were only 14 when Gans died.' Leonard didn't crack a smile. 'I did box him once, back in February of 1919,' said Benny. 'I was training for a four-round bout with Willie Ritchie in San Francisco. The night before the fight, Billy Gibson arranged for me to sleep at Moose Taussig's training camp. Moose ushered me into a long dormitory with many beds in it, all empty. Seemed there were no other fighters staying over that night.Taussig told me, "Take any bed you want. You will find them all comfortable. Young Corbett played the field. Terry McGovern liked that one, and … oh, you gonna take this one? You picked a good one. That's the one Joe Gans slept in." And Moose walked out of the room. I was pretty tired, but once in bed,

I couldn't go to sleep. A slim negro came softly into the dormitory, I knew it was Gans without even looking up. "Who are you, boy?" he asked. "Benny Leonard," I replied, and then foolishly added, "lightweight champion of the world." "Step out, boy," said Gans, "and let's see what you can do. I ain't gonna hurt you. Just put 'em up and let's go." We started to box. There was no referee. We fought and fought, Gans and I, all through the night, and it was a terrific battle. Suddenly Gans raised his hand in a signal to stop. "That will do, boy. Now you go back into bed – *my* bed." And he was gone. When Billy Gibson came around the next morning, he looked at me and said, "What's the matter, couldn't you sleep? First time I ever knew a four-round no-decision fight to worry you so you couldn't sleep!" 'Billy was referring to my fight with Ritchie that night. I didn't dare tell him about my fight with Gans. He would have thought I was nuts. Well, maybe I was. But that *meeting* with Gans will always stand out as the greatest thrill of my life.'[147]

In many ways, Leonard was like Gans in that he was a student of the fight game. Benny would go to the gym even if he didn't have a contest lined up, just to watch other fighters as they trained and sparred … 'Study is the thing that makes a successful fighter nowadays,' said Benny Leonard in an interview with esteemed boxing writer Robert Edgren in 1921. 'We were sitting in a room at the New York Athletic Club, talking over Benny's career,' recalled Edgren. "You have to be a student to get to the top and stay there," went on Benny, "I'm champion and any other lightweight could make a fortune by beating me, yet nothing can induce the best of them to meet me in the ring. Tendler, Jackson and the others know I can beat them, but they don't know why.

"'You have to study three things to be a first-class fighter. First, your opponent's mind and habit of thought, second, your

---

147 Charles S. Biglow *Boxing & Wrestling* November 1957

own mental control of timing and movement, and last, physiology. I learned about the importance of understanding physiology while I was in the army. While I was boxing instructor at Camp Upton, Lieutenant Smith was instructor in Jiu-Jitsu, which he learned in Japan. We worked together and he taught me Jiu-Jitsu. I learned a lot of things about the nerves. There are three knockout points on the head, each where nerves lie near the surface. The nerve telegraphs the brain that you're knocked out, and down you go. If I haven't had a chance to study an opponent before a fight, I study him as well as I can in the early rounds. First his mental limits and then his physical power. I see how quickly he can think, how quick is he to defend and how quick to lead or counter. Then I look for his weak spot.'"[148]

Growing up in Baltimore, Joe Gans had a similar mindset, as recorded by boxing historian Nat Fleischer in his 1938 *Black Dynamite* series. 'From the start of his career, Joe was a tireless student of the finer points of his profession. If he could help it, he never missed an opportunity of seeing the top-notch men of his day go through their paces, whether it was in the gymnasium or in tussles between the ropes. Under Al Herford's management, he was given plenty of chances to indulge his hobby in this respect, and it was due to his close concentration in such matters that he early perfected the polished style and effective punching power that were to win for him the proud title of The Old Master.'

Fleischer also noted that the first time Bob Fitzsimmons appeared in a Baltimore theatre, Joe Gans was on hand to get an eyeful of the proceedings. 'Gans was so fascinated by the skill of the lanky Australian that for weeks following he trailed Bob from town to town in the hope of gaining new tips from watching Fitz step around. Bob was on a 'meeting all-comers' tour then, and Gans

---

148 'On The Ropes' website

saw him put away several opponents in the workmanlike fashion for which the freckled terror was noted. Fitz scored most of those knockouts either with the jolt to the solar plexus that stopped Jim Corbett or an equally effective short right straight to the jaw.

'Where Joe Gans stood head and shoulders over his contemporaries was in his ability to analyse the whys and wherefores of deft moves made by skilled gladiators and put the acquired tricks into combined operation for his own benefit. Nor was it long ere the student developed into the perfect warrior. Gans had intelligence plus – that tells the whole story of his marked efficiency!'[149]

In the September 1992 issue of *The Ring* magazine, Gans and Leonard were matched in a Battle of the Legends, with three experts acting as judges. All three selected Leonard as the winner of this dream match.

Bob Sherrick, a New York-based boxing historian and fight film collector, opined, '[It is] a great match-up between two fighters who dominated entire eras. Gans was one of the best fighters of his day. He was a very methodical guy with a pretty good defence. He was a tough man, but back then most fighters were. The era dictated that. Offensively, though, it would be one or two punches, then grab and hold. By the time Leonard came along, a new style of boxing had evolved. Guys moved more and threw more combinations. And Benny could do it all. Just on the little I've seen, I can understand why he was held in such high esteem. He was a master boxer, he was fast, he could punch and he fought every good fighter of his time. He fought all types of fighters, so he would have been able to cope with Gans. Leonard by 15 rounds decision.'

Hank Kaplan was among boxing's foremost archivists and historians. 'Gans and Leonard were the two greatest lightweights ever,' Kaplan said. 'Gans was the more deliberate of the two. He

---

149 Nat Fleischer *Black Dynamite* 1938

was very economical in everything he did. Defensively, Gans was great. His anticipation enabled him to move his head just enough to avoid big punches. Compared to Gans, Leonard was the more flashy type. He had great speed and athleticism. Leonard was one of the first fighters to take physical fitness seriously. He was also a great student of the game; he'd study his opposition, then do whatever he had to do to win. It's hard to imagine how brilliant a boxing match this would be. Gans would be stalking with his deadly right hand, while Leonard would be boxing and moving in and out. Both would land their shots, but over 15 rounds, Leonard would outpoint Gans.'

Marty Cohen, veteran promoter, manager and trainer, struggled to split them. 'This is a tough one because it's hard to imagine either man losing. Everyone who ever saw Gans said he was a natural, in the same way that, say, Babe Ruth was. He was just good at everything he did. The art of boxing was still in its early stages, and Gans was among the best of his entire era. Leonard was an evolution of Gans; he benefited from fighting when he did. What Gans was to his era, Benny was to his. He could box and punch, and he was smart; he knew every inch of the ring. What set Leonard apart from other champions is that he fought many great fighters of his time. None of them could say they didn't get a chance to beat him. I could see both hitting the deck and getting up. Leonard, however, was a better ring general, and would have been able to take control in the later rounds and win on points.'

Leading sportswriter and artist of the 1920s Robert Edgren wrote, 'Many have asked me whether or not I would consider Benny Leonard in Joe Gans's class as a lightweight champion. Right there is room for endless argument. Except in those athletic events where distances and times show exactly what performances are, it's almost impossible to compare present champions with former title holders. I'll say that Leonard has shown himself easily master of all rivals in his class today and a great lightweight. In many points he is very much like Gans, who is conceded the master boxer of all the great old-time lightweights.

'Leonard has studied anatomy to learn the effect of blows, and has picked up and tried all the best combinations used by other boxers. He practises the delivery of a blow thousands of times until he perfects it in every detail. Gans could hit equally hard with either hand. So can Leonard. But Benny has even a better left than Gans had. He either lands the knockout or starts his man going with left-hand body punches. In one thing Leonard is a greater fighter than Gans was, and entirely different in style. He is endlessly aggressive. Gans was as great a counter-hitter as Fitzsimmons, and was usually satisfied to stand back with both arms raised in guarding position to block or slap aside blows and then use his short and deadly counter strokes. Gans didn't move around much. Leonard has the flashy footwork of a bantamweight.'[150]

'Gans was greatness personified in an era of great fighters,' wrote Johnny Salak. 'He was always the master fighter – cool, exact, deadly, game. It all added up to that intangible something called class. Gans was a master at drawing a lead and getting home first with a counter blow. In later years, one of his successors on the throne, Benny Leonard, gambled in the ring along similar lines. Benny had an accurate right hand that he shot from his chest. Few fighters could judge distance as did Benny. He could left hook with dazzling speed and when he turned the right loose with knockout intention, he usually had the situation gauged to a hair breadth and accomplished his purpose.'[151]

Perhaps the most fitting testament to Gans's greatness as a fighter is the esteem in which he was held by other all-time greats. Sam Langford deemed him the greatest boxer of all time and Bob

150 Robert Edgren *Cincinnati Commercial Tribune* 27 February 1921
151 Johnny Salak *The Ring* September 1950

Fitzsimmons – the first of only two fighters in history to capture undisputed lineal world titles in three of boxing's eight traditional weight divisions – called Gans the cleverest fighter he'd ever seen. Abe Attell gave his opinion that 'Joe Gans was the greatest lightweight that ever entered a ring. In his prime no fighter of his weight was his equal.'[152]

In December 1900, Gans was beaten in two rounds by featherweight champion Terry McGovern in what was panned as a fake. The scandal brought the demise of boxing in Chicago for 25 years. Gans later admitted his part in the unfortunate travesty. The fight had been a lively betting affair. Gans himself, for all his fine qualities, had a pathetic failing for gambling. His backers were likewise men of strong gambling attachments and one can safely surmise that unseemly pressure was brought to bear upon the great boxer to make him do what he did. Gambling was not Gans's only shortcoming; he did not always take the best care of himself, often yielding to various temptations to which his sponsors exposed him.[153]

'To ask whether Gans or Leonard was the best of the lightweights shouldn't be uttered. During Gans's career, fighting was an entirely different sport. Gans fought no fewer than 19 fights over the 20 or more rounds route. Leonard's longest bouts, both with Tendler, were of 15 rounds' duration. When you speak of Leonard, you are discussing one of the most adept ringmen of all time. Leonard never was outscored in a lightweight championship fight.

'There was one big factor in which Leonard was far superior to Gans, and that was physical condition. Benny never went into a ring in defence of his lightweight championship in anything but first-class shape. It was a fetish with him. He never went out of condition between fights. Gans on the other hand rarely was in first-class

---

152 Abe Attell *Baltimore American* 15 August 1910
153 Ted Carroll *The Ring* June 1961

shape. Years ago, I discussed this with John J. McGraw, manager of the Giants, who was a close friend of Joe in their Baltimore days.

'"Gans was a marvel, but he never took care of himself. His sex life drained him; too often he was suffering from disease and how he ever went 42 rounds to beat Nelson on a foul, I never will know. Nor did he know. Had Gans kept in shape, he would have been the greatest fighter in boxing history." So much for comparisons with Leonard, and a dispute which never will be ended satisfactorily because they fought in vastly different eras.'[154]

'Tex Rickard liked Gans,' recalled Fleischer. "I never seen a more clever boxer," said Tex. "His was a different kind of cleverness. I got a kick out of Gans the day that he beat Nelson in 42 rounds on a foul. They were both pretty well battered and coming out of his dressing room, I asked Joe how he felt. 'Not bad, Mr Rickard. Can I go into your office and use the telephone? I want to make a call and I'll pay for it.' I told him to go ahead but to forget the payment. He got on the phone, called up the Western Union telegraph operator and sent a message to his mother. 'Dear mother. Am bringing home the bacon.' 'She's my best friend,' he said, 'she saves my money for me.'"'[155]

Right there was the leveller between those two great champions. Benny Leonard's feeling for his mother is a real case of filial love carried to the point where it supplants all desire for a sweetheart. 'My mother is my sweetheart,' Benny told journalist John Reed. 'She's always taken care of me. I'm lost when she isn't around.'

Joe Gans. Benny Leonard. The best? This author is happy to pick Leonard.

---

154 Charlie Vackner *The Ring* December 1966
155 Nat Fleischer *The Ring* December 1954

CHAPTER THIRTEEN

'CHARLEY WHITE, the Chicago lightweight, has made the modest demand of $25,000 for a ten-rounds no-decision contest with Benny Leonard, the lightweight champion, in response to a request for terms made by J. Frank Black, the New Jersey promoter. When Billy Gibson, manager of the champion, was informed of the terms, he said, "That throws the light on another one of the so-called contenders. I wonder what White thinks the champion should get and how much would be left for the promoter if he is entitled to that sum for a ten-round contest. "This demand should put the public wise to the fact that another of the bunk contenders who has filled the papers with challenges for the title is not sincere, and has no real desire to meet the champion. When I think of how quickly I grabbed the chance to box Freddie Welsh when he was titleholder, sending Leonard against him for a total of $1,400 for three fights, I can't help laughing at the demands being made by these publicity-seekers."'[156]

Benny was due to meet Joe Welling in a rematch in St Louis and the Chicago lad had gone to Hot Springs to prepare for the fight. Joe should have saved himself the train fare. He went the eight rounds with Benny but was hanging on at the finish, newspaper decision to champion Leonard.

---

156 *Olean Evening Herald* New York 26 February 1921

The *Boston Daily Globe* carried this special dispatch from Philadelphia. 'No wonder Benny Leonard has such a kick in his right hand. Benny carries a horseshoe in his sleep-producing mauler. For 25 years, Benny has carried this trademark of his profession. Only a few days ago, Benny's trainer discovered in the centre of his right palm, a birthmark. It was a horseshoe, one inch long and three quarters of an inch wide. At first glance, it looks like a capital C, but after the outline becomes clearer, the impression of the horseshoe is plain. "Gee, I have been accused of carrying a horseshoe in my glove before and now I guess I can't deny it," smiled the champion, as he gazed at the mark that has dented many an opponent."'[157]

The fight game was seeing a new side to Mr Leonard in February of 1921. 'CHAMPION LEONARD IN TOWN' ran a piece in the *Bridgeport Times.* 'Champion Benny Leonard is in Bridgeport today, not on fighting business but for the purpose of giving the "once over" to the Four Marxes, a tabloid musical comedy speciality which is on the bill at Poli's Theatre. Leonard, who is a singer of ability, is expected to sing one or more popular selections at the performance.'[158]

Benny the Baritone, Billy Gibson on piano?

Time for fight business, 6 June 1921, Harrison, New Jersey – 'More than 26,000 boxing fans jammed their way into the old Federal League Park to see Leonard defend the lightweight championship of the world for the third time within six months, against Rocky Kansas, the sensational little Italian from Buffalo. The gate receipts were in excess of $100,000. Every available seat had been sold before Leonard and Kansas entered the ring to the wild shouts of the multitude at an hour unseemly late for those who had hoped to get back to New York by midnight or shortly after ...

———
157 *Boston Daily Globe* 8 August 1921
158 *Bridgeport Times* Connecticut 26 February 1921

'The champion entered the ring a heavy favourite. What little betting there was found Leonard on the long end to retain his title. Ring sharps figured that everything favoured Leonard because it would be necessary for Rocky Kansas to score a knockout in order to win the title. Both boys weighed in under the stipulated 135 pounds at three o'clock in the afternoon.'[159]

'The conqueror of Richie Mitchell and Willie Jackson was the aggressor but his efforts to land on the champion went for naught. Leonard boxed beautifully at times and particularly in the last two rounds he reached the Buffalo boy's face and jaw with heavy smashes. The fourth round was the best the Buffalo challenger had during the mill. In this round Leonard was forced to the ropes twice, and Kansas succeeded in putting across some fast rights and lefts to the face and body. The champion appeared somewhat irritated in this round when Rocky tried to use his famous backhand blow. The fight went 12 rounds with the newspaper vote to champion Benny.'[160]

There was a great deal of activity around Benton Harbour, Michigan, during that first week in June as training camps were erected for lightweight champion Benny Leonard and Sailor Freedman of Chicago, who were to meet in the open-air arena for promoter Floyd Fitzsimmons on Monday, 4 July. A corps of men under the direction if Ike Bernstein were hard at work as the fighters were to begin training two weeks before the fight.

Leonard was not too happy as the fight date approached, as he informed a friend in a letter. Two days before that date, the Battle of the Century was being promoted in Jersey City by Tex Rickard, the heavyweight title bout between champion Jack Dempsey and the idol of France, Georges Carpentier, with thousands travelling to the fight from all points of the compass.

---

159 *Middletown Daily Herald* New York 7 June 1921
160 *New Britain Herald* Connecticut 7 June 1921

'I had my heart set on seeing Dempsey and Carpentier,' wrote Benny, 'but Billy – who is both pal and manager to me – thought I'd better go west and meet this Freedman fellow. I don't care about the $15,000 – what's that in my young life? – but Billy doesn't want to give anyone a chance to say I'm dodging them, so the Freedman fight for me. Incidentally, while I don't know much about this Freedman boy, I'm not going to take chances like I did with Charley White. I'm going to be in condition this time and the fight won't last long if I have my way.'[161] Fighting White in this same arena in July 1920, Benny was left-hooked out of the ring before climbing back in to knock Charley out in round nine.

From Benton Harbour, 22 June, came a report, 'That Benny Leonard, the lightweight champion, is nearing the finish of his fighting career is a fact well known among his intimate friends. In a letter to promoter Fitzsimmons, the champion makes the frank admission that he intends to retire within six months, or "when I have met all the worthwhile opponents in the field. I have two good ears and my nose is just as nature wanted it to be.

'"I have never won any beauty prizes, but I'm proud of the fact that I have exposed these parts to perhaps a million boxing gloves – and still preserve them. I mean to keep them too.

'"I am worth half a million. I have made investments that pay sufficient to keep myself and my family for the rest of our lives. No, the world is mistaken if it thinks Benny is going to go the way of many others in the profession."'[162]

'Benny has been going at such a good clip that few expect the Chicago man to defeat him, but many are hoping for a draw. The sailor has been busily engaged in developing a left hook for the past year or more, figuring that this blow will bother Leonard more than anything else he could use.

---

161 *Fort Wayne Journal Gazette* Indiana 19 June 1921
162 *Racine Journal News* Wisconsin 22 June 1921

'The champion arrived in town 29 June and went through a brisk workout, boxing six rounds, two each with Gene Watson, Teddy Murphy and Mike Snyder and at the end showed no signs of fatigue. Fight experts who watched him were of the opinion that he was in top condition for the coming mill. His judgement of distance was good and his blows invariably went to the mark in his workout. Sailor Freedman today boxed a string of sparring partners, including Soldier Travis, Sammy Frager and Johnny Allen. Manager Herschie Miller is happy with the sailor's preparation.'[163]

The bad news broke on 2 July. 'Benny Leonard, the world lightweight champion, today sent word to Floyd Fitzsimmons, promoter of the fight in which Leonard was to defend his title Monday against Sailor Freedman of Chicago, that he would be unable to go on. Joe Benjamin, Pacific Coast lightweight, will be substituted for Leonard. From Grand Rapids, Michigan, announcement was made early this morning over telephone by E.T. McAuley, secretary of the Michigan state boxing commission, that it had been decided not to permit the substitution of Joe Benjamin of San Francisco for Benny Leonard in his scheduled fight 4 July with Sailor Freedman, and that the fight had been cancelled. Leonard, according to word received here today, was willing to fight Freedman but the Michigan commission decided he was not in fit shape.'[164]

As promoter Fitzsimmons contemplated suicide, Tex Rickard announced that his net profit on the Dempsey–Carpentier fight amounted to $550,000. Rickard was truly the man with the Midas touch …

The Michigan boxing commission was reported to be on its way to Chicago to investigate the illness of Benny Leonard, the lightweight champion who pulled out of a bout in Benton Harbour

———
163 *Burlington Hawk Eye* Iowa 29 June 1921
164 *Quincy Whig Journal* Illinois 3 July 1921

against Sailor Freedman, causing the bout to be cancelled. With fingers crossed, promoter Floyd Fitzsimmons tentatively set a new date for the fight of 16 July. The commission stated that if it was found that Leonard was not ill enough to justify calling off the fight, he would be barred from Michigan for a period. No doubt Benny had a legitimate explanation for the commissioners as he did not go through with the Freedman bout until November, taking the sailor for an eight-round trip in Philadelphia.

It was about this time that Joe Downey was working in Bridgeport, Connecticut, where he was superintendent on the construction of the new Poli Theatre on Main Street. Downey got talking to a reporter from the *Bridgeport Times* one day and the fellow went back to the office and ran this through his typewriter. 'Mister Fight Fan, did you know that Benny Leonard, champion lightweight boxer of the world, was knocked out in his first ring battle? That's what happened to champion Benny and Joseph Downey was one who saw this notable event in Leonard's career. Downey, who is a close friend of Leonard and his manager, Billy Gibson, was recounting the incident yesterday to the writer.

'It happened about 14 years back in Billy Gibson's old Fairmont A. C. in New York. According to Downey, Leonard was a rabid fight fan like the majority of East Side boys. It made it his business to "crash the gates" in the Fairmont at every show. "Couldn't keep him out," said Downey. "Whenever there was a fight, Benny Leonard would be in the rafters or a 'stowaway' in some other part of the house until the fights started. One night, 'Kid' Coleman was on the programme to box, but his opponent failed to appear. It was then the present champion got his opportunity to climb the ladder to fame.

'"Benny pleaded with Gibson to go on and the latter consented. Benny, however, found Coleman too crafty for him, and went out by the kayo route in the third round. That little setback didn't worry

Benny. He came back with a plea for another bout, his request being granted. According to Downey, Leonard showed vast improvement and put up a good fight. He was a persevering youngster," said Downey, "and it's due to these qualities that he made good."'[165]

Freedman had filled his time in waiting for Benny by taking on a visiting Englishman, Ernie Rice, in a 15-round bout at Madison Square Garden. In his first bout in America, Rice had beaten Richie Mitchell, who quit in round four with a broken hand. Ernie was out of luck in his Garden fight with Freedman, suffering a cut eye and taking a beating from the rugged Chicago fighter. The bout ended after 31 seconds of round seven when Rice's seconds threw in the towel. The sailor was sometimes called 'Freedman' or 'Freedman' but whatever you called him, he couldn't beat Benny Leonard when they eventually got together for a no-decision bout in Philadelphia on 22 November 1921.

'Seven thousand followers of fistiana jammed their way into the Ice Palace last night to see Leonard outbox Freedman in eight rounds,' reported Perry Lewis. 'The loser was more aggressive than the titleholder, and much of the time carried the battle to his distinguished opponent, but Benny landed more blows, cleaner blows, and harder blows than did the nautical person. But although the champion won six of the eight rounds, losing the third and getting an even break in the fifth, his showing was a bitter disappointment to his many followers.'[166]

'Every time business gets bad, a boxer goes back. Benny Leonard hasn't been working much,' wrote Henry L. Farrell for United Press. 'The lightweights all pass him up because he's too good. They want a fortune to be knocked off and Benny has to associate with the welters. Last night, Leonard went eight rounds against Sailor Freedman in Philadelphia and they say this morning, "he

165 By Old Sport *Bridgeport Times* Connecticut 1 November 1921
166 Perry Lewis *Philadelphia Inquirer* 23 November 1921

was terrible." The insiders say that he has gone back, that he can't make the weight, that he's afraid of his hands, that his judgement is gone and his speed vanished.'[167]

After that prognosis by the so-called insiders, Benny Leonard should have been thinking about retirement. Tex Rickard liked Benny and he signed him up for the main event at Madison Square Garden to defend his title against Rocky Kansas on 10 November 1922, then watched the fight public scrambling for tickets.

Rocky Kansas was born Rocco Tozzo. He was a chunky powerhouse standing just 5ft 2in, a southpaw slugger from Buffalo in upstate New York. He had boxed Leonard over 12 rounds in June 1921 and he jumped at the title shot when Rickard called his number. Rocky had chalked up 34 knockouts in winning 101 fights and he was determined to make Benny number 35. Tex Rickard only had 15,000 seats in his Garden and on fight night everyone in New York and quite a few from Buffalo were hell-bent on getting into the Gotham arena.

'Policemen, mounted and afoot, battled for hours last night with crowds outside Madison Square Garden, who, because of an oversale of tickets, were barred from the Benny Leonard–Rocky Kansas lightweight championship battle when the fire department closed the doors. To add to the riotous confusion, forged tickets made their appearance and holders of them were driven away. The police made one arrest after two sailors pointed out a man who they said had victimised them of $15. The management announced that holders of *bona fide* tickets who had not been able to get in could get restitution today.'[168]

The guys and gals who couldn't get into the Garden that night were in a worse mood next morning reading the sporting headlines. 'LEONARD SAVES TITLE KNOCKING KANSAS DOWN

---

167 Henry L. Farrell *Fort Wayne News* Indiana 23 November 1921
168 *Hammond Lake County Times* Indiana 11 February 1922

IN ELEVENTH'… 'BENNY LEONARD HAS A HARD JOB KEEPING HIS CROWN' … 'BENNY LEONARD WINS AFTER TAKING LACING FROM ROCKY KANSAS'. 'BUFFALO ITALIAN KNOCKS BRONX BOY'S STOCK DOWN WITH TERRIFIC MAULING' ran the headline on Damon Runyon's ringside review of the evening.

'Benny Leonard, lightweight champion, had Rocky Kansas spread out on the floor as flat as a welcome mat in the 11th round at Madison Square Garden last night. In fact, Rocky's hairy chest gave him something of the aspect of a mat. A left hook to the chin cut Kansas' sturdy legs from under him for a few fleeting seconds, but after he listened to the sing-song of the timekeeper for a brief spell, the Buffalo Italian got up. He remained up for the rest of the 15 rounds. The judges gave the decision to Leonard and no one demurred over the evening's proceedings except a large number of the champion's earnest admirers who had wagered that he would knock Rocky out.'[169]

'Rocky Kansas is not the world's lightweight champion because class most always tells,' wrote Henry L. Farrell. 'Matched against the skill and grace of Benny Leonard, king of the lightweights, the Buffalo Italian ran second in a 15-round bout last night in Madison Square Garden. Scoring a knockdown in the 11th round and earning a wide margin in nine of the 15, Leonard held his title, but he was at times a worried and a badly mussed-up champion.

'The black locks, seldom mussed by any bold challenger, were all on end and his lips were puffed and his face was a crimson smear from a stream that trickled from his nose. It was a piston-like right to the heart that took the steam out of Kansas in the ninth round when it looked all the way like the dumpy little Rocky had a fine chance to win. For eight rounds, Kansas carried the fight to the

---

169 Damon Runyon *Salt Lake City Deseret News* 11 February 1922

champion and the only register that Leonard could get out of vicious right hooks to the jaw was a smile on the face of his target.

'It looked like a knockout in the 11th round and only the iron ribs and steel jaw of the Buffalo boy saved him. The backhand blow, barred in most every place but New York, instead of winning the fight for Kansas, did more than anything else to make him the loser. He missed a right hook in the 11th and tried to swing back with the same motion, but Leonard beat him with a hard left hook to the chin and he dropped for a count of nine. He was a fortunate boy to finish the round.'[170]

'I fought the best fight that I ever fought in my 14 years' experience in the ring last night against Benny Leonard in the Garden,' said Rocky Kansas at the Pennsylvania Hotel today, 'but it wasn't good enough to win. He is the greatest fighter that ever fought in the lightweight class, which is saying something. Benny had me so bewildered in that 11th round when he dropped me on my back that I didn't know what hit me. At any rate I dropped like a log, but I didn't lose my senses completely. I watched the referee moving his hand up and down, but I couldn't hear the counting. I think I might have had a chance to get a decision had I not run foul of that Dempsey-like smash.'

'Dan Rogers, the manager of Kansas, was well pleased with the showing of his protégé. "That boy Leonard is a wonder," said Rogers. "I don't think Dempsey is more popular. What a reception he received when he was introduced. Three hundred fans came down from Buffalo and most of them won plenty of money, as they received all the way from 8 to 5 to 3 to 1 against the chances of his staying the limit. I guess the boys must have cleaned up $100,000.'[171]

The *World* had Vincent Treanor in Leonard's corner to get Benny's story of the fight, with the champion admitting, "I fought

---

170 Henry L. Farrell *Fort Wayne News* Indiana 11 February 1922
171 Alex Sullivan *New York Evening World* 11 February 1922

wrong. I held back my body punches too long. I should have used my left hooks to the body earlier, but 'Gib' kept yelling, 'Left hook, left hook,' and I tried to follow his advice. I hurt my right hand early hitting Rocky on the elbow and I had to save it."

'Thus did Benny Leonard try to excuse himself, strangely, after going through perhaps his hardest and best fight of his career, when he got back to his mother, sisters and brothers last night for the open house celebration that always follows his battles. He had telephoned his mother from his dressing room at the Garden the first-hand news of his victory, as he never fails to do, whether in New York, California or any other place in the country. He couldn't shed his fighting togs too quickly to get out to a waiting automobile, which whisked him to his house on Upper Seventh Avenue. There, he had to submit to the motherly inspection and with only a swollen left eye which he had reduced with hot towels in his dressing room, so mother wouldn't be alarmed, he passed the maternal muster.

'"My boy, you've been working hard again," she said as tears came into her eyes. "Just think, 15 long rounds."

'"Do you know, I enjoyed one of the happiest moments of my life at the Garden," he began saying. "It was in that 11th round, when I knocked Rocky down and the crowd got up and cheered. I don't think I ever heard so much noise before. I had a funny feeling that perhaps they thought I was champion long enough and wanted to see me beaten, but when that roar went up it made me feel great. Even at that moment when a fellow's mind is on his opponent, I was thinking only of the tremendous approval of my work shown by the crowd."'[172]

'It was his wonderful head that gave him his mastery over the challenger,' the *National Police Gazette* wrote of his 1922 title defence vs Rocky Kansas.

---

172 Vincent Treanor *New York Evening World* 11 February 1922

The esteemed wordsmith Heywood Broun was in the Garden that night and was moved to write an essay praising the young champion, the one he called 'The Orthodox Champion'.

'The entire orthodox world owes a debt to Benny Leonard. In all the other arts, philosophies, religions and whatnots, conservation seems to be crumbling before the attacks of the radicals. Benny Leonard remains the white hope of the orthodox. No performer in any art has ever been more correct than Leonard. He follows closely all the best traditions of the past. His left-hand jab could stand without revision in any textbook. The manner in which he feints, ducks, sidesteps and hooks is unimpeachable. The crouch contributed by some of the modernists is not in the repertoire of Leonard. He stands up straight like a gentleman and a champion, and is always ready to hit with either hand.

'Rocky Kansas does nothing according to rule. His fighting style is as formless as the prose of Gertrude Stein. But with the opening gong, Rocky Kansas tore into Leonard. He was gauche and inaccurate but terribly persistent. In the first clinch, Benny's hair was rumpled and a moment later his nose began to bleed. The incident was a shock to us. Here were two young men in the ring and one was quite correct in everything he did and the other was all wrong. And the wrong one was winning. Macaulay turned over twice in his grave when Kansas began to lead with his right hand.

'But traditions are not to be despised. Even though his hair was mussed and his nose bleeding, Benny continued faithful to the established order.

'At last his chance came. The young child of nature who was challenging for the championship dropped his guard and Leonard hooked a powerful and entirely orthodox blow to the conventional point of the jaw. Down went Rocky Kansas. His past life flashed before him during the nine seconds in which he remained on the floor and he wished that he had been more faithful as a child in heeding the advice of his boxing teacher.

'After all, the old masters did know something. There is still a kick in style, and tradition carries a nasty wallop.'[173]

---

173 Heywood Broun *The Fireside Book of Boxing* Edited W. C. Heinz 1961

CHAPTER FOURTEEN

FIGHTING OUT of New Orleans, 24-year-old Pal Moran had put 70 fights in the book and the promoter of the Louisiana Auditorium figured he would make a good match with Benny Leonard. Moran thought so too, and so did Billy Gibson. He had to keep his champion busy and getting well paid for doing so. Billy looked up the train schedules for Louisiana and in no time at all had the tickets booked and Benny packing his fight gear. He liked to travel.

The night of 25 February 1922, world lightweight champion Benny Leonard had to travel a tough ten rounds to come out with the newspaper decision over the durable local man. Pal made a remarkable showing, sticking his chin out to the champion on several occasions and rushing him at times. He had the better of two rounds and held Leonard even in another. Benny fought most of the battle with his left hand, saying afterwards he had injured his right hand hitting Moran on the head in the first round. He seemed fresh after the bout. Moran looked tired but was still strong. The champion weighed in at 139 pounds, 134½ for Moran …

The local fighter won the first round, rushing at Leonard and barely missed with a smashing right to the jaw. Moran spun him around with a right high on the head. Benny seemed over-anxious and was wild with his punches. Pal came out strong for round two, put a hard right to the body, then a right uppercut and a solid right to the face. Benny got in gear and landed hooks to the body that steadied Moran and he took the round.

Round three and Benny was in charge, landing both hands to the body. He spun Moran by the elbow and rocked him with a left hook, then another, and at the bell Pal had a bloody nose. It was Leonard's round and he won rounds four, five and six. There was a good crowd in that night and they cheered Pal through the seventh as he got home a left to the body, a right uppercut and a left hook. Coming out of a clinch, Moran pulled a perfect pivot punch, landing a heavy smash to Leonard's jaw. Benny jabbed twice but Moran hooked to the head and landed a right to the body, and at the bell he had the honours. In the eighth, he fought the champion even and the New York boy had to put in a strong finish through the ninth and tenth to come home a winner. Moran was tired at the final bell but fighting desperately and gamely. The crowd gave both boys a standing ovation and went home happy.

Three weeks later, Benny was back home and booked for Boston for a ten-round date with Johnny Clinton, lightweight champion of New England. It was the first time since the state boxing commission had been set up that a no-decision bout had been allowed. The match was billed as an exhibition and that is what it was. As far as Benny was concerned, they could call it whatever they wanted. He was promised $15,000.

'There were about 4,000 people at the arena, a storm obviously kept a lot of folks at home. Speculators figured on making a harvest but were badly stung and before the main event they were pushing $10 tickets for one dollar. Benny toyed with Clinton most of the way and Johnny didn't try to annoy him. In one round, he did come out of his shell and sent a couple of rights to the jaw. They were open-glove hits and the champion just smiled. Leonard showed enough to make the fans realise he is the great fighter he is credited with being. He did such wonderful feinting that he had Clinton all at sea most of the time.'[174]

New York, 16 June – 'FORTUNE FOR BENNY LEONARD IN MONTH – Lightweight Champion Should Make $250,000 in His Next Three Fights – A new fighting record is about to be hung out to dry by Benny Leonard, prince of the royal family of pugilism, who began today to dust off his armour like a plumed knight in preparation for jousts with three of the toughest opponents in the business within the short space of 32 days. Jack Britton, world's welterweight champion, Lew Tendler of Philadelphia and Rocky Kansas of Buffalo will meet him.

'Three bouts within a month will net Benny at least a quarter of a million dollars, and, if he knocks out Britton, he will step out of the ring the welterweight champion of the world, the fourth fighting man since Napoleon to hold two championships. As Britton will not be down to 135 pounds, Leonard's lightweight coronet will not be in danger. Leonard's summer season will open 26 June at New York's Velodrome with Britton in a no-decision bout. Eight days later he will meet Rocky Kansas at Michigan City, Indiana in an Independence Day battle for his crown, and on 27 July he will be back in New Jersey in a championship go with Lew Feldman, recognised as the most formidable of contenders. After that, he may rest for a while. No modern champion has such a record.'[175]

'Velodromes are steeply banked wooden cycling tracks. The open-air Bronx Velodrome was located on the east side of Broadway at 225th Street in the Marble Hill sections of the Bronx. Constructed in 1920, with seating for 23,000, it was known primarily for banked-track bicycle races of all types, including motorcycle-paced races. In the 1920s, the Velodrome was also the site of a number of major boxing matches, especially by bantamweights (118 pounds).

174   Daniel J. Saunders *The Boston Globe* 20 March 1922
175   *Oakland Tribune* California 16 June 1922

Bantamweight champions Johnny Buff, Abe Goldstein, Joe Lynch and Charley Phil Rosenberg all fought there to enthusiastic audiences.

'But the most important and perhaps the strangest contest in Velodrome history took place on 26 June 1922, a scheduled 15-rounder fought before an overflow house of 26,000. The bout created considerable excitement because the rivals were both current world champions: Benny Leonard, 26-year-old lightweight champion, then at the peak of his form, versus Jack Britton, 37-year-old welterweight titleholder who was well past his prime.'[176]

Benny Leonard tipped the scales at 139¼ pounds at the afternoon weigh-in as Britton scaled 146¼.

The betting was brisk, with Leonard going in a 3 to 1 favourite.

Referee appointed by the New York commission was Patsy Haley. Leonard brought a record of 158–20–8, with 61 knockouts. The veteran, three inches taller at 5ft 8in, showed statistics as 193–40–37, with 30 kayoes …

The opening contest, preceding the main event, saw Joey Leonard, younger brother of the lightweight champ, 130 pounds, take a decision over Sammy Marco, 133½, in a four-round bout. It was Leonard's professional debut. That pleased Benny.

Jack Britton stepped into the ring at 9.35pm, followed two minutes later by the lightweight champion. Both fighters received long rounds of applause. Ring the bell!

Leonard took the offensive in the first round with a left to Jack's nose and the veteran missed a left swing for the body. Both men were cautious, Benny to avoid Britton's left hook and Jack to keep away from the lightweight champion's straight rights. There were few punches of note in the opening three minutes. Things warmed up in round two. A few light blows to the jaw and a few clinches

---

176 Lawrence S. Ritter *East Side, West Side* 1998

before Britton staggered Benny with a right to the jaw. Leonard came back with a series of lefts to the face and a solid right to the jaw turned Jack at the bell.

In the third, a series of lefts to the face had Britton backing around the ring, and Jack attacked the body with right hands. He sent a straight left to the face and Benny was bleeding from a cut upper lip. They exchanged hard lefts and rights at close quarters and Leonard was backed into a corner at the bell. Into round four and Leonard staggered Britton with a hard right to the jaw and followed with a series of lefts to the face. Britton scored with hard lefts to the face and body then forced Benny back to the ropes with a body attack. They were fighting hard at the bell.

Round five and Britton took the offensive, but landed few hard blows. They exchanged lefts and rights at close quarters and the welterweight champion appeared to be having the better of the exchanges. In the sixth, Leonard caught Britton on the jaw with several straight rights and Jack came back with right swings to the head. He was cut in the mouth from a straight left but he had the better of a brisk exchange on the ropes. Round seven and Benny appeared to be taking things easily looking for a chance to land a knockout punch. Britton found his jaw with right and left hooks. They staggered each other with rights to the head and the crowd roared them on …

'The contest was interesting at all stages with both men appearing to be fighting their best. Despite his 37 years, Britton displayed no end of activity and when called upon brought all of his famed ring generalship to bear against his opponent. The result prevented Leonard from achieving his greatest ambition – to become holder of both the lightweight and welterweight world titles. No lightweight champion has ever been able to win the welterweight title. Kid Lavigne, one of the great lightweights of other days, tried it 27 years ago but was stopped by Mysterious Billy Smith.'[177] Round eight opened with both men swapping leather at a brisk pace, going for head and body. Benny worked his left to the head effectively but was shaken twice as Britton hooked his left to the jaw. In a hectic exchange at close quarters, they punched to the body and Britton appeared to be getting the better of his man.

Leonard jumped from his corner in the ninth and forced Britton around the ring with rights to the head, but the old man's defensive work was at its best and he survived to fight back with a stream of lefts to the face to pin Benny in a neutral corner. He tried to fight back with right swings to the head and caught a hard right to the jaw for his trouble. The lightweight champ was shaken in the tenth round with overhand rights to the head and Britton seemed willing to mix it up, giving as good as he got.

Coming out for work in round 11, the little Hebrew sent hard rights and lefts to the head and Britton reeled to the ropes. He threw some back but this was Benny's best round of the fight and the veteran had to take some of those hard right crosses to the jaw before the bell brought relief. The old fox of the ring was craftily defending his welterweight title against the attack of the young lightweight king, who had nothing whatever to lose.

'There were times when Leonard stunned Britton,' observed Nat Fleischer, 'noticeably with powerful right crosses or left hooks to the jaw which sent the welterweight king reeling about the ring. But invariably Leonard hesitated in following what appeared to be a big advantage and the crowd seemed to sense that he wasn't trying to win the bout. At times, after he had Britton going, he missed punches that carried damaging power and Britton was enabled to recover his equilibrium whenever danger threatened …

---

177 *North Adams Transcript* 27 June 1922

'Britton had seven of the first 12 rounds. In the sixth, seventh and eighth rounds, Leonard discarded his caution and carried the fighting to his opponent at a rapid rate. In the 11th, after the crowd had razzed Benny for not following up an advantage he had obtained by crashing a hard blow to Britton's jaw, Leonard opened up and seemed bent on scoring a knockout. He almost succeeded in crushing Britton under the power of his blows in a furious two-handed assault which had the welterweight champion reeling and the crowd in a frenzy of excitement.'[178]

In the 12th round, Benny jabbed to the face and Britton sent hard hooks to the jaw from left and right. He shook Leonard with rights to the body and left hooks to the jaw. They exchanged light punches to the head and body. Britton's defensive work failed to show in this round. He used offensive tactics altogether.

Round 13, unlucky for some. 'Benny's left cheek was cut as he came out for this round and his hair was very much mussed. He rushed Britton across the ring with a left which bounced off Jack's ribs and up to his head. For the next minute, Britton did all the leading. Then, as he blocked Leonard's right swing he pushed Benny away so forcibly that Leonard went down on the floor and rocked there to his shoulder blades. Britton didn't think this an infraction of the rules and he actually let Benny do the apologising. Jack was using a lot of rough stuff now, pulling his glove across Leonard's face, breaking from close quarters and generally mussing Benny up. They stood together fiddling in the centre of the ring when Leonard suddenly hooked a left to the pit of Britton's stomach. Few saw the punch. It was dangerously low.

'Britton began to sink slowly to the ground. As one knee touched the floor, Leonard walked in and hit Britton a left punch on the face. Britton, evidently in pain, made no attempt to protect himself

---

178 Nat Fleischer *Leonard the Magnificent* 1947

or block the punch. Instead, he nodded for his manager to come into the ring. He was reaching to his groin with his left hand. The timekeeper, Ed Purdy, said he had begun to count as soon as Britton's knee touched the floor. He had reached nine when Leonard landed the left punch. Referee Haley stepped between the men and pushed Leonard back. He assisted Britton to rise and escorted him to his corner. The whole thing happened so suddenly that no one knew what had really occurred.

'Charley Leonard, Benny's brother, jumped into the ring to find out how Haley had decided, and Britton's manager also got inside the ropes to see what it was all about. Veteran ring announcer Joe Humphreys, after consulting Haley, told the crowd that Leonard had been disqualified for hitting Britton when down.'[179]

In 1956, Dan Daniel of *The Ring* magazine had started conducting a series looking into odd happenings in the ring. The Leonard–Britton contest was number three. 'What prompted Leonard to do this? Leonard said that Britton had had one knee off the canvas and was not legally down. This hardly hit the cognoscenti as a plausible explanation of how Benny had come to lose the welterweight title on a foul. That Britton could have arisen before the count of ten appeared to be highly improbable.

'The publicity was tremendous, but there was one big discrepancy between it and fact. Leonard didn't want the welterweight title. He was doing very well as champion of an exciting lightweight class. He was quite willing – yes, even eager – to have Britton continue as welterweight champion. For Leonard, the heavier laurels would have meant nothing. Perhaps a bit of added prestige, but nothing in money.

'Then, too, Benny liked Britton personally. Everybody, in fact, liked Britton. He was a real credit to boxing. Now, as a 37-year-old

---

179 Vincent Treanor *New York Evening World* 27 June 1922

veteran, he couldn't have much more to go. Why not let him keep the welterweight title, with what financial returns it meant to him. This, it seemed, was Leonard's reasoning ... Benny was positive he could whip the "old man," perhaps knock him out. But this he didn't want to do. Yet how could Benny not win and at the same time suffer no loss in prestige? No fighter ever has had a keener pride in himself than Leonard. He didn't want to lose even to a heavier rival. And, yet, how could he have his cake and eat it, too? It was a ticklish situation.'

In his summing up, *The Ring* Detective asked, 'Does the evidence point to a deliberate foul? Does it indicate that Benny wanted Britton to keep the welter title? Or is there room for doubt, and the conclusion that Leonard, behind on points, actually did lose his head and perpetrate a foul without meaning to do so? The court hands down this decision – guilty of deliberate foul.'[180]

Mannie Seamon, who trained Benny through his championship years, told the story of the Britton fight in a series for the British *Sunday Empire News* in 1948. I have that series in my files but unfortunately I missed that issue. Fortunately, author Ronald K. Fried, in his fine 1991 book *Corner Men,* was able to tell the story.

'Leonard trained hard and was in great shape for the Britton fight, and I'm sure he would have won. But for some reason which I do not know to this day, he just didn't have to [win]. After the weigh-in, Benny's manager, the late Billy Gibson, told Leonard, "I'm sorry I've got to say this, but you can't win this fight tonight." Leonard started to cry and said, "Gib, I'm in such great condition, and I know I can win. And my friends are betting on me." I'm sure that if Gibson had told him earlier, there would have been no fight.

'But at the New York Velodrome in the Bronx that night, we had the awful sight of the clever Leonard having to stand flat-footed and

---

180 Dan Daniel *The Ring* January 1957

let Britton jab him. Leonard looked so bad that as he was going out for the 13th round, I said, "Benny, you're a little too flat-footed. It looks too bad. You've got to get on your toes and hit this fellow a few punches." Leonard walked out, hit Britton a vicious body punch, and Britton went down. The referee counted seven. Britton tried to get up, but it was obvious he couldn't.

'Then Leonard realised that he had to lose. Ice-cool, he walked over, and when the referee said nine with Britton still on the floor, he hit Britton a right to the head and lost on a foul. Whatever else he had done, he had saved his friends, because 99 per cent of the wagering was on terms of "Foul, no bet."

'And so Seamon explained Benny Leonard's most peculiar performance.'[181]

In his third fight with Jack Britton in New York on 26 June 1922, the jury finds Benny Leonard guilty as charged.

---

181 Ronald K. Fried *Corner Men* 1991

CHAPTER FIFTEEN

'THE LEONARD family started the evening with a bang. Brother Joey, who Benny thinks will be the next lightweight boss, went four laps against Sammy Marco. Joe was given the judge's decision. He is a likely-looking lad and made a big impression in his professional debut. John A. Drake, the old time plunging partner of John W. Gates, watched Joey Leonard very closely from the ringside. "He'll be a good one," he said, "but just like a two-year-old race horse, he's got to learn the game. There's no better place to do it than right in there before a crowd."'[182]

In the main event, the pride and joy of the family, world lightweight champion Benny, had brought disgrace by striking Jack Britton when he was down on the canvas, thereby losing his contest for the world welterweight championship on a disqualification. Brother Charley had been suspended by the New York commission for jumping into the ring while Jack Britton was still kneeling on the canvas.

In press rooms of the city's newspapers, sportswriters hammered their typewriters well into the early hours, furrowed brows trying to figure out what really happened out there in the Bronx Velodrome.

---

182 Richard Freyer *New York Evening World* 27 June 1922

Jack Sheehan, the veteran referee, wrote in his column, 'It always has and I suppose it always will be after an unexpected happening takes place in the ring game to have some of the extra shrewd wink knowingly and pretend to assume an aspect of suspicious discreet silence that there was a "Mule in the Stall," and that the contest was not on the level.

'Coming out of the Velodrome after the Britton and Leonard whirl, I heard one young man advance the opinion that the contest was all cooked up for Britton to be returned a winner, and on the unsupported and unsubstantiated statement of this fellow the cry was taken up by others. I heard the very same thing over on the Jerome Avenue line on my way downtown. I, for one, am clearly of the opinion that the contest was fought out on its merits, and at no time during the period that the men were fighting was there the least hint of frame-up or scandal. I am inclined to the belief that Benny suffered from ring blindness rather than design when he let go the blow that caused him to be sent to his corner in disgrace for the first time in his wonderful fighting career.'[183]

'Says Leonard Wanted to Lose' ran W. O. McGeehan's headline in the *New York Herald*.

'It is my conviction that Leonard did not want to get the verdict from Britton. Why he wanted to lose I do not know, for who can fathom the weird, inscrutable mind of the clean-cut young business man in pugilism? There was a motive, of course, for so self-possessed a business man as Leonard has shown himself to be does not do anything without a motive. I am not going to get a headache for myself puzzling out Benny's motive. However, it was as plain as a new cauliflower ear that Benny did not want to win that bout Monday night.

'Some of the customers were a bit indignant over the affair, but it seemed to me that the weather Monday night was too pleasant

183 Jack Sheehan *The Boston Post* 28 June 1922

to be wasted in indignation. The customers got plenty of fresh air and a beautiful view of a slate-coloured twilight, for the Velodrome boxing arena is delightfully situated. All of the customers were not agitated needlessly over the affair. Mr Arnold Rothstein, whose name was so unjustly associated with that of Mr Abe Attell in connection with the fixing of the Cincinnati–White Sox series, left the arena with an air of philosophical calm which might well be adopted by the rest of the customers.'[184]

'Another one of those things has gone down on fistiana's books for future unfolding,' wrote Henry L. Farrell for *United Press*. 'Perhaps someday, when Jack Britton and Benny Leonard are old and garrulous, they will tell what happened, or what led up to the incident in the 13th round of their fight last night, when Leonard took a swing at Britton while the latter was down, and lost on a foul. The referee was as much in the dark as each of the 25,000, but he spoke for them when he screamed at Leonard, "What in the hell did you do that for?"

'"He wasn't down," said Benny. "He had his knee off the floor."'[185]

'The gentle art of fisticuffs, New York state model,' reported Davis J. Walsh, 'received a body blow more painful than Jack Britton received Monday night, and was fouled more heinously than Jack Britton was fouled when he was smacked with a left hook by Benny Leonard as he knelt on one knee near the end of the 13th round. If Leonard was determined to lose, it wasn't necessary to gain his point by fouling.

'If Leonard was determined to win, he must have known that he couldn't do it by socking a gentleman who was in no legal position to be socked. Leonard is far too wise in ring lore to commit a *faux pas* of that kind, although many of his friends claimed that, in reality, Benny lost his head. If so, it was the first time the lightweight champion had

184 W. O. McGeehan *The Boston Post* 28 June 1922
185 Henry L. Farrell *Madison Wisconsin State Journal* 28 June 1922

exhibited symptoms of ring hysteria. Another and final point made by some of the post-mortem debaters was that Leonard, knowing that he was beaten, preferred to lose on a foul rather than have an official decision go against him. That theory is not altogether impossible … However, those who decry the proceedings as a raw piece of business are in the majority. In making their claim, they point to the fact that Leonard was just starting to show something, that he had taken the 12th round by a wide margin, and that the left hook to the body, on which Britton's claim of foul was disallowed by Haley, had really hurt Jack badly. That, in brief, with Britton on the floor and Haley counting, Leonard was all set to win, but selected the one method by which he was certain of losing.'[186]

Apart from the brief suspension handed out to Benny's brother, Charley, the New York commission took no action on the Leonard–Britton fight. It was consigned to ring history. The champion carried on with business; he had two major fights scheduled for July 1922, Rocky Kansas and Lew Feldman …

Fighting a tough guy like Rocky Kansas on the Independence Day holiday was never going to be easy, but lightweight champion Benny Leonard was fit and raring to go in what would be his fourth contest with the boy from Buffalo. They had gone ten rounds in Rocky's hometown in 1916, Benny taking the newspaper decision. Harrison, New Jersey was the site of the second bout, 12 rounds, with the lightweight champion on top. Rocky got his big moment in February 1922, a crack at the title in Madison Square Garden. Rocky climbed off the deck in round 11 after suffering his first ever knockdown, and was fighting back at the end of the 15th round. Manager Dan Rogers had badgered promoter Floyd Fitzsimmons to get his boy the fight he wanted more than anything, and the big day had arrived.

---

186 Davis J. Walsh *Quincy Daily Herald* Illinois 30 June 1922

CHAPTER FIFTEEN

Everybody, it seemed, had arrived in Michigan City, Indiana. Thousands of fight fans poured into the city. Dust-covered automobiles arrived from all directions shortly after daybreak. The people came by special trains and boats. The main streets of the city were jammed. Farmers from the nearby countryside came in wagons and buggies to give their families their first taste of boxing. Michigan City took on the appearance of an oil town at the height of the boom. Food was at a premium and only obtainable after a long wait. Movie places did a land-office business offering about the only place to rest in town. Kerb-stones and lawns were littered with weary fans.

Yet, with 24 hours to go, there was a threat that the fight might not take place. The decision as to whether the contest would be allowed rested with the officials of Laporte County, in which Michigan City was located, state governor Warren T. McCray declared on the eve of the contest. Following announcement from the governor's office that the contest would be prohibited if it should be adjudged by the Laporte County officials as being a prize fight, the sheriff at Michigan City, William E. Austiss, said it was his belief that the bout would conform to the Indiana statute which prohibits prize fighting but permits boxing contests.[187]

Promoter Fitzsimmons had built his brand new concrete arena in a vast hole scooped out of the Lake Michigan beach, located on the eastern edge of the city. The six-inch elevation for each row of seats makes the back row 25 feet higher than the first. The bleacher section on the east side will accommodate 10,000; seats are painted an inky blue to soften the glare of the sun.

'They tell me Kansas says he is going to take me,' Benny told the *Associated Press*. 'While I know I'm going against the toughest of all the lightweight contenders, I know who is going to win. Yet no

187 *Lincoln Nebraska State Journal* 4 July 1922

champion is invincible always. A sock on the chin is a sock on the chin in anybody's league. And Kansas can hit. I won't weigh heavy. I'll need speed for Kansas can travel fast for ten rounds … He says he has been ahead of me at the end of ten rounds in our last two scraps. He won't be this time.'

Rocky was just as confident, saying, 'I never went into a battle with more confidence than I'm going into this one. To get the title, I'll have to knock Leonard out. Benny is clever. He is fast. He can hit. He is a master boxer. He looks good in there. They say I am cleverly awkward. And I know I can hit. In my recent fights with Tendler, Jackson, Mitchell, Welling, I had them on the floor. I figure I'll have Leonard winged to the canvas – maybe he won't get up.'[188]

At ringside for the *International News Service* was Ed. W. Smith, veteran Chicago sportswriter. 'It usually happens that way – the champion gets the long end of the money and the poor miserable contender gets the short end and a smashed mush and a broken bone or two. Dope ran true to form yesterday afternoon when Benny Leonard, champion of the lightweight boxers of the world, scored a technical knockout over Rocky Kansas of Buffalo in the eighth round when the latter's seconds tossed in the sponge. Net results, Leonard gained all of the honours, and, better still perhaps from his point of view, the money, and the beaten man gained a terrible-looking face and a fracture of the left forearm, received in the third round through one of those futile swings to the head.

'Leonard is a champion. Rocky Kansas is just a great little fellow of the highest type of gameness, a man fit to be in any company, mind you. He has beaten Lew Tendler and is a little pal fit for any red-blooded man to be associated with and be proud to know. But as a boxer of the wonderful Leonard type, well, there

---

188 *Fort Wayne News Sentinel* 4 July 1922

After losing a four-round bout to Willie Ritchie in San Francisco, Leonard won the rematch KO 8 Newark New Jersey April 1919

Film star Benny in episode 11 of The Evil Eye *1 January 1920*

BENNY LEONARD
in
"THE DUEL IN THE AIR
Episode 11
of

In the ring at Michigan City, Indiana to fight Ever Hammer (won) 7 August 1922

Benny with his beloved Ma and sister 18 February 1922

Leonard in training at Budd Lake, New Jersey, sparring with Mike Carrier 21 July 1922

Rocky Kansas on the ropes as Leonard is led back to his corner by the referee. Rocky's manager Dan Rogers threw in the towel in the eight round, 4 July 1922

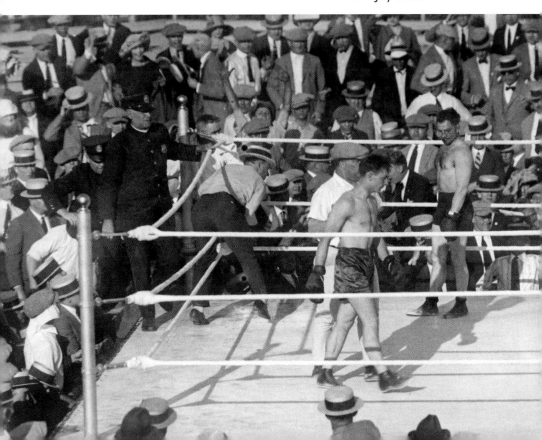

In March 1925 Benny settles in as editor of magazine devoted to American Hygiene

Back page of New York Daily News *24 July 1923: Leonard Wins pts. 15 Lew Tendler*

Benny Leonard in the gym to begin training for his comeback October 1931

Leonard vs Pal Silvers in first fight of comeback in New York October 1931 – referee is Mickey Walker – Leonard won KO2

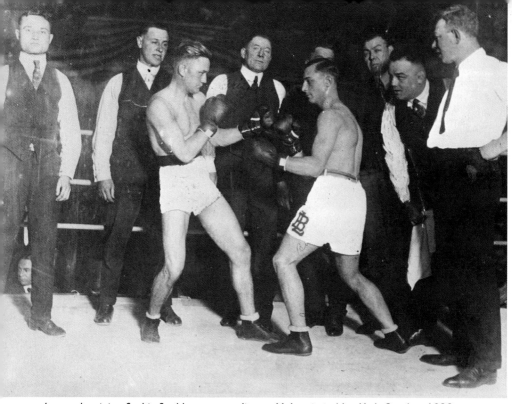

Leonard training for his final bout versus Jimmy McLarnin in New York October 1932

End of the road for Benny, counted out by referee Arthur Donovan as McLarnin scores a sixth-round KO 6 October 1932

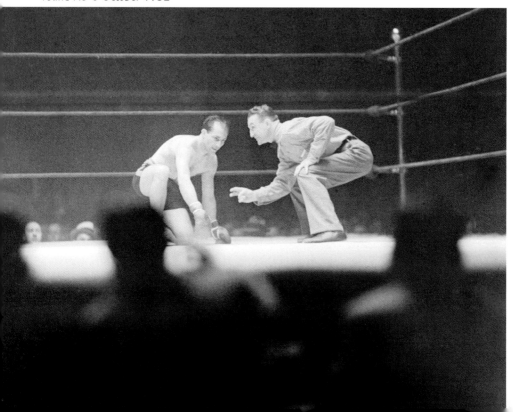

Benny whispers advice to Britain's Tommy Farr who is training to challenge world heavyweight champion Joe Louis in August 1937 – Farr lost 15 rds

Opening of Benny's new restaurant 72nd Street and Broadway – The ex-champ is seen cutting beef for his customers

Opening dinner for 29th Annual Convention Boys Clubs of America in New York 30 May 1935. Among guests were Leonard, sportswriter Grantland Rice and retired heavyweight champion Gene Tunney

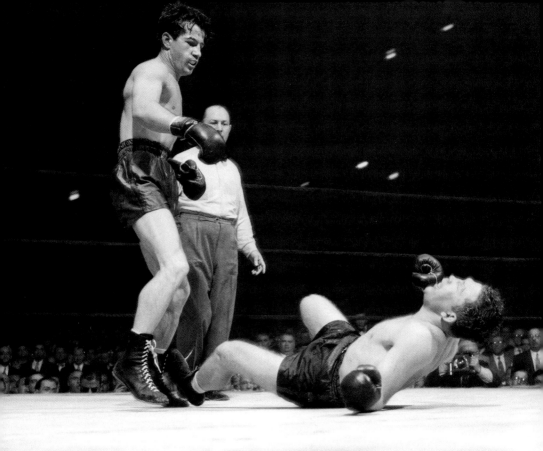

Rocky Graziano floors Freddie Cochrane for a tenth-round stoppage by referee Benny Leonard, Madison Square Garden 24 August 1945

THE LEONARD-WHITE THRILLER

25 Cents
In Canada 30 Cents

JANUARY
1945

the RING

BUY
UNITED STATES
WAR
BONDS
AND
STAMPS

Former Lightweight king,
Lieut. Com. Benny Leonard
of the U. S. Merchant Marine

BOXING OUTLOOK IS BRIGHTER

Former world lightweight champion Benny Leonard on cover of Ring *magazine January 1945*

can be no argument. Benny has it on him a dozen ways and then back again.

'Leonard gave those who predicted a knockout plenty of scare. He fought so carefully and cautiously through the early rounds that they thought he was just going to shade his man and save his hands for Lew Tendler at Jersey City on 27 July. But once that smart Jewish boy saw he had Kansas, he forgot about the hands and let fly. Left hooks and right hand crosses were poked in as fast as lightning. It proves what Leonard has shown in the big majority of his ring triumphs – that he's a great finisher.'[189]

'Such a beautiful thing as the friendship between Benny Leonard and Rocky Kansas,' wrote Henry L. Farrell, 'had to be sacrificed yesterday to satisfy the aching heart of the world's lightweight champion. Because the fans said nasty things about him after he had lost on a foul to Jack Britton and because he had been referred to as a "good fighter" several years ago, Leonard had to go out and clip his little playmate on the chin. In forcing handlers of Kansas to toss in a sponge in the eighth round yesterday in Michigan City, Leonard showed that he is still just as good as he was and wants to be. Leonard apparently reached the point where he decided a continuation of the Leonard–Kansas firm to be unnecessary. So he bumped off Rocky. The Buffalo lightweight is one of the toughest fighters in the ring and when Leonard put him out, he showed that he isn't the helpless victim for Lew Tendler that many thought a week ago.'[190]

'No claim was made at the ringside as far as we heard about Rocky having broken his arm,' wrote Jack Roberts, 'and it was not until we reached Chicago that we heard about the unfortunate accident. From all appearances in the ring, both of Rocky's arms might just as well have been busted – and maybe they were. Going the way he was yesterday, Benny could have licked a dozen Rockys

189 Ed. W. Smith *Salt Lake City Deseret News* 5 July 1922
190 Henry L. Farrell *Indianapolis Times* 5 July 1922

and the hundreds of fans who motored to the Fitsimmons arena could have licked the Indiana legislature after bumping the bumps they call roads down "that-a-way".

'From the third on, Benny loosened up and it was then apparent that Rocky was in for a bad trimming. He slipped to the floor in that session. It may be the old wing was busted then as some say, but he didn't put up any howl and kept "agoing" strong. Benny started the eighth with the evident idea that the fans had received full money's worth and that it was time to pack up the gloves and get out of Indiana as he stormed in a rapid fire rain of head and body blows that smashed down Rocky's resistance and left him standing there wabbly and bloody. The champ was just on the point of putting in the finishing blow when the sponge was thrown into the ring. Benny's hair wasn't even mussed up in the battle and he was cool despite the excessive heat of the day.'[191]

'Check of the attendance at the lightweight championship contest between Benny Leonard and Rocky Kansas yesterday revealed today that the crowd was just above 10,000 with receipts of $59,830. While no official announcement was made, it was reported Leonard got $25,000 and Kansas received $15,000. Leonard, with Billy Gibson, his manager, left today for New York to prepare for his championship engagement with Lew Tendler, the Philadelphia lightweight, to be decided at Jersey City 27 July.

'Kansas, badly upset by his defeat, will return home tonight. He planned to have an x-ray picture made today of his broken arm. The arm was encased in splints after two physicians examined the injury, said today to have been suffered in the third round when Kansas blocked a fast right-hand chop by Leonard. "He is the gamest lightweight," said Leonard of Kansas. "If it is true his arm was broken, his gameness is all the more remarkable.'[192]

---

191 Jack Roberts *Racine Journal News* Wisconsin 5 July 1922
192 *Cincinnati Commercial Tribune* 6 July 1922

It was true, Rocky's arm was broken. 'X-ray pictures of Rocky Kansas' left arm today showed an oblique fracture of the small bone and it probably will be two months before he can return to the ring, according to Dr C.W.K. Briggs of Chicago, who attended the Buffalo lightweight after his injury in his contest with Benny Leonard at Michigan City 4 July.

"'It is a clean break about four inches above the wrist," Dr Briggs said. "Kansas is fortunate that he is big boned and the larger bone of his arm gives [so] much support to the fractured one that it will mend perfectly and be as strong as ever."

'Kansas is on his way heartbroken. Ten days before the contest, he buried his father and the day before the match received word that his mother was dangerously ill. This latest shock, according to his handlers, broke his fighting spirit.'[193]

Chicago newsman Sam P. Hall was in Michigan City for the fight. Before legging it back to the Windy City, Sam wrote, 'The best fighter in the world today, inches for inches, left town early last evening. His name is Benny Leonard and he is the lightweight champion of the world. He probably will retain the same title after he fights Lew Tendler, the Philadelphia southpaw, at Jersey City on the 27th of this month.

'Leonard is on the razor edge right now. Our prediction at this minute is that he will knock Tendler out before the scheduled 12 rounds in Jersey are over. He is able and capable to do such a trick. He wants to do it. He will do it. Leonard boxed a cautious fight with Rocky Kansas, with the Tendler fight in mind. Tendler is a good fighter. On the 27th, he will be battling a great fighter. That's the difference.

'Leonard went back to New York to get ready for the fight. He would rather win than knock over Jack Dempsey. Leonard hates

---

193 *Oakland Tribune* 6 July 1922

Tendler with the bitterest kind of poison that could get into a man's heart over any situation. The day he stands erect in Jersey City and sees Tendler counted out via the volition of his own punches will be Benny's happiest day.

'Every man has his happiest day. Leonard's is still coming. He anticipates having it on the 27th.'[194]

---

194 Sam P. Hall *The Washington Times* 6 July 1922

CHAPTER SIXTEEN

'BENNY LEONARD is a millionaire. He has made it all in the boxing ring. Equipped with a splendid business brain, he would have succeeded in any line of work. But he has built his fortune in the space of ten years with the cleverest set of socking dukes any lightweight champion ever had. Benny doesn't need any more money. He doesn't care for the fistic racket any more. He plans to finish a brilliant career with a more brilliant finish.

'If you had a million dollars, would you be a fighter? Would you try to add a few more thousand to a million-dollar bank account by a game which requires continual training to keep fit to fight? Benny Leonard has more money than he knows what to do with. He lives in a palace. He keeps his parents in luxury. He has tasted of glory until it no longer thrills him. In a month's time, Leonard has contracted to box three of the best ringmen of today: Jack Britton, welter champ, Rocky Kansas, most rugged contender, and Lew Tendler, southpaw body socker. This is the toughest route card any fighter ever bit off. Of the three, he figures on two knockouts. That he will knock Britton out and win the welter title: that he will win on points from the rugged Kansas: and that he will knock Tendler out in five or six rounds. After this, what? That he will retire with his million and glory – a double champion.'[195]

---

195 *The Quincy Daily Herald* Illinois 22 June 1922

So Benny, what do we have? You could have knocked Britton out to take the welter title, but chose not to do so; you beat the rugged Kansas, who suffered a fractured arm. That leaves the tough Philadelphia southpaw who has been after you for some time. There was a night in June 1919 when you fought Johnny Dundee at the Phillies ball park and lefty Lew figured this was a good time. Wrong move Mr Tendler!

From Philadelphia comes an interesting little story. 'According to this tale, Tendler went to the ball park, determined to challenge Leonard when he climbed into the ring. He was frustrated, however, and it is said that the reason he was not allowed to hurl a defi at the champion was that Leonard and his manager threatened to call off the contest with Dundee if Tendler was allowed to climb through the ropes. The reason they are reported to have advanced for their objection was that they did not care to have Tendler "make any capital at Leonard's expense".[196]

Lew Tendler was born in the south Philadelphia Jewish ghetto on 28 September 1898. His father died of a long illness two years after he was born, leaving the family in desperate financial straits. He began selling newspapers by the time he was six. Those were the days of the circulation wars. There were eight Philadelphia dailies, among them the *Ledger, Item, Bulletin, Inquirer* and *Record*. The papers hired tough guys to peddle their papers at prime street locations. Young Tendler was a tough guy growing up and he fought to keep his spot at the intersection of Market and 15th Streets.

'A guy passing by remarked, "Why don't you make some money out of your fighting, you're good at it." Lew thought it was a swell idea. Over to Diamond Lew Bailey's Broadway Athletic Club he went. With the help of a local fight manager named Phil Glassman, who also happened to be the head of the Philadelphia

---

196 *Galveston Daily News* Texas 6 July 1919

Newsboys' Association, a six-round no-decision professional bout was arranged for Tendler to fight Mickey Brown on 6 November 1918 to determine the champion newsboy of the Quaker City.

'Tough looking and well built for his age, Mickey moved around the ring like a veteran. When Lew climbed through the ropes, the audience broke up in derisive laughter. "That bag of bones a boxer?" To the amazement of the crowd, not only was the 102-pound bag of bones on his feet after the final bell, he took the newspaper nod as well.'[197]

Carefully handled by Phil Glassman, within eight months Lew earned $15,000. Their contract was a handshake and throughout his career Tendler never entered the ring unless he first shook Glassman's hand. The tall, rangy southpaw beat Pete Herman in 1916 and a year later Herman was the world bantamweight champion. He beat Johnny Dundee, who would become world junior lightweight champion, future lightweight champion Rocky Kansas, Willie Jackson and George (KO) Chaney. World junior welterweight titleholder Pinky Mitchell and tough Sailor Freedman also lost their four bouts to Tendler. It would be seven years and 79 bouts before Lew finally lost. Then Lew went after Benny Leonard ...

Signing the boys up was not a problem for promoters Herman Taylor and Robert H. Gunniss and the bout was scheduled for 12 August 1921 at the Philadelphia Ball Park. Then the gossip and rumours started, drawing a strong response from veteran promoter Taylor.

'This fight is absolutely on the level,' asserted Taylor, 'and all rumours and reports to the contrary are not only unfounded but downright lies. I have never been connected with a queer bout in all the years that I have been associated with the boxing game in this city and I'm not going to start now.'

---

197 Ken Blady *The Jewish Boxers' Hall of Fame* 1988

'Billy Gibson, manager of Benny Leonard, was in Philadelphia for a few hours last night. He held a long conference with Taylor and Gunniss. Gibson was here to make it clear to the promoters that Leonard is coming to Philadelphia to fight, not waltz. Just before leaving for New York, Gibson made this shot, "Just let the world know that Benny Leonard is the world's lightweight champion. He is a fighting champion. When he meets Lew Tendler, that youth will know he is facing a fighting fighter." Gibson originally planned to remain over until tomorrow to visit Betzwood Farms, the spot selected for Leonard to finish his training. Gibson said that Charlie Leonard, brother of Benny, will look over the Betzwood quarters on Monday.'[198]

'Lew's Sparring Partner Says Title Will Change Hands Next Friday Night' ran a headline piece in the Philly *Inquirer.* "'May I be permitted to speak a little piece," spoke up Eddie O'Keefe in one of the 25 rooms of the Clarence Taubel estate where Lew Tendler is putting in his licks for the greatest battle of his life with Benny Leonard at the Philly Ball Park next Friday night, "then the battle is all over bar the coronation. They tell me that Big Ben isn't alarmed over the reports that little Lew will stop him in the ring, but that's just what's going to happen," said the veteran featherweight. "And I ought to know, for haven't I been stopping enough punches to knock out half a dozen Leonards?"

'Local light-heavyweight Battling Levinsky also placed himself on record as predicting a kayo for the Philadelphian. "Leonard has never been hit in the body since I have seen him fighting and Lew will sock him there. There never was a 'right forward guy' like him. He hits. A glimpse at Tendler hitting the bag proves that. You've never seen a fellow since Ketchel who rapped the fast bag with a double tattoo, have you?"

—

198 *The Philadelphia Inquirer* 30 July 1921

'Tendler joined the group and spoke quietly. "Let me say this. When I knock Leonard down, he isn't going to get up and kid me. He won't step back and fix up his hair on me. Neither will he readjust his tights while he is giving his head a chance to clear. When he gets up, he'll go down again without any kidding or primping. He may whip me but he won't kid me."'[199]

The challenger for Leonard's title received a further build-up from no less than George Engel, Leonard's former trainer and present manager of Harry Greb. 'With all due respect to the lightweight champion's wonderful ability, I think he is making a mighty big mistake if he thinks Tendler is a set-up or anything like that. There have been southpaws and southpaws. Then Lew Tendler came along. This man is no awkward George Chaney, Johnny Wilson, Al McCoy or KO Brown. Lew is Benny Leonard turned around. He can box; his footwork is very good; he can punch and can take a sock; and he is the gamest fighter I ever looked upon. I do not predict that Tendler will beat Leonard. Neither do I pick Benny to emerge the winner. I think this fight will be one of the greatest anyone ever saw and the result will be in doubt until the final bell or until the referee says, "ten and out."'[200]

On Tuesday, 9 August 1921, the bad news broke over the city of Philadelphia. *The Inquirer* had the story, 'CHAMPION'S THUMB KNOCKED OUT; MAY SCRAP IN SIX WEEKS'. On Monday night, the sports editor received this wire from Billy Gibson, Leonard's manager. Benny Leonard suffered a complete dislocation of the carpo-metacarpal bone of his left hand in boxing with Jack Toland in training at Stillman's today. Leonard suffered intense agony, which abated when the bone was set by Dr Sol Rottenberg. A cast was placed on the hand. Rottenberg said Leonard would be forced to be inactive for six weeks at least. The injury occurred in

---

199 Louis H. Jaffe *Philadelphia Evening Public Ledger* 5 August 1921
200 George Engel *Philadelphia Evening Public Ledger* 8 August 1921

the first round. This necessitates cancelling matches with Tendler, Britton, Dundee, Kansas, Freedman and Mel Coogan.

Gibson later sent word that he expected the battle with Tendler to be held within six weeks, as Leonard's injury by that time would be completely healed, he expected.

In the same issue, *The Inquirer* ran a story under Benny Leonard's byline. 'Lew Tendler certainly got a lucky break. He was sure to be bowled over on Friday night if I had not hurt my hand. I am not talking through my hat. I mean every word of it. My left hand is in a plaster cast. I guess I'll be laid up for at least two months, according to what the doctor told me this afternoon, so that means there will be no fight for little Benny. As for Tendler, I'll give him his chance as soon as my hand is better.

'This is how it all happened. I had just boxed four three-minute rounds with my other partners, at Stillman's Gymnasium. Then I took on young Jack Toland of Philadelphia. I had shot two rights to the body against this southpaw and then decided to try out my left. I started it for the jaw, but missed and the blow landed on top of Toland's head. That was the last punch I landed. I knew I was badly hurt. Shooting pains went through my hand and arm. It seemed to me it was paralysed. I never suffered so much in my life as I did for 15 minutes after landing this punch.

'As soon as my trainer, Mannie Seamon, removed the big gloves and the bandages, the left thumb started to swell, and inside of a minute it was three times its normal size. The bone was almost sticking through the flesh. The injury was an expensive one. I figure that the fights arranged for me would bring in more than $125,000, for you know the fight with Tendler was good for $75,000 or even more. Then again, I and Billy Gibson had a lot of our own money tied up in the moving pictures. All this is lost.'

There was surprise at the Tendler headquarters at the Taubel mansion at Delanco, New Jersey. The southpaw was going through his training when manager Phil Glassman broke the news to him. 'Gee, I'm disappointed,' said Lew. 'I want to meet that Benny fellow bad. I know I can knock his block off, and I was all set to do it Friday night. Well, I'll have to pack away the old KO for six weeks.'[201]

Maybe a bit longer than that, Lew.

Richard Freyer had a lovely story in the *New York Evening World* on 19 July 1922. 'Six years ago a 17-year-old Hebrew lad, who made his living selling newspapers at the main depot in Philadelphia, numbered among his customers Benny Leonard, the pugilist who was making rapid strides toward the lightweight championship goal. Leonard won the title a year later.

'Benny was a great drawing card in Philly and made many a trip from New York to engage in bouts in Quakertown. Every time he took the trip the little Hebrew newsboy – Lew Tendler by name – would be right on the job waiting for the train from New York to come in. Benny took a great liking to the lad and always stopped for a few minutes' chat during which he gave Tendler many a point of clean living and other things.

'That was six years ago. But times have changed.

'On the 27th of this month, that same kid is going to meet Benny Leonard in an eight-round bout for the lightweight championship of the world. And the kid is given more than an outside chance to win the title!'

Not everyone wanted to give the kid a chance to become a champion. 'A protest against the holding of the Benny Leonard–Lew Tendler lightweight boxing championship contest at Boyle's Thirty Acres Thursday night was made to Mayor Hague on Tuesday by the Rev. Harvey L. Wyatt, acting for the Society of New Jersey for the prevention of crime, a newly organised ministerial

201 *Philadelphia Inquirer* 9 August 1921

association. Dr Wyatt told the mayor that the Tendler–Leonard affair would be demoralising. He asked the mayor to see to it, if the fight actually did take place, that the law for the punishment of crime was enforced. "The mayor thanked me and said nothing more," Dr Wyatt said later.'[202]

It's more than likely that Mayor Hague already had his ringside ticket in his pocket; he was a fight fan and wouldn't want to miss the Leonard–Tendler fight. Harry Ertle, who would referee the fight, stated afterwards that he got the gloves and that one pair would go to Frank Hague, mayor of Jersey City.

'It was just a year after the Dempsey-Carpentier world heavyweight championship in Jersey City, for which promoter Tex Rickard needed an outdoor venue large enough to hold what he correctly anticipated would be a record crowd, so he built his own open-air arena.

'Frank Hague, mayor of Jersey City, helped Tex Rickard in leasing a plot of land that was known as Boyle's Thirty Acres. The site was named after its owner, John P. Boyle, a paper box manufacturer. Municipal records indicate that despite its euphonious designation, Boyle's acres actually numbered 34. Rickard leased only part of it anyway – namely, a six-and-a-half-acre portion of the property. On this site, the promoter built an enormous wooden octagon-shaped open-air amphitheatre large enough, so he announced, to seat 91,613.

'It took only two months, from the end of April until the end of June, to complete the arena, just hours before the fighters climbed through the ropes. The official name was Rickard's Arena, but from the start everyone chose to call it "Boyle's Thirty Acres", which has been its name in history books ever since. Tickets for Dempsey–Carpentier were scaled from $5.60 to $50 ringside and Rickard took

---

202 *Boston Daily Globe* 26 July 1922

in gate receipts of $1,626,580, boxing's first million dollar gate, a phenomenal sum in those days.'[203]

A year later, when Rickard promoted the world lightweight title fight between champion Benny Leonard and Lew Tendler, he wanted to put the fight in Boyle's Thirty Acres, but it was said that the 'famous arena on the other side of the Hudson must undergo expensive repairs before it can be thrown open to the public again'. The workmen moved in and Tex got his fight on and it drew gate receipts of $367,862, a record at that time for fights below heavyweight, paid by a crowd of 54,685.

The eight-round no-decision bout arranged for Philadelphia, to be promoted by Herman Taylor and Robert Gunniss on 21 July 1921, had become a 12-round no-decision bout to be promoted by Tex Rickard in Jersey City on 27 July 1922. Taylor and Gunniss arranged to attach the receipts for that show to satisfy a claim for $13,480 to reimburse them for their loss in preparing for the contest that never took place ...

Damon Runyon, the Bard of Broadway, had this to say on the coming battle. 'The Leonard–Tendler affair at Boyle's Thirty Acres on Thursday night will be the most spectacular sport event since the day Jack Dempsey and Georges Carpentier met on the same field. We incline to the belief that Leonard ought to beat Tendler, but we are not so sure he will knock him out. Twelve rounds to no decision, with plenty of argument afterwards, would be our first guess at the result.

'If Leonard discovers early that he can handle Tendler without any trouble, he may deposit Lew in the cash register for future reference. You can put that grudge business in the same pigeon hole with the statements that were issued at intervals for months before the match that Leonard would never, never, never give Tendler a

---

203 *Brooklyn Daily Eagle* 2 July 2008

shot at the title. Tendler is the best side-wheeler we ever saw, but we have never seen a side-wheeler that we considered a truly great fighter ...

'Leonard is a great fighter when he wants to fight, of normal style, and the closest student of form could not fail to make him favourite over Tendler. The latter has been outscored and even put down – by fighters who do not class with Leonard. One possible ending of the Leonard–Tendler matter is with Leonard on the floor, and his manager, the honourable Will Gibson, squawking foul in stentorian tones. Tendler's battles often end that way, and while we do not believe Tendler intentionally punches low, the very manner of his punching sends his clouts deep, deep down. When he lets his left go, we doubt if he knows within a foot where it is going.

'The sort of fighter we figure would beat Leonard is a Wolgast, ripping and tearing in without cessation, or a Battling Nelson coming on and on under storms of punches until he discouraged an opponent. Tendler is neither a Wolgast nor a Nelson. If he beats Leonard, he is ten times a better fighter than we can figure him on past performances.'[204]

'Leonard will not be handicapped by the weight,' wrote Louis H. Jaffe. 'He will be robbed of none of his strength when he answers the tingle of the gong in defence of his diadem on the well-known acres owned by Mrs Boyle's husband, so that it would appear that Lew Tendler will have to continue being the foremost contender for Benny's laurels. I watched both Tendler and Leonard in training at their respective camps. At the time, each was close to the lightweight limit and there was little doubt that either would be affected in weighing in at the prescribed poundage. Lew showed that he was strong in his workouts with Tim Droney, while Benny went the challenger two better when he pummelled three of his

---

204 Damon Runyon *The New York American* 27 July 1922

sparring partners, all heavier men, with ease. In fact, Benny had to let up on his shock absorbers in his eight-round workout last Sunday.

'A knockout may decide tonight's contest, but if the contest happens to go the limit, those there will witness one of the greatest exhibitions of lightweight glove-wielding in many moons. Because of his superior cleverness, Leonard is the favourite to win on points in the event that the contest goes the limit.'[205]

'There was much betting in Wall Street yesterday over the coming scrap. Several thousand dollars were placed on the contest. In all the betting Leonard was the favourite, W. L. Darnell & Co. having waged as high as 2½ to 1 that the lightweight champion will receive the consensus of opinion of the newspapers. The firm last night was still offering $15,000 at these odds. Betting interest in this event is more keen than in any fight in some time. Inquiries as well as offers to place money were received in Wall Street yesterday from all over the country, many coming from Chicago and Detroit.'[206]

'Gustave Meyer, Hoboken astrologer, yesterday predicted that Benny Leonard will hold his lightweight boxing championship in his fight tonight against the challenger Lew Tendler. Leonard's victory, according to the astrologer, will be due to the fact that Leonard had the martial planet Mars in friendly aspect to the sun at his birth. Tendler is due to see more stars than he ever saw in all his pugilistic career, and will imagine that his star is setting.'[207]

---

205 Louis H. Jaffe *Philadelphia Evening Public Ledger* 27 July 1922
206 *Washington Times* 27 July 1922
207 *New York Evening World* 27 July 1922

CHAPTER SEVENTEEN

'LEONARD LOSES CHAMPIONSHIP' ran a headline on the sports pages of America in January 1922. A sub-heading declared, 'Is Terribly Punished by Jack McAuliffe, the Unbeaten Lightweight, in a Gruelling Forty-two-Round Battle.'

An editor's note clarified matters for the shell-shocked members of Benny's fan club. 'This is another instalment of an imaginary battle between a champion of yesterday and today. It takes us to Jack McAuliffe and Benny Leonard. McAuliffe never was defeated, but in matching these kings of the lightweight division careful attention is taken to every vantage point of these two boxers in making a decision. Style, hitting, power, cleverness, general-ship, training – the reader will be able to gather on this everlasting argument.

'It must be remembered that Leonard never fought a prize fight. He never has boxed more than ten rounds in any one contest, and most of these amounted to nothing but exhibition bouts. McAuliffe's career was different. He battled to a decision. He fought Jem Carney 74 rounds, Billy Myer 64 rounds, Jimmy Carroll 47 rounds, besides many more.'[208]

Thursday evening, 27 July 1922, Boyle's Thirty Acres, Jersey City. Shortly after 9pm, Benny Leonard, lightweight champion of

---

208 *Indianapolis Star* 8 January 1922

the world, climbed into the ring to face challenger Lew Tendler. The lad from Philadelphia was well aware that no southpaw had ever held the lightweight laurels and if he succeeded tonight he would be making pugilistic history, his name going up there with Jack McAuliffe, Kid Lavigne, Frank Erne, Joe Gans, Battling Nelson, Ad Wolgast, Willie Ritchie, Freddie Welsh and Benny Leonard.

When referee Harry Ertle signalled the timekeeper to ring his bell, it was 9.28pm. Battle was joined as they say. At 23, Tendler was three years younger than Benny, two inches taller and had an inch more on his reach, good advantages over the champion, yet he was short with two rights to the head. Lew landed a light left and they clinched. Sparring around, Tendler hooked a left to the chest and the same hand to the body. He scored with the left again and rammed two sharp rights to the body. Rushing Leonard, Lew slipped and fell to the canvas. He stood up slowly, wiping the dust from his gloves before banging a hard left to the head and Benny was bleeding from a cut on his left eye. They were sparring at the bell and when Leonard sat down, he said the cut was caused by a butt and held a towel to the eye. Trainer Mannie Seamon had work to do.

Round two and Tendler missed two rights and rushed Leonard into a corner. Benny crossed a hard right to the jaw but missed a right and a left. Forcing the fight, Tendler landed a hard left and followed with two uppercuts then a short left. The champion sent a hard right to the head, then two short uppercuts. Tendler scored with right and left and had Benny covering his face with both arms, protecting the cut. Lew threw both hands to the head and blood was running from Leonard's eyebrow. Two rounds to Tendler.

Lefty Lew was out for work early in the third but a wild left missed. They closed and Harry Ertle warned the challenger for hitting in the clinch. Benny complained of Tendler's low punching. Lew had the better of a body exchange and slammed two rights to the jaw. There was another close-quarter exchange and Lew was heard to say, 'Come in and fight.' He rushed Benny to his corner at the bell. It was an even round.

The fourth opened with a two-fisted exchange, Lew landing to the body and Leonard with hard right crosses to the jaw. The champion scored with short uppercuts, Lew answered with a hard uppercut to the body. Benny was spitting blood as he missed with a right and slipped to his knees. Tendler walked away then came back with his left. Leonard sent hard rights to the body before Tendler hammered a left to the body and followed with two right hooks to the head. The challenger was pounding his right to the jaw at the bell. At this point, many newspaper men agreed that the lad from Philadelphia was ahead on points.

As round five opened, the champion was short with a right then set up a body attack. He outfought Tendler in a clinch and concentrated on the body, lefts and rights pounding home. Tendler using his height and reach advantages kept Benny busy, but he missed a long left uppercut. The bell ended a pretty even round …

Before sending Leonard out for round six, manager Gibson, trainer Seamon and brother Charley lit a fire under the champion and he came out and rocked Lew with a right to the jaw, then another right and a left. Tendler missed with a left and Benny chased him along the ropes, scoring two hard rights to the jaw. Lew was warned again by the referee for hitting low and Leonard smashed two rights to the body. Tendler fired three lefts to the head then Benny opened up with lefts and rights and the crowd was in uproar as the New York boy uppercutted Tendler twice and Lew was bleeding from the mouth as the bell rang.

Benny had predicted that he would win in the seventh and he went all out to bring the lanky left-hander to the canvas. Tendler hooked two lefts to the head, but Benny was on fire now and he had the better of a two-fisted exchange. Tendler jabbed rights to the body and hooked his left to the head. Leonard sent two long rights to the jaw and accused Lew of hitting low. Tendler sent lefts to the head and they fought at close range. Benny spat out a tooth then landed an uppercut to the jaw, crossed a left to the body, another right to the jaw and the crowd roared as the champion came back strongly.

Into round eight and Tendler jabbed his right to the head then crossed his left. He landed two lefts to the head in a clinch. Both men swung at long range, Benny scoring to the body and Tendler hooking three times to the jaw. Lefts and rights caught Benny and sent him reeling into the ropes. He looked in trouble as he clung to his attacker and manager Phil Glassman was screaming at Lew to follow up. The champion was talking to Tendler angrily as Lew tried to shake him off. Tendler got away from Leonard then chased him around the ring, yelling to the referee that Benny was holding. Leonard shot a left to the jaw and Lew smiled at the champion as he took a hard left uppercut, then hammered the body. At the bell, Tendler asked Benny, 'How's that?' Leonard replied, 'That was nice work,' as he went to his corner.

In the ninth round both fighters were talking to each other, almost as much as they were punching. Tendler was trying to cash in on his work in the eighth and kept Benny busy with lefts and rights to head and body. He rocked Leonard with a left to the chin and Benny danced away, grinning, then smashed a right to the body. Tendler had the better of infighting at the bell.

Round ten and Tendler missed a right, Leonard hooked two rights to the body, sent another and followed with a right to the jaw. He uppercutted twice to the jaw then hammered both fists to the head. Leonard kept leading and landing with his right and chased Tendler to the ropes. The Philly boy fought back and sent three left hooks to the jaw. He backed away as Benny jumped like a cat, smashing two rights to the jaw to back Lew into the ropes.

The New York crowd were roaring for their boy as he stepped up a gear, with the finish line coming nearer.

The champion had recovered after that bad eighth round and was growing stronger over the last two rounds, feinting Tendler into knots before opening up with lefts and rights to head and body. There were smiles in Benny's corner now. Twelfth and final round and Leonard sunk a right to the stomach. Tendler rushed in, landing lefts to the jaw. Leonard landed wild rights and lefts and had the better of a vicious exchange at close quarters. They danced around. Leonard landed short rights to the jaw, sent both hands to the body and rushed Tendler to the ropes. Leonard missed a right uppercut and hooked two glancing rights to the jaw. It was all Leonard now, another two rights to the jaw. He uppercutted with rights and lefts and they were fighting hard at the gong.

In a report for the *Boston Post*, referee Harry Ertle stated, 'It was Leonard all the way after the first round. If I had had the privilege, I surely would have raised Leonard's glove at the end of the 12th. Of course I can't give an official decision, but as you have asked me to tell the readers of the *Post* my opinion, why, that is it. It was a smashing battle. Both men were in wonderful form and though I have refereed many hard-fought lightweight battles, I don't think I ever had one as fast. I feel Leonard won because he landed the more damaging blows, the harder blows, the cleaner blows. And, besides that, he was a ghost on the defence. At any rate, I want to be present at the next fight if it's at all like the one they had tonight.'[209]

Famed columnist Damon Runyon wrote from ringside, 'When Greek meets Greek, tradition has it that there is a tug of war. Benny Leonard, the lightweight champion of the world, and Lew Tendler, of Philadelphia, demonstrated last night that there can also be plenty of trouble when two fighting sons of Abraham get together.

---

209 Harry Ertle *The Boston Post* 28 July 1922

Leonard, in the opinion of the writer, won from Tendler in their 12-round battle on Boyle's Thirty Acres, but in the earlier rounds the champion was far outfought by the tall and pallid-looking Philadelphian, and had to bring forward all his boxing skill and knowledge in the latter part of the fight to catch up.

'Once in the eighth round, Tendler hit Leonard a solid smash to the chin and the knees of the champion bent in a manner that brought half of the 60,000 men and women up yelling. It looked for a fleeting instant as if Leonard was in serious trouble. Then as fast and as vague as a shadow, Leonard drifted into a tight clinch and held on until the threat had passed.'[210]

Davis J. Walsh, sports editor for INS, had this to say, 'In a roaring two-fisted bout that filled the eye and gladdened the heart, Benny Leonard not only managed to preserve his lightweight title intact by avoiding a knockout, but outscored Lew Tendler, the challenger, last night at Boyle's Thirty Acres after 12 of the most sensational rounds a championship engagement has known in many years. A beaten man until the ninth round with his championship crown hanging at a most surprising and rakish angle, Leonard came back like a bad cheque in the last four to nip Tendler's lead right at the wire. In the final round, he was shooting lefts and rights into Tendler's anatomy. As it was, his margin of superiority was sufficient to convince the majority of critics and spectators at the ringside.'[211]

For *United Press*, Henry L. Farrell observed, 'Lew Tendler, young and slow on the mental trigger, was talked out of the world's lightweight championship last night in Jersey City. With a groggy champion in front of him in the eighth round all set for a knockout punch and with 60,000 frenzied fans on their feet sensing a change in the championship, Tendler allowed the glib tongue of smart Benny

---

210 Damon Runyon *Salt Lake City Deseret News* 28 July 1922
211 Davis J. Walsh *Oakland Tribune* 28 July 1922

Leonard to rob him of the big opportunity of his life. 'The quick brain of Leonard brought him out of his greatest crisis and enabled him to go through 12 of the hardest rounds of his life and earn a decision over his rugged challenger by the slightest of slight margins.

'For five rounds, Tendler had won by a mile margin because the champion could not figure the awkward left-hand style of his opponent. In the sixth round, Leonard stepped out and took the lead for the first time. In the seventh and up to the middle of the eighth, Leonard was the champion of old. Getting restless, he tore into Tendler. Just for a moment, he lapsed and Tendler crashed over a terrific left swing to his jaw. Leonard's knees sagged. His guard dropped and his eyes glazed. His corner was frantic. His legs were going and his arms were heavy, but the brain was still there. "Don't kid yourself, you're not going any place. You'll miss the next one," the groggy champion hissed through a hole in his jaws where a tooth had been knocked out in the third round. Tendler fell for it. Rattled, he tore in with another left swing – and missed. Falling forward, Leonard went into a clinch that held him up until his head cleared. Tendler's big chance was gone. He knew it and acted like it. From then on, it was all Leonard.'[212]

The Philadelphia southpaw had at least one high-ranking supporter in the press row. Writing exclusively for *Universal Service*, former heavyweight champion pugilist of the world James J. Corbett, old Gentleman Jim himself, came out punching at the bell. 'Lew Tendler won the fight by a shade. If it had not been a no-decision affair and I had been the referee, I would hand the crown to him. He fought a surprisingly strong battle and his blows, especially in the early rounds, were far more punishing that the champion's. He is a most worthy contender for the lightweight title. It was the greatest lightweight fight I ever saw.

---

212 Henry L. Farrell *Sandusky Star Journal* 28 July 1922

'They were at it from the first exchanges. They fought without a moment's hesitation. Both roughed it in the clinches, driving their blows to the body and head fiercely. It was a slamming, tearing, honest-to-goodness attempt to knock each other kicking all the way. The champion seemed to have put in a lot of time perfecting a defence against Tendler's much-touted left to the kitchen, as the cultured folk know the stomach, and he profited. He repeatedly blocked the blow, his arm getting down there before the smash came. But when he caught it – and he did – he shook a beam and aft and every which way …

'I wouldn't have missed it for a pile. Judging by the remarks on all sides of me and the constant roar, like a pounding sea all over the great saucer, everybody that got over here wouldn't have either.'[213]

Some years after the Jersey fight, Nat Fleischer had Benny in *The Ring* magazine office and they talked of this and that. 'Do you want to hear what I really said to Tendler when I talked him out of a knockout?' the lightweight champion said. 'I've heard so many versions, Benny,' said Nat, 'that it would be a pleasure to get the real lowdown.'

'I'll tell you, Nat, just what I said,' replied Benny. 'There have been lots of stories printed about that incident, but this is the only one that's absolutely true. He nailed me right on the chin – and boy, how Lew could punch! My head went swimming. My knees buckled under me. I was ready to drop. I saw stars and with the little thinking I could do, I said to myself, "Benny, you're hurt. You're going to get knocked out. Say something to him." So I looked at Lew, and nonchalantly, though I could hardly say the words, I remarked: "That was a peach of a punch, Lew. But if you want to get fresh, I can get fresh, too."

---

213 James J. Corbett *Salt Lake City Deseret News* 28 July 1922

'Lew looked at me in astonishment. He didn't know what to make of it and pulling his right hand off my shoulder, went like that with his hand, meaning for me to shut up. I repeated the statement and this time he replied, "Aw shut up. Come on and fight." He stopped hitting me, gave me an opportunity to regain my senses, and I tell you, it was a life-saver to me. It sounds silly when I tell the story now but it wasn't the least bit silly when it happened. Maybe you wonder why, when I was hurt, my first thought was that I must say something to Tendler. That's because I always talked in the ring. It was something I learned from my great manager, Billy Gibson. I always had something to say even if it was only to repeat the instructions from the referee when we were called to the centre of the ring. Why? Just psychology.'[214]

In his *The Ring* Detective series, Dan Daniel cornered Lew Tendler in Atlantic City, where the old Philadelphia southpaw had his business. 'You are bringing up a sore spot in my career,' laughed Lew. 'For a minute or so, I was the lightweight champion of the world. But I was inexperienced. It was my first shot at a title and I let that wise guy talk me off what I was after. In 1921, Leonard and I, disliking each other intensely, finally signed for a fight in Philadelphia. We put up forfeits of $5,000.

'Leonard announced that he would not be able to go through with it, as he had busted a hand in training. I then claimed the forfeit. They demanded the return of the dough, and I refused. So when we finally got together in Jersey City in 1922, there was no love lost between us.

'Well, you know how the fight went. In the eighth round, some 15 seconds after we got started, Leonard caught me with a right uppercut. I followed with a hard straight right to the head. I think that one hurt. I then smashed a left to the body, and that hurt more.

---

214 Nat Fleischer *The Ring* June 1939

Then, in close, I ripped a left to the jaw. That did it. Leonard was just about out. He grabbed me around the body and held on for dear life. His knees were rubber. I said to myself, "Belt this guy just once more, and you are the champion." I should not have talked so much or listened to talking Benny.

'Leonard said to me, "Hey, you are getting too damned fresh. Just for that, I will nail you in the next round." He kept threatening me, and I said to myself, "What's this all about? Here I have the guy in trouble, and he is threatening me." Benny set the trap with that glib tongue of his, and I walked right in.'[215]

The morning after the fight, the sports pages headlined 'Record Crowd Sees Battle in New Jersey, 54,685.' The old lightweight champ Battling Nelson (1905/06; 1908–10) was sadly not one of them. The durable Dane put 134 bouts in the record book, fighting his way into the Hall of Fame. On the afternoon of the Leonard–Tendler fight, the 'Bat' stowed away under the stands early and just before the fight started sneaked into a prime seat. Alas, he was found without a ticket, and three cops, none too courteously, hustled him to the gates and pushed him outside. So much for fame.

---

215 Dan Daniel *The Ring* September 1959

CHAPTER EIGHTEEN

THIS LEONARD-TENDLER thing was not going away. Firstly, a correction, as noted in the *Fort Wayne News Sentinel* on 6 August 1922. 'The story that Battling Nelson, former lightweight champion, had stowed away under the ring at Jersey City and tried to get into the press row after the big battle was on between Leonard and Tendler, is not right.

'The fact is that Nelson had a ticket with a coupon calling for a $10 seat, but that "Bat" wanted to edge into the press row, claiming he was writing a story for one of the papers in Denmark. The copper at the ringside cared not what "Bat" said, but ordered him out. Then "Bat" pleaded, he told the cop who he was, but the latter only replied, "Never heard of Battling Nelson in my life." That was adding insult to injury for "Bat". Then the big cop grabbed "Bat" by the back of his sweater and dragged him up the aisle and into the $10 section. How different it would have been for the Battler ten years ago.'

A couple of days after the fight, Damon Runyon wrote in the *Washington Times*, 'Leonard won the majority of the votes of the newspaper writers who judged the battle of Boyle's Thirty Acres in a purely unofficial capacity. But they all agreed that he won by a mere breath, which certainly justified the opinion of quite a number of very capable writers who called it a draw.

'Harry Ertle, the referee, and a fine, high-class chap, writing for a newspaper after the fight, expressed the opinion that Leonard won. Under the boxing laws of New Jersey, a referee is not permitted to render a decision, and Ertle's expression of opinion gives rise to the interesting question as to whether it is a violation of the law. It is supposed to be an unofficial decision, but here again comes a question as to whether an official referee can render such a thing as an "unofficial" opinion and remain within legal bounds. Technically, it would seem that Ertle's opinion, however or wherever rendered, must be accepted as official, and therefore, Leonard officially won.

'Ertle made one rather astonishing statement, which we are inclined to think was a slip of his nimble pencil. He said, "It was Leonard all the way after the first round." In the eighth, Tendler had the lightweight championship in his grasp when he hit Leonard on the chin and knocked him crook-legged. The pictures show that Leonard went to the floor. It was only for an instant, but immediately thereafter the champion fell into a tight clinch and backed Tendler all over the ring. You could not say it was all Leonard from the first unless you threw out the eighth, and even then there were rounds between the first and the 12th when Benny was going none too well.'[216]

'After 15 revenue agents closeted with the receipts in a private room in Jersey City had finished their work, the following official figures were given out: paid admissions 44,920; gross receipts $364,548; net receipts $298,267.20; Leonard's share $90,760; Tendler's share $55,584. According to these figures, promoter Tex Rickard made $151,923 on the extravaganza at Boyle's Thirty Acres. Announcement of the attendance came as a surprise, for it had been generally believed that around 70,000 had swarmed into the great pine saucer.

---

216 Damon Runyon *Washington Times* 30 July 1922

'Of 21 newspapermen and experts engaged to give their opinions of the fight in New York newspapers, 16 agreed that Leonard won, but with only a few exceptions that it was by a slight margin – a shade. Four declared it a draw and one picked Tendler the winner by a shade. Interestingly, out of five Philadelphia papers, four said Leonard and one Tendler, this paper being the *Evening Bulletin*.

'Discussion is still at fever heat, and it was everywhere agreed a wonderful fight.'[217]

'What everyone now is trying to determine is whether he [Leonard] is right up in the class of Benny at his best, or whether the champion is seeing the end of his days as a legitimate lightweight. His showing against Rocky Kansas when he was not required to make weight defined him as A-1. But last Thursday night, he looked frail and it is an even guess whether his fatal right lacked steam or whether Tendler's ability to take wallops is equal to that of the well-remembered Battling Nelson. If this is the case, it is a new quality acquired by Lew, who in the past has been known to go to the floor when hit by men inferior to himself.

'Leonard, by the way, is likely to run up against another stiff proposition next Saturday in Floyd Fitzsimmons's big Michigan City arena when he goes against Ever Hammer, the blonde lightweight who gave Leonard a hard battle out west two or three years ago. Hammer is the Harry Greb type of mauler and has gained in strength and in skill since last he met the champion. Hammer says that his motto is "box a fighter and fight a boxer". Putting Leonard in the boxer class, Hammer says he intends to keep on top of him every minute and make him look like Harry Greb made Tommy Gibbons look. Since July of last year, he has fought 14 battles and won them all – three via the knockout route. Good as Hammer may be, however, the chances are that with no

---

217 Thomas L. Cummiskey *Dubuque Telegraph Herald* Iowa 30 July 1922

necessity of tipping the beam at 135 pounds, Leonard will be in every way his old self.'[218]

'Victories over Richie Mitchell and Charley White put the old confidence in my bones,' said Hammer. 'That left hook of mine isn't bad. It may upset the dope like it did Mitchell and White.'[219]

In his summing up of the fight, Ed. W. Smith stated, 'Leonard, it is very well known, likes to box with boxers. He is a great boxer himself and he likes the orthodox fellow who steps out with some degree of politeness and with regard to what the boxing book says. We'll say this right here that once the summer air vibrates with the opening bell, there isn't a thing polite or nice about Ever Hammer. His Scandinavian blood fairly boils and seethes with the task at hand. He is out for blood in a figurative way and it takes a champion to stop him in his wild quest.'[220]

Trainer Mannie Seamon 'spoke glowingly of Leonard's 1916 Kansas City bout against Ever Hammer, in Hammer's home town. Leonard called it "the fight I can never forget". Early in the fight, Seamon remembered, Leonard was "smashed, bashed, belted and hammered all over the ring. Only his superb condition and ring generalship at crucial times saved him from a knockout." After Leonard knocked out Hammer in the 12th round, he said of his aptly named opponent, "If, like Mannie says, we're made out of the things we eat, that guy must have been weaned on trip hammers!"'[221]

So you have to ask why Leonard was meeting a tough guy like Hammer, just nine days after his hard 12-round battle with Lew Tendler, from which Benny emerged with a nasty cut by his right eye. The *Associated Press* reported two days before the fight, 'Because of the danger of re-opening the cut over his right eye, received

---

218 Sparrow McGann *Oakland Tribune* 30 July 1922
219 *Washington Times* 30 July 1922
220 Ed. W. Smith *Logansport Pharos Tribune* 5 August 1922
221 Ronald K. Fried *Corner Men* 1991

in the match with Lew Tendler, Benny Leonard, lightweight champion, will do no boxing in preparation for his ten-round contest with Hammer, the challenger from Chicago, here next Saturday afternoon. This was the announcement of Billy Gibson, manager of the champion today, after he examined the injury. The most dangerous wound is in the eyebrow, the other cut is in the lid. This is nearly healed.'[222]

Benny was well aware of his situation, giving a statement to the press which they printed on the morning of the fight. 'He had better not open this cut over my right eye. If he does, he will be a sorry fellow.'

All roads led to Floyd Fitzsimmons's new arena, which rose out of the Indiana dunes and was crammed with a carnival crowd of more than 8,000 that sun-drenched afternoon in July of 1922. When Benny walked into the ring at 6.10pm wearing a patch over his right eye, Billy Gibson and Mannie Seamon had their fingers crossed and a silent prayer moved their lips. A mighty roar broke from the crowd as the Swede from Chicago and the Hebrew from Harlem answered the opening bell.

Hammer was first to score, a left to the body. Leonard sent a left to the body then the same punch to the head. Benny jabbed to the Swede's face. He was very cautious, measuring his blows. Hammer landed a solid left to the nose and the same fist went south and caused Benny to hold on. In a fast exchange to the head Leonard got home heavy punches, and they were fighting strongly at the bell. Leonard's round.

Out for round two and Hammer was trying for the patch over Benny's eye. Leonard jabbed to the face and a right uppercut hurt Hammer. He stormed back but Benny was keeping him at bay with the left. Hammer landed a left to the nose and rushed to the

---

222 *Biddeford Daily Journal* Maine 3 August 1922

ropes, but Benny pulled him back to the centre of the ring. Leonard continued to fight cautiously and successfully blocked Hammer's efforts to reach the patch on his eye. A hard, stiff left to the body and the same hand to the face from Leonard, then a solid right to the jaw, staggered the Chicago man. Benny's left was working overtime at the bell.

Leonard was two rounds up coming out for the third and Hammer stormed in, firing with both hands. Benny missed with a right and Hammer's left fist sent the patch flying from the champion's eye. Now Benny looked worried as he felt the blood run down his cheek. He drove Hammer back to the ropes and the Swede planted another left in Benny's eye. Leonard tried with left and right but Ever covered up and Benny did little damage. The Swede stuck another left in Leonard's bad eye and Benny was happy to hear the bell end Hammer's first round.

Hammer rushed from his corner and fought furiously, trying to follow up his advantage. He planted a left to the body and the New Yorker held. They clinched and Benny scored with a stiff uppercut that stopped Hammer in his tracks. The Chicago man jumped in throwing lefts and rights inside and referee Miller had his hands full keeping them apart. Hammer staggered Benny with a stiff left and right, then a hard right to the ear. The champion was fighting hard but took three hard jabs to the face. He was bleeding from the eye and his mouth at the bell. It looked like an even round.

As Benny came up for round five, Hammer closed in and hurt him with a stiff punch over the heart. Leonard fought back and stunned his man with right and left that visibly hurt him. He drove the Swede to the ropes, his left jab going like a piston. Hammer was holding in the clinches as though he was tiring. In an exchange of body blows at the end of the round, Leonard had the advantage.

Round six and Hammer was more cautious. Benny had him hanging on with short left jabs to the face. Leonard took his man to the ropes, where he outpunched him, scoring lefts and rights to have Hammer holding and bringing the referee in to break them up. The Chicago fighter was attempting to stand off and box but he was in with a boxing master and his swings were wild. Benny smashed a hard right to the face as the round ended and the crowd roared as he walked back to his corner …

When Benny was no longer able to protect his damaged eye, he let down his guard and opened up with both hands, staggering Hammer with two-fisted attacks. The Swede was hanging on desperately through rounds seven and eight. The champion was hammering his man as the seventh ended and in the eighth Leonard had his foe at his mercy, the left jab going like a machine gun and following rights leaving Ever reeling before the storm. With the big crowd going crazy, the champion was coming in a winner.

Round nine and Hammer was more cautious, Leonard wading in trying to finish the Swede as he had six years before. But Hammer caught Benny with his guard down and landed a savage right to the head, causing blood to stream from the eye injury. Leonard fought back furiously and Hammer reeled from a battery of lefts and rights. He was glad to hear the bell.

Coming up for the tenth and final round, the crowd was on its feet, yelling their heads off as the fighters battled for a finish. Leonard was in charge now, kidding Hammer to stand up and fight while the Swede was trying to last out the round, last out the fight still on his feet. It looked bad for Hammer as Benny threw lefts and rights at his opponent, trying to bring him down on his face. But the man from Chicago was still there as the bell ended his torment. He knew he was running second to the champion, but he was happy to walk to his corner at the bell.

Talking to the press after the fight, Hammer said, 'Leonard is the greatest lightweight in the world. I fought a hard battle but could not solve him. I hope to meet him at some future date.'

The champion declared, 'My eye bothered me slightly in the early rounds because I had it on my mind. However, when the patch came off I knew there was no more use worrying about it, and I forgot that there was anything wrong during the remainder of the fight.'[223]

'They All Get It Sooner Or Later', 'The Observer' headed his piece in the *Philadelphia Evening Public Ledger*. Before Benny Leonard became champion, he was very careful to avoid a blow that would mar his personal appearance. He was decidedly uncomfortable if his hair was mussed and the thought of cauliflower ears was horrifying. The champion has been fortunate in sidestepping and blocking blows that would spread his nose east and west. He has sported black eyes and cut lips, but has suffered no permanent disfiguration.

'Leonard makes a very natty appearance in his civilian clothes. He is quite a handsome chap and refined looking. One would take him rather for a businessman than a boxer. At that, he has shown impressive business ability. Now Benny has a new wrinkle. He isn't worrying so much about his hair as he is about his mouth. Leonard's teeth are coming out, but are being forced out by boxing gloves instead of chicken bones. One tooth was clipped at the gum by a Tendler right jab and another by an Ever Hammer jolt. The dentist will get quite a cut from Leonard's purse, for the champion is anxious for the best job the profession can produce. Benny so far has been lucky to escape the facial contour of the average boxer, but sooner or later the disfiguration will come if he stays long enough in the game.'[224]

Veteran Doc Almy, in his 'Boxing Gossip' column in the *Boston Post* on 8 August 1922, wrote, 'According to one of the New York papers, Benny Leonard is not the millionaire king of the ring,

---

223 J. L. O'Sullivan *Fort Wayne News Sentinel* Indiana 8 August 1922
224 The Observer *Philadelphia Evening Public Ledger* 8 August 1922

in fact hardly comes under the head of being comfortably rich. Leonard is quoted as admitting that Wall Street and horses had corralled the greater part of the fortune he has made with his fists. Leonard plans to take a month's vacation in the Adirondacks, and will then fight the winner of the Charley White and Bobby Barrett bout, following which he will go to Europe and battle Ernie Rice, lightweight champion of England. "I'm going to fight all I can and get the sugar while the getting is good," said Leonard. "I don't care what becomes of my title as long as the nimble dollars keep rolling in.'"

CHAPTER NINETEEN

'CHICAGO'S SOCIETY gathered up its skirts tonight and invaded the famous stock yards to watch Benny Leonard, world's lightweight champion, in his contest with Pinky Mitchell, the Milwaukee challenger, staked for charity. The fighting Irish from the stock yards district hemmed in the fashionably gowned society matrons from Chicago's gold coast, jamming every seat in the Dexter Pavilion, at 42nd and Halsted Streets. Society's first introduction to boxing was in full thrills. Polite ears attuned to tea table gossip were shocked with the raucous shouts of "bust him in the beezer, Benny," and similar other cries from the frantic boxing fans.

'Tonight's bouts, staged without interference, probably will be the last in Chicago for some time as the city administration wants a test made of the state law prohibiting the sport. James C. Mullen, promoter of tonight's charity show, had arranged to be arrested on a charge of violating the stringent law, and if convicted planned to carry the contest to the state supreme court, which will be asked to pass on the validity of the statute.'[225]

The Mitchell family from the Wisconsin city of Milwaukee were out in force. Promoter-manager Billy, brother Richie and younger

---

225 *Nebraska State Journal* 30 May 1923

brother Myron, who liked to be called Pinky. Richie had twice been knocked out by Benny and was now loudly predicting that Pinky would do what he had twice failed to do, and beat Benny Leonard. The younger Mitchell was actually a better boxer than Richie, just 24 years old, and had won 36 of his 47 fights. The Mitchell money was riding on him tonight. Pinky had been matched with Leonard in January 1922, but an attack of bursitis put Mitchell out of action on the morning of the fight, forcing him to cancel the bout. Leonard's lightweight title would have been at stake in that one and Pinky would have had to knock Benny out to claim his title in the no-decision bout.

By the time of the Chicago fight with Leonard, Pinky had a title of his own. 'Mike Collins, who managed Pinky at various times, was the publisher of a Minneapolis weekly called the *Boxing Blade*. He offered to conduct a poll among his readers to pick "the best man in the world at 140 pounds" and provided a $2,000 championship belt when the National Boxing Association decided to recognise the newly created junior welterweight division in 1922. To nobody's surprise, Mitchell topped the voting and was officially proclaimed world champion on 15 November 1922. It was the first and only time that a world champion had been crowned by a boxing publication with official support.'[226]

Leonard actually refused to weigh in for the contest and expressed no interest in the title which, according to Judge A. J. Hedding, would still be retained by Mitchell. Leonard's title was not at stake in the Mitchell bout. It was Benny's first fight in ten months after he suffered from infected teeth – the result of his fight with Ever Hammer in August 1922. They were paying him $25,000 to see if the kid was as good as his older brother, the one he had knocked out twice.

---

226 Bert Blewett *A–Z of World Boxing* 1996

'In the first round, Leonard and Mitchell feinted for at least 30 seconds before the champion led with a left hook to the chin. Mitchell, boxing defensively, declined to lead. Leonard connected solidly with two lefts and a right to the chin. Mitchell remained on the defensive in the second, forcing Leonard to do all the leading, but neither landed effectively. In the third, Leonard reached Mitchell with a right-hand punch to the chin and received two solid rights to the chin in return. Leonard shook Mitchell with a jolting right to the chin in the fourth and Mitchell returned it only to receive a left and right to the head.

'Leonard was ahead and boxing nicely in the fifth but Mitchell backed out of danger, still on the defensive. Leonard started the seventh landing a left to the chin and Mitchell forced him into the ropes for an exciting rally, but did no damage. Mitchell opened up in the eighth and traded light left hands with the champion. Leonard missed in his attempt to hook a left to the body. Mitchell had Leonard backing away and in danger in the ninth round as a result of landing four right smashes to the chin. In the tenth, Leonard came out of his corner and backed Mitchell into the ropes. Leonard ripped over a right to the chin, flooring Mitchell. Mitchell attempted to get up and drew a leg under him and resting on his right knee. Leonard attempted to punch him but referee Miller waved him away and counted the challenger out in the centre of the ring.'[227]

'It was the contention of the Mitchell faction that Leonard hit Pinky while he was still resting on one knee, but their claim of foul was denied by referee Miller, who contended Mitchell had assumed a fighting pose after a short count and should have protected himself from the vicious right-hand finishing punch Leonard shot over five seconds before the final bell would have sounded. The contest was

227 *Nebraska State Journal* 30 May 1923

billed as a ten-round no-decision affair, but referee Miller raised Leonard's right arm and turned to carry Mitchell to his corner. It was then Richie Mitchell sprang into the ring and slammed away at the referee. Billy Gibson, Leonard's manager, Charley Leonard, Benny's brother, and Herschie and Harry Miller, brothers of the referee, quickly engaged in the rough and tumble fighting. Police restored order after 15 minutes and rushed the referee to a taxicab and down town.'[228]

London boxing writer Gilbert Odd recorded his version of what happened. 'The tenth, of course, is the whole story of the fight. Referee Dave Miller moved over to part them and grabbing Pinky's arm pulled him back. Miller was still holding Pinky's arm at this time when, quick as a flash, out shot Leonard's right and caught his opponent flush on the jaw.

'Mitchell went down like a log, groping on the canvas. He crawled to one knee as the referee started to count. At "two" he slightly raised his other knee off the canvas and Benny, standing a few inches away, stepped in and shot his right to Pinky's jaw for the second time. Again, the Milwaukee boy crumpled to the floor and although badly dazed, worked himself into a position, with his knees resting on the canvas while the count proceeded. Then, to the amazement of everyone, Dave Miller ceased counting at "five", lifted Mitchell up and carried him to his corner, thus intimating that he had called a halt in the battle.

'The gong was about to sound when Dave Miller innocently saved the gamblers who had taken long odds at the last minute that Leonard would stop his opponent. But apart from that, how come the referee overlooked the punch that Leonard threw at Mitchell's chin when the referee was still holding the Milwaukee boy's arm? This was the blow that tumbled Pinky for the first time, but even

---

228 *Portsmouth Daily Times* 30 May 1923

so he had got one knee off the canvas at the count of two and was in the act of raising the other one when Leonard struck again. Miller would appear to have erred when he suddenly stopped the bout. Pinky was terribly wobbly and another punch might have put him away for good, but the bell would have come to his rescue. Had he been on his feet when the final gong sounded, Miller must have given him the verdict on points, in which case the long-shot gamblers would have lost their money.'[229]

On 31 May, the *Madison Wisconsin State Journal* reported, 'Rumours declare that someone cleaned up big on the Leonard–Mitchell bout. Thousands of dollars were bet that Mitchell would not last ten rounds. Referee Miller stopped the fight on an alleged technical knockout 25 seconds before the finish and opinions differ as to whether he was all right or all wrong. Richie Mitchell was the first to protest about this. Society on the whole stood the racket very well. There were many screams and a few faints but the social leaders, such as members of the Armour and Field families, were not noted to blink an eyelash. Earlier, they had seen a prelim fighter's ear virtually torn off. It was suspected that most of the dowagers and debutants through the post bellum melee in the ring part of the show. But if society wants to see any more fights, it probably will have to go to New York or some such place as Shelby, Montana.

'Pinky Mitchell may have been knocked out in the closing seconds of his bout with Benny Leonard at Chicago Tuesday night, and blue coats may have resorted to swinging their clubs to quell a riot, but just the same Pinky is still the junior welterweight champion of the world.

'The scrap was billed as a championship affair, and it would have been such if Leonard had agreed to step on the scales at three o'clock on the afternoon of the fight. As matters were, Leonard

229 Gilbert E. Odd *Was The Referee Right?* 1952

first refused to weigh in and Pink followed suit. Automatically, the refusal of Leonard to tip the beam took the championship flavour from the bout. Leonard was hog fat and weighing in the neighbourhood of 145 pounds.'[230]

From Chicago 31 May, '"Boxing is a dead sport," Mayor William E. Dever declared tonight when informed that James Mullen, promoter of last Tuesday's engagement between Leonard and Mitchell had failed to appear in court to face a charge of promoting a prize fight. City authorities claimed Mullen had agreed to test the stringent provisions of the Illinois anti-prize fight law by allowing himself to be arrested and carrying the case to the Supreme Court. Mullen's case continued for a week, but John Gallagher, who was a spectator at the fight, was arrested and charged with looking at the match, and this may be a test case.'[231]

'The Chicago chapter of the National Sports Alliance announced it has taken steps to have the three Mitchell brothers, Richie and Pinky, boxers, and Billy, manager, blamed for the riot, barred from all bouts in Illinois. It also requested the New York chapter to make a similar action.'[232]

'It was too bad that Milwaukeeans had to come to Chicago and disrupt a clean sport,' said Benny Leonard after the bout. 'It was no more than could be expected, for the same pair created a rumpus in New York when I knocked out Richie Mitchell at Miss Ann Morgan's benefit for the poor children of France.'

Pinky Mitchell told the press, 'It was the rawest thing that ever happened to me. While I admit I was dazed when I got up the second time, when Leonard hit me I was still far from out and the referee had no business in stopping the fight and should also have sent Leonard to his corner. Miller held my arm after breaking us

---

230 *Madison Wisconsin State Journal* 31 May 1923

231 *Burlington Hawk Eye* Iowa 1 June 1923

232 *Appleton Post Crescent* Wisconsin 1 June 1923

from a clinch and before I could jerk it away, Leonard clipped me with his right. He would never have done that had my arm been free to protect my jaw. I would have no excuse to offer if I had lost fair and square and my only desire is to get Leonard again. I've got his measure. He's not as great as he's painted to be and I'll lick him for sure if I ever get him in the ring again.'[233]

A somewhat disturbing report came out of Chicago on 9 June to the effect that the charity linked to the $55,000 fight between Leonard and Mitchell 'profited to the extent of $24.35 for the West Side Boys' Club. The proceeds were under $25 after expenses were paid, according to promoter James Mullen. Small wonder that Billy Gibson, Leonard's manager, telegraphed from New York that Leonard was willing to return to Chicago and box for nothing for the benefit of the club. Gibson said Leonard had a better offer from Tex Rickard but "wanted to help the game in Chicago" and so came here under the impression that the bout would draw about $100,000.'[234]

Two days later, Billy Mitchell weighed in with a similar offer from brother Pinky that he was willing to box without remuneration at a benefit for the West Side Boys' Club, providing Benny Leonard was his opponent. '"It appears to me that Benny's offer is purely bunk, or that his offer might have a string tied to it having for an easy bout," said Billy Mitchell, manager of his boxer brother.'[235]

The Mitchell fight brought bad reviews for the champion. 'LEONARD LOSES PUBLIC FAVOUR' ran a headline in the *New Castle News*, Pennsylvania, with *International News Service* sports editor Davis J. Walsh writing, 'Broadway and its habitués have turned thumbs down on Benny Leonard, the esteemed lightweight champion, following his rather dubious performance

233 Gilbert E. Odd *Was the Referee Right?* 1952
234 *Canton Daily News* Ohio 9 June 1923
235 *Titusville Herald* Pennsylvania 12 June 1923

against Pinky Mitchell and the subsequent testimony of men who witnessed the affair. Leonard, they aver, is absolutely thru and declare that the first contender with a punch to happen along will "take" him like a suicide takes poison …

'This is an old story that has been exhumed many times in the last several years, yet the existing reports have a very plausible ring; for example, Pal Moore, the bantamweight, declares that Leonard boxed like a wooden man against Mitchell and would have been easy for Charley White or Lew Tendler on the night in question. Not quite so unbiased, perhaps, is the word of White himself. Writing to a friend, White declared that he, "would have knocked Leonard out inside of ten rounds or he wouldn't have asked for a nickel for his services".

'The seemingly permanent retrogression in Leonard is his loss of speed. Gone is the dazzling footwork, the change of pace and the ability to feint an opponent silly; instead he now stands back on his flat feet and places all reliance in his punch. The change in style has brought Leonard, a great champion, down to the level of many challengers and the punishment he has taken during the last 12 months is hardly compatible with his reputation.'[236]

From the Illinois State capitol, Springfield, 20 June, 'Inquest on the death of the proposed boxing bill was held by the senate, sitting as a coroner's jury yesterday, and the verdict, that it was murdered by the Chicago "100,000 benefit show" that netted charity $24.25, was adopted by a vote of 14 to 28.

'The riotous performance staged at the close of the Benny Leonard–Pinky Mitchell fight was termed a plot engendered by Wisconsin promoters who saw a vanishing of fat profits if Illinois boxing fans were given the privilege of enjoying the sport at home. Senator Adolph Marks said the Leonard–Mitchell roughhouse was

---

236 Davis J. Walsh *New Castle News* PA. 8 June 1923

a plot of Wisconsin promoters and pointed out that the Mitchell brothers, in the thick of the milling, hailed from the Badger State.'[237]

Later in the month, Benny's press was a bit better. 'Benny Leonard of New York, world's lightweight champion, will defend his title in a 15-round match with Lew Tendler, Philadelphia southpaw, at the new Yankee's stadium on the night of 23 July. The boxers, together with their managers, late Tuesday signed contracts for the bout with the newly organised Cromwell Athletic Club, which has obtained ring privileges at the American League park. Financial terms, it was understood, called for the champion to receive 37½ per cent of the gross receipts and Tendler 12½ per cent. Club officials estimated that the fight would attract a gate of $400,000 and on this basis Leonard would receive about $150,000 for the defence of his crown and Tendler $50,000.

'The match was made as a result of a protracted period of negotiation and after spirited bidding for it by several metropolitan promoters. Tex Rickard, Madison Square Garden promoter, and Tom O'Rourke, Polo Grounds matchmaker, both were dickering for the match besides the Cromwell Club, of which Jimmy Johnston is the matchmaker. The last possible obstacle in the way of the match, it was said, was removed Monday night when ringside critics accorded Tendler a decisive verdict over Pal Moran of New Orleans, in a no-decision affray at Philadelphia.'[238]

New York, 23 June – 'The New Jersey boxing commission Friday notified the New York Athletic Commission that it would suspend Benny Leonard unless he fulfilled his unexpired contract to meet Charley White. The Leonard–White match was called off after the champion received an injury to his mouth which kept him out of the ring for some time. Meanwhile, his manager, Billy Gibson, has matched him to meet Lew Tendler at the Yankee Stadium 23

---

237 *Muscatine Journal and News Tribune* 20 June 1923
238 *Racine Journal News* Wisconsin 20 June 1923

July. White wants Leonard to box him first. Gibson claims that his charge's contract with White last October was revocable at the champion's pleasure, but the Chicagoan denies this statement.'[239]

After a meeting, the New York commission declined to uphold the New Jersey suspension of Leonard, stating that it found nothing in the White–Leonard contract to prevent either boxer from engaging in other contests and thus cleared the way for the championship match at the Yankee Stadium between Leonard and Tendler. After he had been informed of the New York body's decision, Newton A. K. Bugbee, director of the New Jersey commission, issued a statement saying, 'Leonard must respect his contract to box White in New Jersey before meeting Tendler. If he does not he and his manager Billy Gibson will be suspended indefinitely in this state.' Meanwhile, the Cromwell A. C. announced that Leonard and Tendler had posted forfeits of $10,000 each to guarantee a fulfilment of the contract for their 15-round decision match.

It was a somewhat happier champion who set off for his training camp in the sleepy village of Tannersville, New York. He had work to do.

---

239 *Canton Daily News* Ohio 23 June 1923

CHAPTER TWENTY

AT RINGSIDE for the *Philadelphia Inquirer* that July night in 1923, Gordon Mackay wrote, 'Headliner on the fistic programme provided for the 35,000 fans at the Phillie's Ball Park last night, the top-notch and biggest crowd that ever witnessed battling in this vicinity, Benny Leonard, lightweight champion of the world, outpointed Alex Hart in a dismal bout that went the limit of eight rounds. Mr Leonard some months ago donned the sock and buskin and started to elevate the stage. A short time ago, however, he left the drama flat and devoted his time and talents exclusively to the task of leaving his fighting opponents the same way.

'Last night's affair against Hart was a woeful thing to witness. Perhaps Benny did not care to besmear Alex's features over his face owing to the fact that Hart is to be married this week. Maybe, too, that the presence of Lew Tendler among the multitude on hand kept Benny from exerting all his skill and abilities, because Ben and Lew are to wrangle sometime this month in a bout that should settle definitely the best lightweight in all the broad domains of Uncle Sam.'[240]

The champion was a popular performer in Philly, the Hart bout being his 29th outing in the City of Brotherly Love, most of them

---

240 Gordon Mackay *The Philadelphia Inquirer* 10 July 1923

no-decision bouts. In April 1920, boxing matches were permitted to be eight no-decision rounds and a boxing commission was proposed to regulate the sport. After debate, a state athletic commission was established and bouts were allowed to be ten rounds, with official decisions rendered on 1 December 1923.

'Whether the cause, the Messrs Leonard and Hart did nothing to electrify the assembled thousands. Alex tried hard enough and he also intended to stay the limit if possible. But whatever the reason, whatever the cause, Leonard did not look good. His physical condition was superb, but his talents were awry. He missed punches that ordinarily he could land with his eyes closed. He had no zip or steam in his slams.'[241]

A worthy opponent, Hart listed three world champions among his victims: Johnny Dundee, Joe Dundee and Jimmy Goodrich. Sadly, Alex committed suicide in August 1934, aged 35.

'Benny Hertz, popular Carteret, New Jersey, lightweight boxer, is assisting Benny Leonard in preparing for the latter's second engagement with Lew Tendler. Tendler is conceded to be the strongest contender for Leonard's title at the present time. Hertz, now under the wing of Mannie Seamon, trainer of Leonard, has been added to the champion's camp for the purpose of developing the latter's speed. The remainder of the champion's sparring partners are southpaw boxers. Before leaving for Leonard's camp at Tannersville, Hertz worked out daily at Seamons's gymnasium in New York city.'[242]

Another visitor to Benny's camp is his mother. 'If Benny Leonard whips Lew Tendler at the Yankee Stadium on 23 July, when they meet in a 15-round encounter for the world's lightweight championship, he will give a big portion of the credit to his mother, who, at his training camp near Tannersville, New York, is the

241 Gordon Mackay *The Philadelphia Inquirer* 10 July 1923
242 *Perth Amboy Evening News* New Jersey 10 July 1923

devoted guardian of his health and comfort. The champion has never been separated from his mother for any length of training for important bouts, she never leaves him. Mrs Leonard personally supervises the preparation of his food and nothing reaches his table that she has not approved.

'The champion's mother is the embodiment of cheerfulness and optimism and if the strain of work and training begins to tell on the little champion, she is the first to detect and fight it. A little "mothering" and Benny apparently forgets his troubles. Mrs Leonard believes her warrior son is invincible in the ring and imparts this spirit of absolute confidence to everybody at the champion's training quarters. She seldom watches her boy while he is thumping his sparring partners and has never seen him, nor will she ever see him, in a ring battle. She is too gentle in spirit to enjoy seeing men pummel each other, even though they are wearing padded gloves. She remarked the other day, "Benny will win, of course, but I do hope he won't hurt Mr Tendler too badly."'[243]

'Leonard's stand in defence of his lightweight title has a sombre psychological background for him. He has been listening to the dull thud of falling champions for the last six months. In May, he saw his old pal Johnny Dundee relinquish the world's junior lightweight championship to Jack Bernstein. The stroke of the battle had hardly lifted when Johnny Kilbane, featherweight title holder, was enveloped in the resin dust of defeat – knocked out by the Frenchman Criqui. Then up stepped Jimmy Wilde, world's flyweight champion, to receive the axe at the hands of Pancho Villa, the brown terror from the Philippines. Benny might have been excused if he had paraphrased Shelley's line and remarked to himself: "With these kings gone, can I be far behind?"'[244]

243 *Chester Times* Pennsylvania 10 July 1923
244 *Bridgeport Telegram* 10 July 1923

'Leonard laughed when he was reminded that 1923 has been a jinx year for champions. "Well, I've thought about that," he admitted, talking to Max Case, "but you can tell my friends that Leonard is one champion that will get by." In his fights with Mitchell and his last bout with Tendler, Leonard was in bad straits, but is said to have saved himself by talking his opponent out of their advantage. The writer asked him about this, particularly of the eighth round of his fight with Tendler. In this fight, it will be recalled, Leonard is supposed to have talked the Philadelphian out of the fight after Tendler had him groggy with a terrific punch to the jaw.

"'Why, that is all foolish," Leonard exclaimed. "If I was in such a groggy condition as they say I was, then I could not very well have been in condition to talk to him. He clipped me a good punch on the jaw. I said to him, 'That was a good punch, Lew,' but as for talking him out of the fight that is foolish."

'The champion ridiculed reports that he was doing secret training. "It's funny how those rumours start," he said. "It rained here one or two days and I could not work in the open as I had been doing. So I pitched my ring in a ballroom of a hotel here. The place was so small that not many people could come in. Only said few were able to see me work and as a result I was training behind closed doors." Leonard said he had no intention of retiring after the Tendler bout. "Nothing of the sort," he said. "I'm only starting. Why, I'm only a young kid yet."[245]

'The spectacle of a world's champion boxer training in the grand ballroom of the hotel here, reputedly the most exclusive hostelry in the Catskill Mountains, has excited comment today among the oldest inhabitants of Greene County. Benny Leonard it was who upset the best traditions of this staid village when he marched in three sparring partners to do his first day's work indoors because

---

245 Max Case *Naugatuck Daily News* Connecticut 18 July 1923

of the rain. Three hundred vacationers saw Leonard go through his paces.

'The ballroom was lighted as it is when a dance is in progress. Trainer Mannie Seamon roped off an imaginary ring and society rubbed elbows with Catskill farmers while Leonard went through his workout. Willie Davis, Sid Terris and Sammy Berne in turn, for three rounds each, were on the receiving end of Benny's jabs and jolts. Then Leonard skipped the ropes for ten minutes and topped off with body exercises.'[246]

'For a champion who is about to defend his title against admittedly his most dangerous contender, Benny Leonard today is unusually carefree and exuberant. To say that he is confident of the outcome of his bout with Lew Tendler at the Yankee Stadium in New York next Monday would be superfluous. "Of course I will win," Leonard said, and then explained his showing in his bout with Tendler in July of last year.

'"You know southpaws are very peculiar. I've been fighting right-handers all my life and the first time I fought Tendler, I was a bit confused and puzzled. But I have had a year's time to scheme out the tactics of a southpaw. I know how they fight and I know how Tendler fights. Tendler is a good strong fellow. He is no easy man to beat and will take plenty of punishment. But still I will beat him."

'Leonard has not been given over to extravagant promises in the past. But his confidence was based on a knowledge of his opponent's ability and his own physical condition. The champion appeared trim and fit. The many weeks he has been working in open camp in this Catskills resort, favoured with every natural advantage, have aided in rounding him to the peak of physical perfection. "I feel fine, better than I have felt in a long time. I am in great shape. Today I weigh 136 pounds and it won't be a difficult task for me

---

246 *Danville Bee* Virginia 4 July 1923

to make the prescribed weight of 135 pounds on the afternoon of the fight.'"[247]

'New York 14 July – Benny Leonard is training at Tannersville N.Y. for his Lew Tendler fight in Yankee Stadium on 23 July. After a visit to his camp, promoter Jimmy Johnston said, "The champion looks fine. It isn't often that Leonard talks in advance of a fight – that is, talks about his hopes and expectations – but Benny told me that he expects to knock out Tendler."'[248]

'Benny Leonard is using golf in his training for the Lew Tendler match. Up in the Catskills these afternoons, he is socking the little white ball around the course, thereby defying the traditions of old-timers who say golf will prove the ruination of a ball player or fighter. The old-timers point to Jimmy Wilde, who played 18 holes the day before he met Pancho Villa and was knocked out.

'But it wasn't golf that beat Jimmy Wilde, it was Villa.'[249]

'In the parlance of the ring the promoters of the fight say, it is a natural,' reported Henry L. Farrell. 'They point to an advance sale of nearly $300,000 and they reasonably sound off the expectation of a gate of a half million dollars. In their last fight, one of the best of all lightweight fights, Tendler had his mental apparatus stopped by the fast vocal mechanism of the champion and he pulled up when one or two good socks would have had Benny on the floor for keeps. Leonard's fighting equipment goes beyond his shoulders, and Tendler has never shown the ability to think fast as a great fighter should. It is the brain factor in Leonard's favour that is making the champion a 9 to 5 favourite in the betting to retain his title.'[250]

Reporting from New York on fight day, 24 July 1923, Harry Newman recorded, 'While Benny Leonard and Lew Tendler were

---

247 *Athens Messenger* Ohio 18 July 1923
248 *Oakland Tribune* 15 July 1923
249 *Clinton Daily Clintonian,* Indiana 16 July 1923
250 Henry L. Farrell *Sandusky Star Journal* Ohio 19 July 1923

weighing in at 2pm this afternoon in accordance with the rules of the state athletic commission for their championship battle tonight, someone pulled a monumental blunder. The result of this was to cast suspicion in every direction. Indeed it gave good reason to believe there was something wrong with the match. The blunder had to do with the absolute exclusion of newspapermen from the room in which the two principals were weighing in.

'Under the articles for the match, Leonard and Tendler were obliged to weigh 135 pounds on the afternoon of the contest. The fighters duly appeared on the scene and were immediately ushered into the suite of the Cromwell A. C. at 25 West 43rd Street. It was then all the newspapermen were given the air. Not a soul was permitted to remain save several members of the boxing commission, Messrs Dayer, McCormack and the secretary Dan Skillings. The newspapermen made several assaults on the closed gate but without avail. They were told they could not see Leonard and Tendler on the scales, that the weights would be announced in due time.

'After quite a wait, word was sent out that Leonard weighed exactly 134 pounds, while Tendler scaled 133½ pounds. It is an unusual procedure to bar newspapermen from weighing-in ceremonies. All of which led the boxing writers to suspect that everything was not on the up-and-up with this big titular affair. There have been murmurings for some time that both principals would have some difficulty in making anything near 135 pounds.'[251]

One of the waiting newsmen voiced his feelings on the matter, telling his colleagues, 'If I put Jack Dempsey on that scale right now, he would weigh 135 pounds!' Bill McGeehan ended his fight report for the *Philadelphia Inquirer*, writing, 'While Tendler is one of the toughest, he also is one of the most sluggish and the most

---

251 Harry Newman *Sioux City Journal* 24 July 1923

awkward of the lightweights, if these two young men can be called lightweights.'

The fact that this is such a big-money bonanza leads to a somewhat unique situation that does not come out until years later. The way it happens is, three days before the fight, Billy Gibson says to Leonard that Tendler is about three pounds overweight and having a tough time getting down to the lightweight poundage. Benny is also struggling a bit with his weight and Gibson says to him at his Tannersville training camp, 'Why make the worst of it for the sake of taking his forfeit? You go in at the natural weight and we'll forget the forfeit. Jimmy Johnston assures me that he and boxing commissioner Walter Hooke will take care of the matter.'"

Benny later recalls that he is exactly 135 pounds at the time but he is delighted that he no longer has to worry about holding his weight. Now Johnston and Hooke set about rigging up a false weigh-in unknown to the sportswriters who are expecting to see the official weighing ceremony at Philadelphia Jack O'Brien's gym. The secret weigh-in is held in Johnston's office at 25 West 43rd Street and Deputy Commissioner Hooke announces to the enraged reporters when they finally track him down, 'I weighed both boxers in Johnston's office and the official weights were Leonard 134 and Tendler 134.'

Many years later, Leonard reveals that at 2pm on the afternoon of the fight he weighs 137½ and Tendler hits the scales at 138, and Tendler verifies the statement that on the big day they are both over the class limit of 135 pounds …

'To all indications, New York's greatest fight crowd was packed in the Yankee Stadium tonight to see Benny Leonard and Lew Tendler quarrel out the lightweight championship,' wrote James Crusinberry. 'Long before the sun sank behind the three-decked grandstand, the two dollar boys had filled the big but distant bleachers. There were 20,000 of them; many came armed with field glasses. The bleacher seats were not reserved. It was a case of first come, first seated, and the gang began surging in at five o'clock when the gates were opened. A great many had lunch boxes with them. Those who didn't bring their own raided the hot dog stands.

'The fight promoters had a brass band on hand to furnish entertainment for the early comers. The band was placed out in front of the bleachers. By eight o'clock, it had played "*Yes, we have no bananas*" 16 times! Just before eight o'clock, there was an unusual rush at the gates and it was learned three trainloads of Philadelphia fans had just arrived. Of course, they were a noisy lot and came to root for their prominent fellow citizen, Tendler.

'There was great commotion out in the bleachers just before the first preliminary and an investigation disclosed that Harry Wills, prominent resident of Harlem, was making his entrance. He towered above the throng around him as he walked to his seat, hat in hand, bowing acknowledgement of the applause. Harry has a lot of admirers among the two dollar boys who hope someday to see him fighting Jack Dempsey.'[252]

'Mannie and I scheme out three or four days in advance my plan of battle,' reported Benny. 'It will surprise you undoubtedly to know that four days before I fought Tendler in the Yankee Stadium I took Mannie, or better still, Mannie took me, behind closed doors. He enacted the role of Tendler, the Philadelphia southpaw, and I learned more about southpaws in the half hour or so that I spent with Mannie than during the whole months of training with a quartet of southpaws.'[253]

While the vast crowd of 58,519, who paid $452,648, a record for a non-heavyweight fight, were looking for their seats, veteran ring announcer Joe Humphreys was yelling out the names of the

---

252 James Crusinberry *Sioux City Journal* 24 July 1923
253 Ronald K. Fried *Corner Men* 1991

officials appointed by the boxing commission – judges Billy 'Kid' McPartland and Charles F. Mathieson and referee Andy Griffin.

The bell for round one brought the fighters from their corners and brought a roar from the crowd that must have been heard in Jersey City. Tendler missed a right chop at Leonard's head, they feinted, fenced, then Leonard hooked a right lightly to the head. Tendler looked in better condition than Leonard. He was brown and swarthy. Leonard's face looked drawn. They clinched and as their bodies came together they tried fiercely to hurt each other with short blows. Tendler drove Benny to the ropes and chugged his left to Leonard's body. As they came away from the ropes, a red streak showed along Benny's shoulder. It was a rope burn. At the bell, the round looked even.

Round two and the champion landed a straight left to Tendler's chin and as they closed in Tendler beat Benny about the body. Leonard got Tendler around the neck with his left arm and pummelled him with his right. Leonard clipped Tendler on the head with a solid right then repeated and as Tendler drew in close, he smashed him a right uppercut. Working both hands, Benny punched Tendler soundly as the round closed. Leonard's round.

They clinched as the bell rang for the third round. Leonard worked his right hand up against Tendler's jaw with good effect time and again. Now they began fighting. Tendler hammered Leonard about the body and also with an uppercut. Tendler turned to walk away from Leonard and Leonard fairly ran in chasing him, only to miss as the ropes stopped Lew's flight. Tendler jabbed twice with his right then got his left hand home to Benny's head. He jolted Leonard's head back with an uppercut. They came close together and Leonard stopped Tendler's rush with a body punch and a smash to the jaw that staggered Lew.

'Leonard got going good in the fourth round when he rocked Tendler with a left hook to the head and body. A right hook to the jaw and a right uppercut to the same place had Tendler so baffled he wasn't sure where he was. Leonard never looked better in his whole career. He was in splendid condition and from the very first bell it was apparent that he had learned well the way to stand off and beat the awkward left-hand style of his opponent. In his timing and judgement of distance, Leonard was perfection. In his boxing, he was a picture. In his generalship, he was a master.'[254]

In a clinch in the fifth, Leonard again punished Tendler with uppercuts. Tendler wiped his mouth with his glove to conceal the blood. Tendler hooked two lefts to Leonard's head as they came out of the clinch. Leonard jabbed him three times and again chased him across the ring as Tendler turned and walked away. Tendler rushed at Leonard head down and the smash he got under the chin must have made him see more stars than were visible in the skies. Leonard was not trying much of his famous footwork. He was standing solidly and punching with Tendler. At times, he boxed with his right hand extended in imitation of Tendler, a queer 'side-wheel' style ...

'Jab-jab-jab-jab. That's the staccato beat of Benny Leonard's left glove, as rhythmic as the tap of a woodpecker's bill, picking out boxing points last night on the pale profile of Lew Tendler, a tall youth from Philadelphia, with legs like scissors. Jab-jab-jab-jab-jab. That's Benny Leonard of the Bronx, New York, defending his title of lightweight champion of the world thru 15 long rounds to a decision against the man rated the most formidable of his contenders. Occasionally the incessant jab-jab was varied by a "kuh-blump" as if a woodsman had laid an axe against a hollow tree. That was Leonard's right hand falling against the chin of the tall Philadelphian.'[255]

Round six. After a tame opening, Leonard jabbed Tendler twice on the chin with his left. Tendler missed Leonard with a right

254 Henry L. Farrell *Chester Times* Pennsylvania 24 July 1923
255 Damon Runyon *Davenport Democrat and Leader* Iowa 24 July 1923

lead and Leonard side-stepped and left Tendler to fall over the middle rope. They touched gloves as Tendler recovered his feet, then Leonard chucked him under the chin with a right. Leonard landed three more rights. It was all Leonard's round.

'Leonard not only outfought the contender, but even beat him on those rare occasions when they stood up and slugged. The Leonard left had Tendler baffled from the very start. As the slow-thinking Philadelphian seemed to be contemplating shooting out a punch, Leonard would lead two, and they stung. Had Tendler not been about the toughest of them all, he would have crumpled before that rain of blows, first to the head, then to the body and then back to the head. The huge nose of Tendler, jutting out like a promontory, was red and bruised as the fight went on. Yet it always pointed at Leonard like the nose of a pointer, excepting when Leonard swung him around with rights or lefts to the chin.'[256]

Leonard jabbed Tendler with his left as the seventh opened then made Lew gasp and cringe with a right to the body. Tendler hooked his left to Benny's jaw but Leonard made him grunt with another body punch as they came together in a clinch. Leonard drove Tendler to the ropes in a neutral corner and gave him a sound slugging with both hands to head and body. Leonard seemed able to swing Tendler around as he pleased in the clinches. This was another round for Leonard. Tendler was not fighting up to his Jersey City form.

Before they answered the bell, Gibson talked earnestly to Benny and over in the other corner Glassman was whispering to Tendler. They pawed and jabbed and clinched in the early part of the eighth. The referee warned Tendler against wrestling. Leonard got Tendler in close to him and punched his jaw with a right uppercut. A couple of short right-hand body punches made Lew's mouth pop

---

256 W. O. McGeehan *The Washington Post* 24 July 1923

open. Leonard blocked a lead by Tendler and smashed Lew under the heart. As the bell rang, Leonard whaled Tendler on the chin with a right.

'There have been greater battles in ring history. Many title bouts have supplied thrills in greater quantity and quality, but this latest test for the lightweights was to tradition in every respect held before a tremendous outpouring of men and women interested in the strenuous sport, between two of the greatest lightweights of the ring today. The clash furnished enough excitement and spectacular moments for even the most exacting fans. Tendler earned the plaudits of the crowd by a truly great stand. The challenger fought a different battle than on the occasion a year ago when he last sought to wrest the title from Leonard in their bout at Jersey City. There was not the reckless aggressiveness Tendler flashed a year ago associated with his work last night. Still, unquestionably he fought up to his best. He tried with every ounce of his strength and every trick of the trade at his command to supplant Leonard as champion.'[257]

Leonard was dancing as the ninth opened, 'stepping' as he speared Tendler with his left. Tendler drove for Benny's body and Griffin warned him the punch was too low. Tendler dropped himself over the middle rope, missing a punch. Leonard punched him hard with uppercuts in a clinch after Tendler recovered his footing. Leonard outboxed Tendler all through the round, although Lew got one hard right to the face in at the bell. Again, Leonard's round.

Leonard cut a gash under Tendler's left eye with a left jab in the tenth. He was slipping Tendler's punches with his hand and folding up Tendler's rushes. Benny spat a little blood from bruised lips as he stood still and blocked Tendler's smashes. Then he crossed a right to Tendler's jaw and made Lew do the clinging vine act. He had Tendler totally befuddled.

---

257 *New York Times* 25 July 1923

The crowd began clapping their hands, the pugilistic crowd's sign of dissatisfaction as the 11th came on.

Then the crowd became curiously silent for a moment. Leonard jabbed and jabbed with his left to Tendler's face and hooked a right hard to Tendler's body. Tendler danced, his left poised until someone in the crowd yelled, 'Why don't you let it go, Lew?' Tendler finally did let it go, landing lightly on Leonard's chin. Leonard caught him with one and swung him around, Tendler almost falling. It was a tame round and all Leonard's.

'Tendler in his left-hand swinging looked clumsy when compared to the agile and graceful sharp-shooting champion. There was scarcely a round in which Tendler was out in front. Leonard picked off nearly every lead of the awkward left-hander and smacked him good and plenty when old Lew stumbled along missing like a novice at nearly every step. From the very outset, it was apparent Leonard was in there to give Lew a good licking. Several times during the journey, Leonard had Tendler on the verge of a knockout but to the credit of the Philadelphian he never whimpered even when the champion landed telling chops to the chin. He invariably recovered to fight his way back against the severe odds.

'From the 12th round on, it did not seem that Tendler could weather the rough passage. At the start of the 13th, Leonard ripped a smashing left to Tendler's stomach and then in a fierce exchange in which Leonard had the better, Tendler went to his knees. It did not seem to be from any one particular punch that Lew went down, but just a flurry of socks in a wild grapple in which Lew sank to his knees. He never took a count but bounded up and went to fighting back as hard as he knew how, but could make no impression against the clever Leonard.'[258]

---

258 Harry Newman *Sioux City Journal* 24 July 1923

In the 15th and final round, Lew was still trying with a right but missing just as often. Benny ripped a left and right to the face and then hooked a left to the body. Benny drove Lew to the ropes, plastering him with lefts to the body and rights to the face. Benny hit Lew on the jaw, sending him reeling across the ring. It looked like curtains for Lew but he held on. The big crowd was on its feet as Benny staggered Lew again with lefts and rights to the body and he was trying for a knockout, but Lew held on. Lew rocked Leonard with a wild swing to the head at the bell. Then Joe Humphreys, from the referees' and judges' stand, crawled into the ring and held up Leonard's right arm. Leonard grinned. Benny posed with Tendler for a final snapshot before he left the ring.

Benny was so far ahead and was handling Tendler so easily that there were some who thought he didn't want to knock Lew out. At breakfast in the hotel next morning, he held out both hands as evidence of the force with which he had struck. They were puffed and angry-looking. The skin on his knuckles was scuffed and peeled back.

'That guy has the hardest chin I ever hit,' said Benny …

CHAPTER TWENTY-ONE

WRITING FROM New York the day after the big fight, Max Kase put lightweight champion Benny Leonard on a pedestal. 'The Old Master – that old title which has rested unused on the pugilistic shelf since the great Joe Gans passed on – may now in all propriety be hauled out, dusted off and placed firmly on the brow of Benny Leonard. Never in his palmiest days did the marvellous negro lightweight display anything that would overshadow the dazzling exhibition of the lightweight champion last night before 60,000 fans in the Yankee Stadium, in decisively winning over Lew Tendler of Philadelphia in 15 rounds.

'Leonard's victory places him absolutely in a class by himself as far as the present-day lightweights are concerned. Tendler, without a doubt, a great lightweight, was so decisively whipped that he himself was the first to concede it.

'"You're a better man than I am Benny, and that's from the heart," he declared a few seconds after the final bell rang, as he and the champion stood in the middle of the ring, patting each other on the back. Later, in his dressing room, Lew told reporters, "Benny is the greatest fighter the world has ever known in my estimation. He made me do things I didn't want to do. I never could get going because he always seemed to know what I planned and prevented me from doing it."'[259]

---

259 Max Kase *Logansport Pharos Tribune* Indiana 24 July 1923

W. O. McGeehan ended his report for the *Washington Post* in a lighter vein. 'Of the lightweight championship battle, we read that Leonard would have had less trouble in getting Tendler down if he had not had so much trouble in keeping his own trunks up.

'That a boxer after months of rigid training should in the test be hampered by loose tights is indeed a sad consideration. But Benny Leonard is of the stoic school. Even when one hand was drafted by propriety, that other kept remodelling Tendler's facial contours. Not by accident was man given two arms with which to ward off adversities.'

According to Heywood Broun, who covered the fight for the *New York World*, 'The wonder is that Tendler still had a head. Rights and lefts, hooks and jabs rocked him from the beginning. Water cascaded from the top of the Philadelphian's pompadour as if he had been Old Faithful, the Geyser. Now his head went back. Next it sagged, but mostly was doubled from side to side as Leonard landed first with one hand and then with the other. Distinctly this was highbrow entertainment, for it was boxing developed to its most lofty phase as a fine art. The only trouble was that it was not a contest between two masters. The participants were professor and pupil.'

Boxing writer Hype Igoe had this to say in the *New York World*, 'They will tell tomorrow and tomorrow that our Benny played it safety first but what I'm seeing before me is something vastly more thrilling than the wild eighth-round climax of their first fight. This is artistry, mastery. It is a plan of intelligent battle expertly executed. This is the finest of matadors working the cape against a brave bull.

'From any angle of boxing, it is the finest job these old eyes have ever glimpsed, and I have been watching them since the turn of the century, almost. Oh, friends, I don't ever expect to see it duplicated, not until I begin to braid my long white grogans in three plaits. Benny, you are a beaut!'[260]

---

260 Hype Igoe *New York World* 24 July 1923

Damon Runyon, in his column a couple of days after the fight, wrote, 'Jim Dougherty, "The Baron of Leiperville," referee of the Dempsey–Gibbons fight at Shelby, saw the Leonard–Tendler battle Monday night. "Leonard has the finest ring mind of any fighter I ever saw," Dougherty said to the writer after the fight. "He has brains. He knows what he is doing, why he is doing it. In addition to his amazing boxing mentality, he is a thorough ring mechanic. He is beyond any lightweight I've ever seen, and I've seen them all for the past 30 years. I knew Gans as well as any man," said the Baron. "He trained at my place many times. I saw him in a lot of fights. Leonard would have whipped him as easily as Leonard whipped Tendler. As for Nelson and Wolgast, Leonard as he stands today is head and shoulders above them at their best. Leonard is a great fighter – a real great fighter."'[261]

Writing a few weeks before the Tendler fight, Arthur Housman noted, 'Benny Leonard has mapped out an ambitious programme this year. First, Leonard has been booked for a series of five fights with more or less eminent contenders. Secondly, he intends to make a drive for literary honours, and thirdly, he has accepted an offer to go on tour with a music production.

'After these fights, Leonard has plans to retire – for some months at least. Soon after that, he will publish his autobiography, which he will call "Six Years a Champion". In September, he will take the road with a Broadway musical comedy, under Shubert management, and will continue as a thespian for at least three months.'[262]

Two of the fights have been accounted for – Alex Hart and Lew Tendler. Two of the other three, versus Charley White and Sailor Freedman, never got off the ground, which left Mickey Walker, the 'Toy Bulldog' now in possession of the welterweight title, the Mick having relieved Jack Britton of same. A week before taking up the

261 Damon Runyon *Davenport Democrat and Leader* 25 July 1923
262 Arthur Housman *New Castle News* Pennsylvania 27 June 1923

challenge of Tendler, Benny had instructed manager Billy Gibson to undertake negotiations for a world's welterweight championship bout against Mickey Walker.

'Gibson returning yesterday from a trip to Leonard's training quarters at Tannersville, NY, made the statement, "Benny is eager to tackle Walker and is confident he can gain the welterweight title."' [263]

'Benny Leonard, world's lightweight champion, is planning a vacation from ring activity through the indoor season, according to an announcement from the champion's training camp at Tannersville, NY, where he is preparing for the 15-round battle in which he will defend his crown against Johnny Dundee, veteran Italian holder of the world's featherweight title, at the Yankee Stadium on 5 September. The approaching contest will be Leonard's last ring appearance at New York until next outdoor season, if the champion follows the plans he has announced. Leonard is ambitious to make a name for himself behind the floodlights and he intends returning to the stage when the outdoor season closes.

'In addition to the bout with Dundee, Leonard will engage in two other matches. He is scheduled to box Johnny Mendelson of Milwaukee in an eight-round bout in Philadelphia on 7 September, and on 15 September he is scheduled to box Charley O'Connell at Cleveland. Leonard is eager to engage Mickey Walker, world's welterweight champion, in a title match and he has instructed manager Billy Gibson to continue negotiations for such a match.

'Dundee is proceeding with his training at his home in Orange, New Jersey. The featherweight titleholder, like Leonard, is ambitious to hold two ring titles and despite his many years of ring activity, feels confident he can outpoint Leonard with the champion down to 135 pounds.'[264]

---

263 *New Britain Herald* Connecticut 17 July 1923
264 *Biddeford Daily Journal* Maine 28 August 1923

Jimmy Johnston, promoter of the Leonard–Dundee bout and the man known as the 'Boy Bandit', was very high on Dundee, as he informed the press a week before the fight.

'In the world's boxing history, the prize ring has never seen the equal of Dundee,' he said. 'He is leathery, elusive, a punishing type of boxer-fighter combination, the most spectacular and colourful man in any class in the ring today, as well as the most popular boxer of all time and one of the greatest the world has ever seen. Although the great Leonard has fought Dundee eight times, he has yet to solve the mysterious style of this miracle man of the ring. And it is this inability to solve Dundee's peculiar style that makes the interest in the Leonard–Dundee battle so great despite the fact that they have met so many times before.'[265]

'New York, 27 August 1923 – Johnny Dundee, featherweight champion of the world, meets Eddie 'Kid' Wagner at Shetzline Ball Park, Philadelphia tonight, and a tremendous risk he is taking. Not that Wagner is likely to knock Dundee 40 ways for Sunday or even to win the popular decision, but let's be Job's comforter for a while. When Dundee signed to meet this speedy trick from Quakertown he knew that a broken hand, an arm, a leg, yea, a neck, might spoil his chance to annex the lightweight title at the Yankee Stadium on 5 September when he meets Benny Leonard. Dundee figures to outpoint Wagner, but then there is always the chance of being injured, and, splendid little gambler that he is, he has no lurking fear of black men, jinx birds or hoodoo hounds.'[266]

Well, the worst happened.

'Eddie 'Kid' Wagner, bustling young mauler of this Quaker City, swung to the heights of fistic fame last night, when he decisively defeated Johnny Dundee, featherweight champion of fistiana, in eight rounds in the stellar bout at Shetzline Park. Twelve thousand

---

265 *Cincinnati Commercial Tribune* 26 August 1923
266 *New Britain Herald* Connecticut 27 August 1923

spectators saw the upset as Wagner won every round bar the first, which was an even affair. Not only did the Philadelphian outfight, outgeneral and conquer the champion, but he left the marks of his prowess in the shape of a damaged left eye that Dundee will tote into training for several days as he prepares for his coming titular battle with Benny Leonard, lightweight champion.

'Few among those who withstood the attacks of the weeping heavens, fitful gusts of rain sweeping the amphitheatre during the main melee, expected such an outcome as Wagner's doughty fists provided last night. Wagner dominated the feud every minute after the first round. He developed a rattling left hand that he stuck tantalisingly into Dundee's face, over and anon, coupled with a speedy right swing that rarely failed to find a resting place on the Italian's face and body. Dundee appeared for this little ripple on his fistic career unprepared for a scrap with such a dauntless youngster as Wagner proved last night. He was fat, unquestionably so, the flesh rolling in little billows over his trunks. His footwork, usually of the lightning speed variety, was totally absent last night. Wagner was given an ovation when he left the ring in triumph, while a swelling chorus of boos bade farewell to the champion.'[267]

'Before a special meeting of the New York State Athletic Commission this afternoon, Johnny Dundee protested vigorously against the postponement by promoter Jimmy Johnston of the Italian's scheduled match tonight at the Yankee Stadium with the lightweight champion, but after hearing all the evidence in the situation, the boxing solons upheld Johnston and sanctioned the cancellation.

'The commission ruled that Johnston was within his rights in taking advantage in the event either of the principals was defeated in any other engagement before the title match. Dundee left this

---

267 Gordon Mackay *The Philadelphia Inquirer* 28 August 1923

loophole open to the promoter as a result of his recent defeat by Eddie 'Kid' Wagner in Philadelphia.

'But the question arises, Why did Johnston wait until the 11th hour before he took such action when he knew Dundee lost a battle ten days ago? Was this because he learned that Leonard could not make the weight and acted then? Dundee's attitude, meanwhile, may result in abandonment of the match altogether. After Johnston's proposal to stage the bout at the Stadium on 28 September, Dundee told the commission he would give an answer on Friday. To newspapermen later, he flatly declared he would not go through with the match at all. Billy Gibson, Leonard's manager, however, agreed to the postponement date. Dundee declared he would claim the title and Leonard's weight forfeit of $5,000, but the commission advised him that he had no grounds upon which to base such action.'[268]

With that settled, lightweight champion Benny Leonard prepared for his fight with Johnny Mendelson in Philadelphia on 7 September, an eight-round no-decision bout with the understanding that should Mendelson stop the champion inside the distance he would be entitled to claim the title. In the event, Benny won seven of the rounds, the fifth being called even. Mendelson proved that he had both the strength and courage to take all that the champion handed out, and it was the consensus of opinion that he gave Leonard a better fight than Lew Tendler did in New York.

In February 1924, Sparrow McGann was writing from New York, 'Among the many so-called great ring battles that are expected to occur in the outdoor arena next summer, there is one and one only that promises to be a real out-and-out scrap, worth anything the promoters have to pay to stage it. The reference is to the proposed Benny Leonard–Mickey Walker battle. Here is a

---

268 Gordon Mackay *The Philadelphia Inquirer* 6 September 1923

battle for you! Even the most ardent admirers of Benny Leonard would not give odds on his defeating the young Jersey wildcat.

'Make no mistake about Mickey Walker, boys. He is a real scrapper and a real champ in every respect, except a willingness to risk his title in comparatively small-money bouts. Facing the Kerreighhead lad in the ring, Benny Leonard would have 15 of the most active rounds he ever went through, assuming both fighters stayed with each other that long. The outlook is that Benny will meet Walker for the welter title and then retire to an actor's career, win or lose, with his reputation as an undefeated lightweight champ an honour which no one has attained since the days of old Jack McAuliffe.

'If either Benny or Mickey want any money this summer, it is absolutely necessary that they get together. So Leonard has no opposition in his lightweight class. Same for Mickey Walker in the welter division. A meeting between Leonard and Walker is a logical issue from a financial and sporting standpoint and present indications make it seem certain they will get together.[269]

'There was one thing that bothered Benny,' Fleischer wrote in his Leonard biography. 'Every time he fought, the picture of his ma fretting at home acted as a disturbing element. When he knocked out Richie Mitchell in the Garden, he came home to find his mother being treated by the family physician, who informed him that Mrs Leiner had fainted when she heard about the knockdown he had suffered and that for more than an hour she was in a serious condition. "Benny," said the doctor, "you'll have to consider your mother. It is getting to be a serious problem. She worries too much when you fight and if you don't want her health to fail, you'll have to give up the ring."

---

269 Sparrow McGann *Canton Daily News* Ohio 17 February 1924

'That didn't help Benny mentally. He knew about his ma's feelings because she had frequently pleaded with him to quit fighting, but he realised that there was no other vocation in which he could earn what he could in boxing and he also figured that he owed an obligation to the game that had enabled him to rise to the heights. "Just one or two more fights, ma, and I'll hang 'em up for good," he told her, but she knew better.'[270]

For some time following the second fight with Lew Tendler, it was common knowledge that Leonard was having great difficulty remaining in the lightweight class. Hence, following the mill, Billy Gibson decided to let nature take its course and urged Benny to fight welterweights.

Mickey Walker had just won the welter title from Jack Britton and a fight with the popular Jersey 'Toy Bulldog' would be good for a $750,000 gross. Gibson and Tex Rickard went after Leonard in an effort to sew up the match. Rickard offered a flat guarantee of $300,000 with a large percentage privilege and Leonard went into training.

But it wasn't working too well.

It was a year since the Mendelson fight and he'd been used to fighting regularly. Benny knew he wasn't right for Walker, not yet at least. He told Gibson and his manager agreed to get him a tune-up fight with a live contender. Benny felt happier when Gibson signed him to face Pal Moran over ten rounds in Cleveland on 11 August 1924.

Promoters Matt Hinkel and Tommy McGinty knew Moran had already given Leonard two difficult bouts, which is why they selected him. None of the other current lightweights stood out as being worthy opponents for Leonard for he had knocked out or badly beaten all of them. Try as he might in their east Chicago and

---

270 Nat Fleischer *Leonard the Magnificent* 1947

New Orleans battles, however, Benny could do no more than barely outpoint the combative Southerner.

At ringside in Cleveland, Vince Dolan reported, 'The old saying of childhood days "as easy as falling off a log" is about the most appropriate title one could give the Benny Leonard–Pal Moran skit at Olympic Arena, this city last night, in the presence of 18,000 fans. Leonard, the dashing Valentino of the prize ring, handed Pal Moran the most decisive beating that famous New Orleans Italian has been the recipient of since he first started plying the leathers for a living. The champion won every round, most of them by a margin so wide that everybody felt sorry for Moran. But the New Orleans boy stayed the limit. He was still trying to punch when the final bell sounded, but his blows were harmless.'[271]

'It cost me more than $100,000 to win from Pal Moran, New Orleans lightweight, in Cleveland the other night,' Benny Leonard wrote for the *Lowell Sun*. 'And it was worth it! I cracked my left thumb in the third round. As a result of that injury, I will not be able to fight Mickey Walker in New York this month. I may not be able to fight him before next spring. The Walker fight would have brought me more than $100,000. I got less than $12,000 for winning from Moran.

'I can hear the critics say, "How foolish of Leonard to run the risk of losing the Walker match just to pick up a few thousand by meeting a set-up." Well, I'm a Jewish boy and I don't exactly cringe at the sight of money. But I didn't take on Moran with the idea of adding to my bank roll. I needed a fight, a good, spirited fight that would put me on edge for Walker. I knew Walker was tough, carried too many guns, was heavier, and besides, I wanted to win his title.

'The result assured me I haven't gone back. I found my footwork as good as ever and my punching as sharp and hard as in days gone

271 Vince Dolan *Canton Daily News* Ohio 12 August 1924

by. I had some doubts as to my ability to whip Walker before; now I have none whatever. My thumb will heal in a month or so. After that, I will continue actively in the ring. I will be in perfect trim when I do meet Walker and I will beat him.'[272]

Syndicated columnist Frank G. Menke was picking Leonard to beat Walker. 'Just why most citizens reckon that Mickey Walker is certain to knock Benny Leonard into a prolonged coma is a mystery.

'Walker isn't a terrific hitter.

'Leonard can take terrific punishment.

'Walker, against a large collection of bozos, has not compiled anything remotely approaching a kayo record.

'Leonard has met Charley White, Richie Mitchell, Pinky Mitchell, Rocky Kansas, Pal Moran and a score of other lusty swingers – and none ever has put him to sleep.

'Why then the theory that Walker can do it? Those who count on Walker to win with a knockout seem to forget, momentarily, that Walker is not a true marksman. He can hurt when he hits – but he doesn't hit so often. He swings his punches, rather than shoots them straight. And a swinger isn't going to accomplish a lot with Leonard. Between the two men, Leonard is the truer hitter, and infinitely the harder hitter. He isn't in the habit of dropping his man with a punch. He can't hit that hard. But he sprays forth jolting blows and unless his foeman is made of concrete, those punches eventually take all the keenness for further warfare right out of the foeman.

'So, when the last blow has been dealt, the announcer will step forward, hold aloft a hand, and clarion, "The winner and the new welterweight champion – Benny Leonard."'[273]

Writer Sparrow McGann had a different slant on the Walker fight. 'Hint Leonard Ran Out of Bout For Welter Title with

272 Benny Leonard *Lowell Sun* Mass. 15 August 1924
273 Frank G. Menke *Steubenville Herald Star* Ohio 22 August 1924

Walker. Lightweight champ used dislocated thumb yarn to escape titular battle with rugged Irish battler. The bout originally was to have been fought next Wednesday, 20 August, but when the match was made Leonard already had an agreement to meet Pal Moran in Cleveland. After it was over, while the champion was still in the ring, a physician who had sat at the ringside throughout the battle was called to the fighter's side. He at once got out his splints and did up the thumb in a manner to indicate it had been cracked in two places. Later, it was established there was no break. One opinion is said to have been that Leonard's thumb was dislocated at the terminal joint. Another is said to have gone this one better and had both thumbs injured.

'Anyway, the whole incident has set the fans talking, the more so because this is not the first time Leonard has had his hands injured when a bout was pending. He gave that as a reason for pulling out of his first match with Lew Tendler and has called the good old injured hand alibi into play when for one reason or another he failed to knock an opponent kicking. Then there was talk that Benny decided in the course of his bout with Moran that he needed more time in which to get ready for a tough bird like Mickey Walker. This is generally credited as plausible and almost everyone thinks that if Leonard did find himself too rusty, he was right in not hurrying to meet Walker.'[274]

'Some weeks ago,' wrote Joe Williams, 'Leonard signed to meet Mickey Walker for the welterweight title. As you know, the bout fell through because Leonard splintered a fairly valuable thumb on the corrugated head of Pal Moran. I saw the champion on the scales the day before the Moran fight. He weighed an ounce or no more than 140 pounds. "I can make it with hard work," Leonard assured as he stepped off the scales. "But the trouble is there is no

---

274 Sparrow McGann *Davenport Democrat and Leader* Iowa 22 August 1924

outstanding challenger among the lightweights – no contender that would pack 'em in at the gate. That's why I agreed to battle Walker.'"

Gibson proceeded to tell an amazing story of how he and Leonard had capitalised on the widespread belief that the champion was 'heavy'. One of Leonard's notable knockout victories was scored at the expense of Johnny Kilbane in three rounds in 1917 at Philadelphia. This was shortly after Leonard had won the championship from Freddie Welsh.

'Contrary to custom, Leonard agreed to fight Welsh at 135 instead of 133. This created the impression that Leonard could not make 133 pounds. Kilbane figured the champion would be weak at the low weight and took him on. Leonard came in at 133½ and handed the Irishman his first knockout. Gibson claims Lew Tendler was hoodwinked in similar fashion.

'Tendler would have had none of Leonard's game if he had known the champion could do the weight. We helped him along in his pet delusion by weighing in heavy for one of the Johnny Dundee fights over in Jersey. Leonard wore his bathrobe on the scales. In the pockets of the robe, he concealed two lead weights. The scales registered 139½ pounds. As a matter of truth, Leonard weighed less than 136 pounds.'[275]

275 Joe Williams *Athens Sunday Messenger* Ohio 17 August 1924

CHAPTER TWENTY-TWO

'"BILLY, WE'VE been through a lot of scenery in the past seven years," Benny was saying to his manager. "We've both made money in our partnership, but I've decided the time has come when we must break it. I've fought my last fight. I'm afraid I've reached the end of my trail, Billy, and I want to retire as the world's undefeated lightweight champion."

'Gibson looked sadly at the boy whom he had cherished as he had his own son. Tears came to his eyes as he replied, "Benny, you're doing the right thing. I've got no regrets. I'm happy that you are doing this not because as you say, you've reached the end of the rope – far from it – but because the love for your mother has brought you to this decision. I know what you think of her, Benny. She's your best pal. Stick to her and your decision.

'"There isn't a lightweight in this world who is your equal even now and we both know it. You're retiring with more money than any lightweight champion ever had and you're taking this with you while you've still got your full health. I know that you're leaving the ring with the best wishes of a million people going with you."

'Only one thing remained. Benny wanted to bring additional joy to his mother. He was eager to make her happy by having it appear that she, not he, had been responsible for the position Benny was taking. Turning to Gibson, he said, "Billy, let's keep this a secret until ma makes it public. Let me call my pal, Francis Albertanti, of the *New York Telegram* and give him the story to publish."[276]

Gibson agreed with Benny, and Albertanti was called to Leonard's home for an interview with Ma Leiner and there she gave him the beat that in a few hours was spread to all parts of the world – 'Benny Leonard's Ma Announces His Retirement.'

It was two months later that Benny's letter was published in the Australian newspaper the *Sydney Referee* and Benny had added something – 'a little story that has never been told before. It will help you to understand'.

'Billy Gibson called me on the telephone not long ago. "I've got something important to tell you, Benny," he said. 'When I went down to meet him, he told me this. "You know, Benny, you ought to quit fighting." I looked at Gib and laughed. "Don't you think I can fight any more?" I asked. "Why, I am just beginning to learn how to fight." He told me it wasn't that. "It's your mother, Benny." I saw a watery look in Gib's eyes. I asked him what he meant by that. "I tell you, Benny," he said. "I met your mother yesterday. She cried like a baby. She told me I was the only one that could do anything to stop you from boxing. I tell you, Benny, the way you love your mother, you will have to stop fighting. The shock of another fight or two will be too much for her."

'Well, I looked at Gibson's face. I saw a tear drop out of his good Irish eye. I couldn't speak. Through my mind just one thought ran. It was the character of the man who was my manager and pal Gibson who was asking me to stop fighting – I, the champion of the world, who earns thousands of dollars for Gibson when I box – because it would break my mother's heart to have her son, Benny, fight. This shows that Billy Gibson thinks more of friendship than of gold.'[277]

276 Nat Fleischer *Leonard the Magnificent* 1947
277 Benny Leonard *The Sydney Referee* Australia 25 March 1925

Henry L. Farrell 'wrote of plans for the organisation of a tournament to find the successor to Benny Leonard, world's lightweight champion, were being considered today by the New York boxing commission. Leonard announced last night that he was retiring from the ring in deference to the wishes of his mother. Mrs Leiner was seriously ill at Atlantic City several months ago, and it was intimated at that time by Bill Gibson, the champion's manager, that she had called the family together and made Benny promise that he never would fight again. "I am not giving up boxing for glory, or because I can't make the weight, but I am retiring for the love of my mother. She is in bad health and I fear that she could not bear the strain if I fought again," Leonard said in a long statement.'[278]

'In recent months, the retired champion has confined his activities to the stage and screen and is about to start on a long vaudeville engagement. Illness overtook him in a New York theatre recently and he swooned as he retired to the wings after he had finished his act. He is not fully recovered yet. Leonard is retiring from the ring in good financial circumstances and with a foundation for a stage career laid by months of preparation. Thus he is following in the footsteps of another noted pugilist, James J. Corbett.'[279]

'Who is the next lightweight champion? Benny Leonard is still lightweight monarch of the world, but it appears to be the common belief that it is impossible for him to do 135 pounds, the lightweight limit, although this is of course denied by Leonard and those around him. Moreover, Benny has formally retired and there is a possibility, of course, that the retirement is *bona fide*. Now they are planning an elimination tournament to determine who Leonard's successor shall be. The fact seems to be that the East Side of New York has

278 Henry L. Farrell *Madison Wisconsin State Journal* 16 January 1925
279 *Davenport Democrat and Leader* Iowa 16 January 1925

developed another Jewish boy who is destined to climb to the purple heights of pugilism. Both Leonard and Sid Terris come from that section of the city east of Fifth Avenue. Benny first saw the light of day in the upper reaches of the East Side. Terris comes from that section known as the "lower East Side". Probably Benny Leonard, were he asked to describe the man who is destined to step into his classic shoes, would say, "Well, I'd like him to be a Jewish boy from the East Side."

'That is quite the way the unsettled lightweight situation is likely to turn out. It will either be a Jewish boy from the so-called "lower East Side", or a sparkling youth from Chicago who will push Benny Leonard into the shadows and usurp the limelight that goes with the lightweight championship of the world. When Sid Terris and Sammy Mandell get together, Benny Leonard will find himself up against the last trench. It will be necessary for him to step out and go over the top against the winner of that affair.'[280]

'Benny Leonard, retired king of the lightweights, started a fight with his letter of farewell. Into the ring climb the National Association of Boxing Clubs, the New York State Athletic Commission and the Madison Square Garden Boxing Association, the latter comprising George L. (Tex) Rickard, all determined to find a successor to Leonard. Rickard is quoted as having said that he will recognise the winner of the bout between Sammy Mandell and Sid Terris at the Garden on 6 February as the title holder and to the successful one will go a diamond-studded belt emblematic of the honour.'[281]

On that Friday night at the Garden, Sid Terris, bright hope of the East Side, ran a poor second to Sammy Mandell of Rockford, Illinois, who gave the New Yorker the licking of his life, winning all but round five of the 12-round bout. Mandell's victory virtually

---

280 *Biddeford Daily Journal* Maine 7 February 1925
281 *Lowell Sun* Massachusetts 17 January 1925

CHAPTER TWENTY-TWO

stamped him as the new lightweight champion but he had to beat Rocky Kansas to gain recognition as the press boys were still pushing their tributes to Benny Leonard through their typewriters and running out of superlatives just as fast.

A leader writer in the *Alton Evening Telegram*, Illinois, titled his piece 'A Real Man'. 'Benny Leonard, champion lightweight boxer and the best there is in that line, is a real man. Who but a real man could return from a line of effort that was yielding and would yield him great profits, and give as his reason that his mother worried too much about him staying in the fighting game?

'When Benny Leonard gives up fighting, it is just like it would be if John D. Rockefeller quit the oil business or E. H. Gary quit the steel business. It would be just like some famed surgeon ceasing to practise surgery, or a great lawyer closing his office because a mother happened to disapprove. Benny Leonard shows to the world he deserved every bit of the admiration the world gave him as the best lightweight fighter. He was the best in more ways than one, and his announcement of his plan to quit and the reason therefor proves it.'[282]

Syndicated sportswriter Sparrow McGann headed his tribute simply, 'GREATEST in RING HISTORY – Benny Leonard's retirement was the big incident of the week and of course all the fans and all the experts are talking and arguing as to whether or not this great lightweight king was the greatest of all lightweights. There are various opinions. This writer is not going to give any opinion. He is going to cite facts and let the fans judge for themselves. What will the facts show? They will prove that Benny sent more opponents to sleep than any lightweight in ring history. That ought to be good enough for Leonard and probably it is.

---

282 *Alton Evening Telegram* Illinois 17 January 1925

'It might also be stated that Benny is the one lightweight champion since Jack McAuliffe's day who retired undefeated.

'Leonard will be a loss to the game not only because of his drawing power, but because of his gentlemanly instincts and his ideal family life. There is no question that he was a great champion in every sense of the word, and there never was any question as to his fighting ability. He has a following in the theatre which will not diminish for some years. For Leonard will carry with him in his theatrical tours the prestige of a champion who retired undefeated after he had given every contender one and frequently more than one chance at his title.'[283]

'It is high time that Jack Dempsey, champion of the heavyweights, and Benny Leonard, champion of the lightweights, either closed their traps or their careers.' This was Joe Williams getting stuff off his chest. 'Dempsey tells interviewers, in one self-sacrificial breath, he will fight as soon as a logical opponent in whom "the public is interested" is developed. In the next breath, he talks of retiring. Leonard is lacking in originality. In much the same language he says precisely the same thing, only oftener.

'We have great admiration for Leonard the fighter, and Leonard the man. But we are convinced Leonard is using his position as lightweight champion solely as a means to further his theatrical interests. Our quarrel with Leonard is he insists on posing as a superlative genius – an Alexander with no more beaks to bust. The cold truth is, enough opposition exists in the lightweight ranks to keep Leonard busy for a whole year.

'A stilling stagnation is coming over the heavyweight and lightweight divisions. Dempsey and Leonard should do one of two things. Either make good their threat to retire or start fighting.'[284]

283 Sparrow McGann *Davenport Democrat and Leader* Iowa 18 January 1925
284 Joe Williams *Charleston Daily Mail* West Virginia 18 January 1925

At Dubuque, Iowa, 'A musical revue in which numerous fine vaudeville features are introduced with a wonderful background of scenery and a comely supporting chorus of singing and dancing girls will open an engagement at the Majestic Theatre today. All this to see plus additional attraction that is expected to prove a big hit is a film *Flying Fists*, in which the famous Benny Leonard, lightweight ring champion of the world, is the star actor. Benny is qualifying as a film star and shows his fighting wares promiscuously in the picture. The show runs three times today, Sunday, but during the week will run twice daily, matinee and night.'[285]

'Leonard's first venture into film-land was in the 1924 picture *Flying Fists*. It was a three-reel film with considerable romance. He had no trouble in making headway in the fistic portion of the film but when it came to acting sentimental scenes, that was a horse of another colour. Having never previously been in love, Benny floundered in his lovemaking to the gorgeous Diana Allen, and so poor a lover was Leonard that director Lawrence C. Windon had to spend three weeks instructing the lightweight king in the proper technique.

'The picture, like many other films in which world champions were the heroes, was a flop. In that respect, Benny had fine company for Dempsey's picture didn't make any more of a hit with the public. Following his first retirement, Leonard appeared in several other Hollywood screen scenes. On several occasions while visiting Hollywood, he appeared with Charlie Chaplin. Chaplin, an ardent boxing enthusiast, put the gloves on with the champ and when the British comedian made the short *Tough Luck*, in which he used ten-ounce gloves on one of the characters, Benny helped supervise that portion of the picture.

'Benny also went into vaudeville, where he gave boxing exhibitions and told of his ring experiences. As a performer on

---

285 *Dubuque Telegraph Herald* Iowa 15 February 1925

the legitimate stage, Benny was far more successful than in the movies. His popularity continued and, being a good storyteller, he was besieged with vaudeville offers, which he accepted. He travelled to all parts of the country and added a considerable sum to his income.

'He was still the champ to the fight fans and wherever he appeared, they came out in large numbers.'[286]

Benny still loved Hollywood and appeared in eight films between 1920 and 1925. He also received one credit as a writer.

From New York, Davis J. Walsh penned a column, 'Benny Leonard has not fought his last fight, regardless of his signed statement to that effect, a statement in which pathos and mother love ran along on a high octave. This declaration was made today by close friends who split no infinitives in predicting that the diffident, retiring young man would be seen in a local ring next summer for one last shot at the big, important money. The occasion, they said, would bring Leonard and Mickey Walker together in their long-deferred battle for the welterweight title and that Benjamin would be recompensed thereby to the matter of $200,000.

'"Benny was entirely sincere when he retired from the lightweight title," one of his local intimates declared. "He knows he cannot make the weight and be strong. He knows also that his mother seriously objects to him continuing in the fighting game indefinitely. But she can be won over. Benny has had to do it for other fights and he can do it again. There is entirely too much money for him in a Walker match to be left lying around idle."

'If Leonard can get $200,000 for his end, and there is plenty of loose money which says he can, it would smack of fistic heresy for him to refuse. For less than an hour's activity in the ring, he can

---

286 Nat Fleischer *Leonard the Magnificent* 1947

thus make more money than in a year and a half on the vaudeville stage, provided theatrical audiences continue to evince sufficient interest in his act.'[287]

'Just why Benny should be counting so much on the screen is hard to figure,' wrote Fair Play. 'He has one or two very costly experiences in that direction and found himself so definitely appraised as no rival at all of Doug Fairbanks and Valentino that only his fighting spirit probably has led him to make another stab. Then again, someone else may be putting up the money. Which would make all the difference in the world, of course. Speaking of pictures, they do say that Jack Dempsey as a movie hero is not turning them away at the box office of the film houses. Dempsey draws best when he appears as his normal and natural role as a bruiser. When he puts paint on his cheeks and rouge upon his lips and looks with languishing eyes upon the girl in the case, he fills everyone with a gnawing desire to hurl half portions of brick through the screen.'[288]

'The mother song which Benny Leonard sang earlier in the year has lost its melody for the lad who amassed a fortune as world's lightweight champion. According to a statement issued Friday by Billy Gibson, who piloted Leonard into the world's title and the accompanying position of affluence and independence Benny enjoys, Leonard is to return to the ring. "Benny Leonard is planning to re-enter the ring immediately and defend his world lightweight championship before the end of the current season," said the statement issued by Billy Gibson. Quoting Leonard, the statement from Gibson says, "I wish it broadcast that matchmakers desiring my services are advised to communicate with my manager Billy Gibson. For the past three weeks, I have been receiving many tempting offers to return to the ring. I will be ready to box in

287 Davis J. Walsh *Athens Messenger* Ohio 19 February 1925
288 Fair Play *Canton Daily News* Ohio 27 August 1924

September. I have been doing light but regular training for the past six weeks.'"[289]

Three months later, Benny was still in the gym weighing his options. Veteran scribe Robert Edgren wrote from New York, 'Again, the story is out that Benny Leonard wants to fight and has been talking it over with Tex Rickard. Benny retired as lightweight champion a year ago. At that time, Benny was without serious rivalry in the class. There was no one in sight who could give him anything better than a few rounds of light exercise. As champion, Benny had whipped all rivals for seven years. He was growing a bit heavy and found difficulty in getting down to the lightweight limit, although he could do it for a championship bout.

'Benny talked of going after the welterweight title. He tried it when Jack Britton was champion and lost on a foul in the 12th round. Benny was matched with champion Mickey Walker, and luckily for Benny he hurt his thumb in another match and the bout fell through. Leonard was a great lightweight, but Walker was just as good a welterweight, and younger. There is little doubt that Walker would have beaten Leonard. Benny's present ambition, if he can overcome his mother's desire to have him stay retired, is to come back as a welterweight and, after two or three bouts to get his fighting hand and eye working together, fight Walker. It would be a remarkable thing if Benny Leonard, who began fighting in 1912 and is now 29, could return to the game and beat the welterweight champion, who happens to be the hardest-hitting welterweight champion, and the best all-round fighting man seen in that class in many years.'[290]

Benny Leonard and Mickey Walker never fought in the ring …

---

289 *Evening Independent* Massillon Ohio 22 August 1925
290 Robert Edgren *Canton Daily News* Ohio 26 November 1925

CHAPTER TWENTY-THREE

'BENJAMIN LEINER – MOST POPULAR AMERICAN JEW by Maurice Abrams;

Philadelphia Jewish Exponent, 19 June 1925 – This article is the second of a series on a number of prominent Jews and their activities. Benjamin Leiner, better known as Benny Leonard, is the retired lightweight champion of the world. Mr Abrams here presents a most human portrait of the man who did effective work in subduing anti-semitism in America. – THE EDITOR

'Literature, theatre and politics were being discussed. This young gentleman listened attentively, nodding now and then, infrequently commenting in a straightforward, unaffected fashion, giving the impression that the subjects discussed had constituted a great part of his life's activities. The man who had attracted my attention by his simplicity now gave me cause for greater admiration as he expressed his views. Leaning over to my neighbour, I whispered, "Who is that chap?" The answer was a hearty, though amazed, chuckle. "What, you don't know Benny? That's Benny Leonard, the undefeated lightweight boxing champion of the world."

'Now the ordinary mortal's idea of a prize fighter is something of a cross between a wild bull and the foreman of a piano-hoisting crew. But here is Benny Leonard, the hero of many a tough scuffle. He has none of the earmarks of the professional boxer. He is a polished individual, a tasteful dresser, carries himself with that graceful elegance which marks the man of the world. His tread is light and his gait carries the rhythmic sway of one of those Grecian athletes sculptured by Phidias.

'His extraordinary success in the ring is in no small measure due to Benny's intense study of the human anatomy. Leonard knows the exact location and specific utility of every muscle in the human body. In other words, Leonard is not the usual combination of beef and brawn, without brains. He has the utility of a panther, the unflinching eye of a prairie Indian and the most perfect control over every nerve in his body. At the Keith vaudeville house, where Benny is now appearing, I interviewed him. While smearing on the paint and arching his brows under the pencil, Benny mused along quietly on his ambitions in life. "I have two ambitions in life now. My main interest is physical culture and along with that is my interest in the stage. The two will go together, because when I am on stage I talk and demonstrate certain phases of physical exercise. My ambition is to teach the American people that exercise is a delightful thing and that it should be contemplated as a pleasure instead of a necessity." Why should Benny Leonard with an independent fortune be concerned about the health of America? His vaudeville contract alone insures him a comfortable living. Leonard's one dominant passion, his only ambition, is raising the health standard of America …

'As I left the champion, I recalled Arthur Brisbane's remark in his famous "TODAY" column, that "Benny Leonard has done more to down anti-Semitism in America than any other person or organisation."'[291]

In his Leonard biography Nat Fleischer wrote, 'Benny brought a bright new chapter into pugilism. His gentlemanly manners

---

291 Maurice Abrams *Philadelphia Jewish Exponent* 19 June 1925

gained for him a horde of friends. Among them, Nathan Strauss, the philanthropist, and Arthur Brisbane, editor of the Hearst organisation. They were so fond of Benny that they even went to see him train at his camp, an event that was widely heralded in all the New York papers. Mr Strauss, who aided the Free Milk Fund of Mrs Hearst, saw in Leonard a great advertisement for the Jewish people and he helped him in many ways. Their acquaintance-ship ripened into a most pleasing friendship.'[292]

In his excellent 1997 book *When Boxing Was a Jewish Sport*, Allen Bodner calls Leonard 'the greatest and most beloved Jewish boxer ever. It is practically impossible for a prize fighter to remain morally and ethically unscathed throughout a career, but Leonard came close. He was a model of personal decorum and a visible and committed Jew. Of all the Jewish boxers, Leonard remains the one most admired by both fans and other boxers. Herbert Goldman, a boxing historian, has an interesting insight into Benny Leonard's role. "Benny Leonard had a very distinct and sharp sense that he was representing the Jewish community. Abe Attell threw a number of fights, and then later on he got involved in the World Series scam in 1919 with Arnold Rothstein. Maybe because of that, Benny had a sharp sense of this. He was a hero to the Jewish population at large in a way that no Jew before him – and I don't think any Jewish fighter after him – ever was.

"'A woman I knew named Kitty Donor was a headliner in vaudeville. She was a male impersonator, which in those days was very popular. She had an affair with Benny. Went on for some time in the 1920s. But he never came close to marrying Kitty. And she thought one of the reasons was that she was not Jewish. Benny had a very strong sense of what he meant to the Jewish people."'[293]

---

292 Nat Fleischer *Leonard the Magnificent* 1947
293 Allen Bodner *When Boxing Was a Jewish Sport* 1997

Novelist and screenwriter Budd Schulberg was raised in a household where Benny Leonard was a super hero. 'The Great Benny Leonard. That's how he was always referred to in our household. There was the Great Houdini, the Great Caruso *and* the Great Benny Leonard.

'In 1920, when my father B.P. was organising one of our pioneer film companies, he was a passionate fight fan. An habitué of the old Garden on Madison Square, his favourite fighter had been the Jewish lightweight Benjamin Leiner, who fought under the *nom-de-boxe* of Benny Leonard. B.P. knew Benny Leonard personally. All up-and-coming young Jews in New York knew Benny Leonard personally.

'They would take time off from their lunch hour or their afternoon activity to watch him train. They bet hundreds and often thousands of dollars on him in stirring contests against Rocky Kansas, Ever Hammer, Willie Ritchie, Joe Welling. He was only 5ft 6in, and his best fighting weight was a few pounds over 130, but he was one of those picture-book fighters who come along once or twice in a generation, a master boxer with a knockout punch, a poised technician who came into the ring with his hair plastered down and combed back with a part in the middle, in the approved style of the day, and whose boast was that no matter whom he fought, "I never even get my hair mussed!" To see him climb into the ring sporting the six-pointed Jewish star on his fighting trunks was to anticipate sweet revenge for all the bloody noses, split lips and mocking laughter at pale little Jewish boys who had run the neighbourhood gauntlet.'[294]

Al Lurie of the *Philadelphia Jewish Exponent* captured a sense of Leonard's appeal. 'Leonard's years as lightweight champion of the world between 1917 and 1925 made him "the most famous Jew in America, beloved by thin-faced little Jewish boys who, in

---

294 Budd Schulberg *Sports Illustrated* May 1980

their poverty, dreamed of themselves as champions of the world".'
More than inspiration and pride, Leonard also offered hope of their
own acceptance as Americans. As Lurie put it, 'When a people is
beaten, persecuted and frustrated, it finds more than mere solace in
its champions. Thus, when Benny Leonard reached the heights in
boxing, he aided not only himself, but the entire American-Jewish
community. When Leonard was accepted and admired by the entire
fair-minded American community, the Jews of America felt they,
themselves, were being accepted and admired. Leonard, therefore,
symbolised all Jewry. And he knew it.

'Leonard's contemporaries also recognised that the great
champion was both a hero to Jews and a positive force in fostering
Jewish acceptance by mainstream America.'[295]

'In a 1923 edition of the Chicago Yiddish *Daily Jewish Courier*,
one writer observed that in the United States, "Jewish strength"
commands more respect than "Jewish intellect". As he put it, "The
Benny Leonards will never arouse any hatred or envy among their
non-Jewish colleagues: they will receive honour and respect from
their American admirers. American youth always respects the brave
sons of their homelands; they will even respect Jews who are of
foreign birth because their physical prowess is in conformity with
one aspect of American culture and increases the prestige of the
nation."'[296]

The Jewish Daily Bulletin on 25 March 1925 commented on
Jewish pugilists, noting that New York's *New Warheit* pays its
respects particularly to the retired Jewish champion Benny Leonard,
and draws the following analogy between him and Einstein. 'He
is, perhaps, even greater than Einstein, for when Einstein was in
America only thousands knew him but Benny is known by millions.
It is said that only 12 people or at the most 12 times 12 the world

---

295 Al Lurie *The Philadelphia Jewish Exponent* May 1947
296 Peter Levine *Ellis Island to Ebbets Field* 1992

over understand Einstein, but Benny is being understood by tens of millions in America, and just as we need a country so as to be the equal of other people's, so we must have a fist to become their peers.'

So, while the most popular American Jew was enjoying his retirement, Buffalo promoter Charley Murray was chasing the former lightweight champion for his signature on a contract to box former victim and present incumbent on the throne, Rocky Kansas. For the *New York World* News Service, Hype Igoe was writing, 'Charley Murray was packing his old carpet bag with bonuses, articles of agreement and statements of facts and figures for Leonard's perusal when Murray will have presented them to him in person in California. Murray is going all the way to the coast to clinch the matter, fully convinced that he will get the former champion's signature for a bout, which in a Buffalo ball park would draw close to $1,000,000.

'Leonard has solemnly vowed that he would never again draw on a fighting glove, having promised his mother that he would forsake the ring for her sake. But Murray believes that the lure, the spirit of combat is so strong within Leonard that he can't resist it further. There is this significant fact about the whole business.

'From the moment the title passed from Jimmy Goodrich to Kansas, Leonard began real serious training out in California. He was outworking Dempsey, who had gone back to gymnasium toils in anticipation of a little ring work this summer. Just what Leonard's plans in the matter were, he guarded carefully. He simply passed the whole business off with the remark that he wished to keep fit, and that his strenuous gymnasium work was a somewhat delayed part of his health routine. Leonard has always declared that he didn't want to be a roly-poly former champion of the world. That was his excuse for all the bag-punching and rope-skipping in which he has indulged.'[297]

—
297 Hype Igoe *Cincinatti Commercial Tribune* 8 February 1926

'Reports have been sent out from New York to the effect that Leonard would meet Kansas in an open-air show in New York some time during the coming summer. Benny at the present time is making a vaudeville tour of the country and it is all good advertising for him, and Benny is a good enough showman to know the benefit of such talk. Despite the advertising arising from the controversy, Benny Leonard is not seeking notoriety but is sticking close to his show work.

'During a talk in his dressing room, Benny made it plain that he is not anxious to return to the ring, although he likes boxing for the sport and exercise he gets out of it. "Many have approached me lately regarding a match with Rocky Kansas for the title," said the retired champion, "but I have not even given it serious consideration. I have beaten Kansas three times and feel that the public would not want to see us in the ring again. As I said before, I do not wish to enter the ring again, not because of all that sob stuff about mother, but for the very good reason that I wish to retire from the game.

"If the public should ask me to come back and meet the best lightweight in the world, I would do so for the reason that it was the public, or rather boxing fans, who made me and I owe it to them to do their bidding. So that is where the matter rests – entirely with the fans. If they want me to come back I will do so, otherwise not."[298]

'For seven years after Benny gave up his crown, he never drew on the gloves in a ring engagement, except now and then in exhibitions. He had invested a considerable amount in various business ventures and in stocks. He owned an automobile accessory business in Harlem, several apartment houses in New Jersey, an interest in a dress manufacturing plant and, in addition, he owned stocks.'[299]

'In June, they were at it again. Close friends of Benny Leonard declare that Benny definitely has decided to return to the ring

---

298 *Afton Star Valley Independent* Wyoming 5 March 1916
299 Nat Fleischer *Leonard the Magnificent* 1947

and wants to meet Pete Latzo, the new world's welterweight champion, in August. "He has given up all hope of again fighting as a lightweight," says the informant. "Benny wanted a match with Mickey Walker, but Latzo shunted Mickey out of the picture. Public and official announcement of Benny's return to the ring will be made almost any day now."'[300]

That day never dawned.

In February of 1927, George Joel was writing in the *Jewish Sport News* of the *Chicago Sentinel*. 'For the tenth time since Benny Leonard took his boxing gloves off and hung them on the wall, he is promising to return to the ring. These outbursts are seasonal and so far have amounted to nothing. We are inclined to believe that the latest threat will peter out and Benny will remain the undefeated, retired lightweight champion of the world. The other instances wherein Leonard promised to return, his reasons were usually based on a desire to fight but each time Mrs Leonard ("my mother") prevailed and Benny remained in retirement.

'Now Benny says he is coming back because there are no Jewish prize fighting champions. Undoubtedly his intentions are of the highest, but if he puts them into execution the result will be appalling.

'Call it a platitude or anything you wish but the old saying "They never come back" holds true and even Benny with his great ability will be unable to overcome the handicap of a five-year lay-off. We say this despite the fact that Leonard has kept himself in excellent condition. For a fighter, there is but one way to remain fit and that is to fight and fight often. Benny Leonard enjoys a reputation among the followers of the cauliflower industry that no other battler in our times has reached and he will keep that reputation only so long as he remains outside the ring.'[301]

---

300 *Salt Lake Tribune* 6 June 1926
301 George Joel *Chicago Sentinel* 25 February 1927

'Leonard's lament is worth an airing. "Do you know why most fighters go broke? I'll tell you. They're poor kids to begin with or they wouldn't be fighters. Then, all of a sudden, they've got money. Once they're on top, their relatives quit working. All they want from him is rent money, eating money and the price of a new set of tyres. Whose advice can the fighter ask? The advice of the one closest to him, his manager. The first thing he told me to do when I won the title was to buy racehorses. So I did. Six of them. They couldn't win a race. They couldn't even place or show. But they could eat. The trainer had his own ideas of how to put the tap on a champion. And then there were the jockeys' fees and the entry fees and all the other stable expenses. And naturally the bets, whenever one of my horses ran. If I'd been having any fun out of it, if I'd had even one winner, I might have kept on. But I quit. It just wasn't worth it to me, so I practically gave my horses away. I had to. Who'd pay me anything for them?"'

Benny's compulsive generosity further depleted the cash stakes. 'I drop into a restaurant for lunch. I'm all alone. But not for long. Pretty soon I have a dozen guys around. Naturally, I pick up the check. Or, if, as rarely happens, I get through the meal alone, can I give the waiter an ordinary tip? Of course not. If I don't give him a five-dollar tip, he tells everybody, "Benny Leonard is a cheapskate."'[302]

'Although at different times in his career Irving Rudd worked as publicity director for the Brooklyn Dodgers and for Yonkers Raceway, he began his trade promoting local fight cards in Queens and Brooklyn. Growing up in the Brownsville section of Brooklyn in the 1920s, Irving recalled that in his neighbourhood, Leonard was a "deity". Given the chance to interview the great champion for his school newspaper, Rudd remembered going backstage at a

---

302 Gerald Suster *Lightning Strikes* 1994

New York vaudeville theatre to talk to him. There, he also received Benny's photograph, on which Leonard had written, "To My Friend Irving Rudd. If anyone wants to hit you, just send for me. Your friend, Benny Leonard." Needless to say, the next day at the local candy store, Irving was the envy of all his friends.'[303]

In March 1923, *Time* magazine ran an item headed 'Personality'. 'Too much emphasis continues to be put on what is, after all, only one part of the actor's equipment – personality. The real battlefield of personality is, of course, musical comedy. Any number of good tunes, clever librettos, gorgeous settings, avail nothing without personality in the cast. A comedian is about as laughable as an undertaker without it. A curious instance of that quality on the musical stage is Benny Leonard, champion boxer turned matinee idol, in the Winter Garden. It is not only the physique which he so delights in displaying, not alone the slapstick ingenuities of his scenes. It is the curious quality of personal magnetism shooting across the footlights into the hearts of every fluttering little gum-chewer in the audience.'

---

303 Peter Levine *Ellis Island to Ebbets Field* 1992

CHAPTER TWENTY-FOUR

BY THE end of September 1929, the American stock market on New York City's Wall Street was riding the wave of a decade of intoxicating growth. The Roaring Twenties had seen millions of ordinary Americans caught up in the excitement of owning shares and making money. Social historian Cecil Roberts observed, 'Everyone was playing the market. Stocks soared dizzily. I found it hard not to be engulfed. I had invested my American earnings in good stock. Should I sell for a profit? Everyone said, "Hang on – it's a rising market."'

On the last day of his visit to New York City, Roberts went to the hotel barber shop for a haircut. As the barber finished and brushed his collar, he said softly, 'Buy Standard Gas. I've doubled. It's good for another double.' Roberts was stunned. As he made his way back to his room he said to himself, 'If the hysteria has reached the barber level, something must soon happen.'[304]

It did. On Monday, 3 October the New York stock market started to fall. Throughout the month, the value of stocks and shares continued to drop alarmingly. On Monday, 21 October six million shares changed hands, the largest number in the history of the exchange. Three days later, on what would become known as

---

304 Cecil Roberts *And So To America* 1946

Black Thursday, the bottom fell out. The Great Crash had begun. On the floor of the exchange there was pandemonium, with jobbers trying to buy or sell stocks and shares caught in the middle.

On Tuesday, 29 October the Great Crash came to a dreadful conclusion in what the *New York Times* described as 'the most disastrous day' in the American stock market's history. On Black Thursday, between eight and nine billion dollars had been wiped off the value of shares. Investors were ruined. The banks, which had been so eager to lend money to fund the share buying, shut up shop. Businesses found themselves without credit and company closures followed by the thousand.

'Comedian Eddie Cantor lost everything but his sense of humour. He told his radio audience, "They're not calling it the stock market any longer. They're calling it the stuck market. Everyone's stuck. Well, except my uncle. He got a good break. He died in September."

'Groucho Marx lost $400,000, while heavyweight boxer Jack Dempsey, one of the first multi-millionaire sportsmen, lost 1.5 million dollars.'[305]

Another big loser was Benny Leonard. Although just 28 years old, Benny had yielded to the pressures of his seriously ill mother and retired as undefeated lightweight champion of the world. 'The hard-earned million bucks Benny made as a fistic conjurer was initially spent wisely. He became part-owner of a hockey team in Pittsburgh and opened a recreation and self-defence summer camp for Jewish children. He even tried the stage, appearing in the Philadelphia musical *Battling Butler* in 1927.

'"Friends tell me how to make money. Just invest a little with them. I invested $20,000 in a tyre company. You know what happened, don't you? The tyres blew out and I lost it all." In 1930, Benny became the boxing coach at the School of Business of the

---

305 Cecil Roberts *And So To America* 1946

College of the City of New York. However, when the stock market crashed in 1929, Benny lost everything.'[306]

In August 1931, Benny was interviewed by *Time* magazine. 'A clean-cut little man with sleepy eyelids, confident, protruding under lip and well-defined paunch, he continued to be a familiar figure about training camps, gymnasiums and other haunts of pugilists. Before every important fight, he gave his expert opinion on who would win. In 1926, he allowed himself to be interviewed by *Colliers* magazine. Said he, "My mother has pledged me against return to the ring. They [promoters] know I've always kept my word. I'll certainly keep it with my mother. Unless you're a champion or a near champion, it's the dirtiest game in the world."

'Last week, aged 35 and four months, weighing what he said was 149 pounds and what some observers estimated as high as 165, Benny Leonard announced his return to the ring. His one-time manager, Billy Gibson, was in a private sanatorium, but Leonard has taken up with a new one – crafty Jack Kearns, one-time manager of Jack Dempsey, present manager of Mickey Walker. Manager Kearns planned a fight between Benny Leonard and Dave Shade in Chicago this month, which the Illinois Boxing Commission promptly refused to sanction. Promoter Jimmy Johnston remembered he had a seven-year contract for a fight between Leonard and Walker, and hoped to utilise it …

'Said Benny Leonard: "I have lost some money. Who hasn't? But I still have plenty. One thing that had a lot to do with my decision to come back was the insistence of my friends."

'From Benny Leonard's mother, who still lives in Manhattan, nothing was heard.'

Veteran writer/cartoonist Robert Edgren was weighing up the comeback news. 'Now we have Jack Dempsey about to start a year of

---

306 Ken Blady *The Jewish Boxers' Hall of Fame* 1988

hammering 'em down in four-round bouts, Benny Leonard trying to come back for more ring money. Benny Leonard is in better shape. Trying a comeback, the ex-lightweight champion can find plenty of men his weight to mix with. But probably he'll be sent against tip-overs at least until he gets his hand in. Leonard can come back if anyone can. He fought with his head. He'll still have the headwork after half a dozen years, and as he always kept in good shape he'll probably be able to develop enough of the old speed, endurance and punches, and come back the way he used to. He'll do pretty well among the lads of today.

'Not that I think he'll fight his way to any more championships. There's hardly a chance of that. A fighter has to keep up to date, keep on going forward. He can't stand still without going back. And Benny has been standing still six years. Jack Kearns, who claims to have Leonard signed up for five years, must think Benny will be good for more than one comeback appearance. But as usual, Kearns is claiming a lot. He says Benny will reclaim the lightweight title and beat Canzoneri; also take the welter title and claim Walker's resigned middleweight crown. First, it's very doubtful that Leonard can make the lightweight limit now without weakening himself beyond all possibility of putting up a good fight – and very doubtful he could beat Canzoneri, at 135 anyway.

'However, title talk kicked aside, Benny Leonard may come back and do some good fighting and make some money, if he is on the level with this. He announced a comeback several times before and it was just a little boost for the vaudeville act. The thing that makes it look likely is that Kearns has him. Old Billy Gibson wouldn't have let Benny fight again, even if Benny had lost some of his money in the stock market, as reported.'[307]

---

307 Robert Edgren *Moorhead Daily News* Minnesota 17 August 1931

Top trainer Ray Arcel had known Benny Leonard since he used to hang around Billy Grupp's Gymnasium and Athletic Club at 116th Street on Eighth Avenue. 'Leonard was just as great as can be,' Arcel recalled. 'He used to talk to me and I used to ask him a million dumb questions, and he would show me. And naturally, I absorbed all his knowledge. His main asset was his ability to think. He had the sharpest mind. He was the one fighter that I saw who could make you do things *he* wanted you to do. He could feint you into knots. He was a master of the feint.'

Arcel didn't train Leonard in the early days but he was around the gyms all the time and he knew Gene Tunney, who was also managed by Gibson. Recalling Tunney's loss to Harry Greb in 1922, Arcel said, 'This is the only fight Tunney ever lost, and he took a bad licking. And Tunney kept harping, "Get that guy back for me." And he kept calling Gibson every day, "Did you make the match?" So Gibson finally called Leonard up, "Ben, do me a favour. Go up in the gym. Gene is working out. He's tearing the bags down. And he's fighting for a return match with Greb. Go up there, look at him, influence him to take his time. 'Cause I don't want to make the match yet." So Benny went over there and, of course, when Leonard walked into a gymnasium everybody stopped working. And he walked over to Gene, and Gene was punching the bag and Leonard stood there looking at him and he says, "How are you, Gene?" Tunney kept punching the bag and he said, "I'm all right, Ben, I'm trying to get in shape. I'm gonna knock that Greb out."

'Leonard says, "You're throwing a right hand. Where you gonna hit him with a right hand? On the chin? You ain't never gonna hit Greb on the chin with a right hand. If you're gonna hit Greb with a right hand, the place to try to hit him is in the body. Try to do *that*!" And he says, "Take your time. The longer you wait to fight Greb, the better it is for you. Because this guy dissipates. He drinks,

THE GREAT BENNY LEONARD

he runs around with women." And Tunney had such a great respect for Leonard that he took advantage of that knowledge. And the second fight, Tunney destroyed Greb. He *destroyed* him. He really did. *Body* punches. He took Leonard's advice.'[308]

Arcel would later recall, 'When it was whispered around that Leonard, the lightweight champion, was training at the old Stillman's Gym up on 125th Street, the gym was mobbed. At first, there was no admission charge and you couldn't move in the place. But then it got so crowded, whenever Leonard was there, they started charging 15 cents. Leonard even had a private dressing room. They built a wall around the only toilet seat in the gym. Anybody who had to go had to knock on the door and if Leonard was in there, he had to let the guy in. The other fighters dressed in a little room. When they got through working out, they would sit and talk about their experiences. Leonard would come in there and tell the kids, "Think, think. Learn how to think."

'Leonard would tell them, "You've got to talk to yourself. 'I'm going to jab this guy' or 'I'm going to hook this guy.'" How could you obtain knowledge in a better way than from the master himself? Kids would walk out of that gymnasium and say, "Benny Leonard told me." Not only the kids but the guys who worked with the fighters. We learned all those tricks by listening to what was Leonard's main stock in trade: to teach.'[309]

'Into Stillman's Gym one day early in 1931 came Benny Leonard,' recalled Ray Arcel. 'I had known him for years and he had been one of my idols from the earliest days. We had always been great friends and on this day we chatted about affairs in general. Then, very quietly, Benny made a remark that stunned me. "Ray," he said, "I'm going to come back, and I want you to handle me." When I recovered, I did all I could to dissuade him. Although he

308 Ronald K. Fried *Corner Men* 1991
309 Dave Anderson *Ringmasters* 1991

was one of the greatest lightweights ever, I felt sure that age and inactivity for years would be unconquerable opponents.

'But Benny said that he had had bad luck financially – like most people in America at that time – and that he had always kept pretty fit. At last, against my inclinations, I agreed to go with him.' Arcel at that time was partners with Whitey Bimstein, but he said, 'I worked with Benny alone because Leonard was a very peculiar fella, and Whitey had a different disposition than me.'[310]

'Shortly after Tunney relinquished his heavyweight title and retired from the ring in 1928, Billy Gibson's life started to unravel. In 1930, at the age of 54, after a legal finding that the death of his wife had affected his sanity, Gibson was declared mentally incompetent and institutionalised. Although eventually released from the hospital, he would not regain full control of his own affairs until 1947. Six months later, on 21 July, the ex-manager and former political bigwig was found dead in his room, aged 71, at the Hotel Paris at West End Avenue and 97th Street in Manhattan.'[311]

'BENNY IS COMING BACK. A couple of months ago, we noticed at Gus Wilson's Gymnasium at Orangeburg a young man weighing 177 pounds. He was the possessor of a rather sizeable professorial paunch. There was, however, in his keen athlete's face, topped by carefully combed slick black hair, something that did not belong to the none-too-impressive physique of this young man of 35. The other day, we dropped in again at the Wilson Health Farm. In the open-air ring, somebody was shadow-boxing. Watching the graceful footwork of the fisticuffs artist, we mentioned to our companion, "That fellow looks like Benny Leonard." It was indeed Leonard, greatest Jewish boxer of all time, retired undefeated lightweight champion of the world. The transformation of Benny Leonard from a paunchy, phlegmatic-looking individual into a

---

310 John Jarrett *Champ in the Corner The Ray Arcel Story* 2007
311 Lawrence S. Ritter *East Side, West Side* 1998

155-pound aggressive fighter startled us more than somewhat. When Benny quit the ring six years ago, he startled the sports world. His claim that he was quitting to please his mother was scoffed at. Cynics branded it a publicity stunt. "When the purse is big enough, he'll be back." Apparently Leonard had meant it. He spurned fabulous offers for a comeback and devoted himself to coaching, hockey promoting, the teaching of physical culture at New York University and other such enterprises which gave evidence of his definite withdrawal from boxing. 'Another visitor to Wilson's place was Sammy Goldman, manager of lightweight champion Tony Canzoneri. "You're a sucker if you don't come back," said Goldman. "You can do 147 pounds easy, and you'd beat Young Jack Thompson, the welterweight champion, as sure as four fingers and a thumb make a fist. Then your end for a McLarnin fight would crowd $100,000."[312]

'Arcel's first task was to bring Leonard's weight down from an initial 175 pounds. They managed it after a fashion. "I knew he had nothing, he was washed up, but he was dead broke. He retired with a million dollars and he thought that was all the money in the world. Well, it was in 1925. I knew he wasn't going to make the money he was hoping to make, either. Maybe at the beginning, maybe as a novelty for the same people who had gone to see him in vaudeville, to see what he had been. But after that, I couldn't see it lasting long."

'Arcel set out a programme calling for Leonard to fight twice a month for something between $400 and $500 a bout, or 25 per cent of the gate, whichever was more. He also devised a training regime that would give his charge the necessary workouts but simultaneously expose him to young gym fighters who would learn something from their sparring. What I wanted was for Benny to

---

312 Harry Conzel *Chicago Sentinel* 10 July 1931

be as much a teacher as he was a boxer in training for a match. Other managers agreed, seeing little to lose by matching their up-and-coming fighters against someone with Leonard's reputation. They knew Benny couldn't hurt their boys, and they would have exposure."'[313]

The great Benny Leonard comeback started on 6 October 1931 with a ten-round bout against Pal Silvers at the Queensboro Stadium, Long Island, New York. 'Leonard started his comeback campaign with a knockout victory over Pal Silvers of Brooklyn with the jeers of a crowd of 15,000 as the principal accompaniment. Leonard floored Silvers in the second round of their ten-round bout last night and Silvers stayed down for the full count, although most experts thought the blows were anything but hard. At the count of ten Silvers bounced to his feet, apparently unhurt and ready to continue. Referee Arthur Donovan waved him to his corner and lifted Leonard's hand as the winner. Benny, a bit plump around the waistline, showed the effects of his seven-year layoff from the ring.'[314]

Arcel never commented on suspicions of a fix or who might have been in on it, stressing instead how embarrassed both he and Leonard were by the Silvers bout.

Nat Fleischer recorded the fight in *The Ring* magazine. 'Leonard walked into the ring to the acclaim of a returned hero, but he left with the hisses of those thousands. The less said about the fight the better. Silvers, after outclassing Leonard in the opening round in which four straight lefts in a row had Benny's face smeared with blood, apparently suddenly figured that it wouldn't do to make Leonard look bad. Instead of following up his advantage in the second round, he forgot how to fight and left himself open to severe criticism. When he received three light blows on the jaw and went

313 Donald Dewey *Ray Arcel A Boxing Biography* 2012
314 *Washington Court House Herald* 7 October 1931

down after first locating a soft spot, he acted like one who was dead to the world. But when Arthur Donovan, the referee, had counted ten, up leaped Pal and, dashing about the ring, sought to continue the "battle". What a fiasco that was!'

A couple of days after the Silvers bout, 'Benny Leonard said today that he would box on 27 October. He said he would continue his attempt to come back as a middleweight despite the ruling of the New York boxing commission that he could not go through with his proposed fight here in Madison Square Garden against Paulie Walker. The commission took the position Leonard was not in shape for a comeback campaign.'[315]

Benny Leonard wins. Boston, 28 October – Benny Leonard, former lightweight champion, floored Vittorio Livana, Italian middleweight, four times before knocking him out with a right to the jaw in the third round of a bout here last night.[316]

Burlington, Vermont, 7 November – Benny Leonard wandered along the comeback trail today burdened by a draw verdict. He fought Kayo Casper, Burlington middleweight, here last night and Casper had him gasping. But Leonard showed he was still a master of defence and ducked to a draw.[317]

Baltimore, 24 November 1931 – Benny Leonard, seeking to come back as a welterweight in the ring he graced for seven years as the lightweight champion only to retire undefeated in 1925, took the fifth of his opponents in stride last night, scoring an easy decision over Buster Brown of Baltimore. Leonard showed the old-time ring generalship that won him his crown, stabbing and jabbing Brown at will, and left the ring practically unmarked. Brown carried the fight to Benny but couldn't land more than a half dozen solid licks throughout the ten rounds. The former

---

315 *New Castle News* Pennsylvania 8 October 1931
316 *Brandon Daily Sun* Manitoba 28 October 1932
317 *Cedar Rapids Evening Gazette* Iowa 7 November 1931

champion had a six-pound advantage in the weights, 149 to Brown's 143.[318]

Edward J. Neil was in New York for the *Associated Press* on 1 March for Benny's opening bout in 1932. 'Down the splintery aisle of a rickety little fight club, St Nicholas Arena, stalked an old, familiar figure in an old, raggedy bath robe – Benny Leonard, undefeated lightweight champion of the world. It was "Benneh", coming back to seek the glory he knew more than ten years ago. His comeback started last summer, but last night was the first genuine test. Climbing in through the other side of the ring was Bill McMahon from the West Side, young rough and tough, undismayed. Leonard bowed. Lew Tendler, fat, wallowing, was there to shake his hand. From the ringside yelled Willie Jackson, who once dropped Benny with a single punch; Johnny Dundee, who fought him a dozen times, all old men now as far as the ring is concerned. The bell rang and Benny sidled out, thick about the body but not fat, for all the world like the old Leonard except for the front of his head, where the hair was carefully combed to disguise its thinness.

'McMahon rushed in, wild swinging youth, and up went both of Benny's arms, catching the punches. They danced in the open, Benny lightly posed on his toes, and left jabs spattered all over the young Irishman's features. So it went, with slight variations, through ten rounds, the old man of the ring boxing beautifully, out-manoeuvring, out-thinking the eager Irishman, holding him tight when danger threatened. But it was a shaky Leonard in spots, a Leonard that tired easily, but even so, Benny won eight of the ten rounds, though several were very close. He weighed 151¾ pounds, McMahon weighed 149. Although referee Gunboat Smith voted the match a draw, the judges gave Benny the award.'[319]

---

318 *Oakland Tribune* 24 November 1931
319 *Wisconsin Rapids Daily Tribune* 1 March 1932

'If Benny Leonard comes back, he will be a miracle of sports and a mighty popular one. Leonard has more friends in the metropolitan area than any boxer. Tommy Loughran is popular. So is Jimmy McLarnin. But "Bennah" Leonard – well, that's something else again. Just for example: Leonard slipped and fell during the bout with Billy McMahon last night. A photographer closed in and snapped the prostrate Benny. Leonard enthusiasts nearly mobbed him and almost broke his camera. Police intervened.'[320]

'Referring to critics as "busybodies", Benny Leonard today expressed himself as determined to continue his comeback march. "The fact that I was held to a draw by Kayo Casper in Burlington Friday night does not mean my finish," Leonard said. "That fight gave me the right edge to enable me to continue my climb to my determined goal – that of the middleweight championship. I yet will surprise those friends and others who so strongly are advising me to quit the ring."'[321]

'One guy hoping to see Benny Leonard back in the ring, hoping to see Benny coming out of the other corner, was welterweight contender Jimmy McLarnin. In Oakland, California to watch the auto races, the Vancouver-Irishman had been tentatively matched with Benny for a Milk Fund show in New York, but that one is out now following the former champion's recent unsatisfactory showings.

'Jimmy believes Benny would have done much better had he not chosen Jack Kearns as his manager. "Kearns is poison with the New York boxing commission," says Jimmy, "and none of his fighters get a break in the big city. Leonard will not be allowed to appear at Madison Square Garden and that is the only spot one can get real money in the winter season. However, Kearns tried to force the issue and rush him along too fast. Benny was accused of

---

320 *Nevada State Journal* 2 March 1932
321 *New Castle News* Pennsylvania 9 November 1931

having Silver in the bag when they met recently but I know that one was on the level."'[322]

Leonard, in an interview with Wilbur Wood, stated that, 'Jack Kearns was never my manager. There was nothing between us but friendship. Kearns and Teddy Hayes [trainer] merely wanted to do anything they could to help me make a comeback. I engaged Hayes as my trainer for a time but there never was any contract, or even any sort of an agreement with Kearns that he was to manage me.'[323]

322 *Oakland Tribune* 12 November 1931
323 Wilbur Wood *Ring* magazine October 1932

CHAPTER TWENTY-FIVE

UNITED PRESS correspondent Dixon Stewart in his 'Speaking of Sports' column, noted, 'Benny Leonard is fast learning the truth of the old prize ring axiom that fighters never come back. For Benny's touted comeback campaign has developed into a virtual tragedy. Benny has made two ring appearances with the net result that he has forfeited much of his reputation for sagacity and boxing skill, and has already been barred from performing in four important states – New York, Pennsylvania, Massachusetts and Illinois.

'Benny lost his money in the stock market and now he is losing his reputation in the ring. If he continues as he has in his first two bouts, he soon not only will have no place to fight but the ring fans will remember him as a fat, pudgy middleweight who won bouts with "invisible punches," rather than as the greatest lightweight of all times.'[324]

Benny was determined to show his critics he still had something left and Arcel booked him for his second bout at St Nick's Arena over ten rounds with Buster Brown. 'After a shaky first round, Benny took eight of the nine rounds, with Brown holding him even in the fourth. The old champ still showed a distressing tendency to trip over his own feet. Buster took

---

324 Dixon Stewart *Fayetteville Daily Democrat* 27 November 1931

considerable punishment over the last five rounds but Benny couldn't get him down.'[325]

'Oddly enough,' observed veteran writer Ted Carroll, 'Leonard was one of the great fighters who never had a nickname, being unique in this respect. Colourful appellations long have been part and parcel of the boxing industry. Perhaps one reason no nickname ever was given to Leonard was that Benny was so superb a ringman he was above any title that could have been created for him. His very name, Benny Leonard, became synonymous with perfection.'[326]

Veteran scribe Hype Igoe, using his 'poetic licence', referred to Benny as the 'White Joe Gans' that was. Leonard was in with New York middleweight Mike Sarko at the Ridgewood Grove. 'Sarko knows now why Benny Leonard was a great world's lightweight champion. Mike was six years old when Leonard won the world title. He was 14 when Benny retired undefeated. If Mike lives to be 100, and Benny is still sticking around, Mike won't be able to outbox the "White Joe Gans" that was.

'Mike took all the liberties a youngster might be expected to seek against an "old champion" and stood blinking in his corner at the end of the six-round bout as he heard Leonard's name bawled forth as "the win-nah!". In the fifth round Benny even tried an old trick, suddenly looking down at Sarko's ring shoes and whispering, "Your laces are undone" but Mike didn't bite and Benny had to laugh at his own joke. But he did have a right hand ready to turn off the sunshine if Mike had looked down!"'[327]

Leonard didn't need any tricks three weeks later when he met Willie (Cannonball) Garafola. In the fourth round, he had Willie off to the showers after three visits to the canvas. Next!

---

325 *Bakersfield Californian* 12 April 1932
326 Ted Carroll *The Ring* magazine July 1947
327 Hype Igoe *Indiana Evening Gazette* 20 April 1932

It was Marty Goldman on a Monday night in Newark and it was all over in round two. Marty fell face-forward after taking a hard right and referee Gene Roman counted to ten. One week later it was Paterson, New Jersey with Jimmy Abbott on the ropes, bleeding from a cut eye, taking a lacing before referee Danny Sullivan called it off in round six. Andy Saviola gave Leonard a run for his money before he was awarded the decision. By then, Benny's right eye was cut and almost closed. Rough business, this!

Benny was off to Philadelphia in the morning with a patch over his eye to box local boy Billy Angelo ten rounds at the Phillies ball park. The veteran champion was too clever for the kid and eased to a decision victory. At the final bell, Billy had learned something and Benny still had the patch over his eye.[328]

'Leonard registered another victory on his comeback trail when he tangled with rugged Bronx battler Eddie Shapiro in the eight rounds main event at the Coney Island Stadium. A crowd of 4,000 was on hand when the battle started, but a rain storm which increased in proportion as the bout progressed drove away a greater part of that number and there were less than 1,000 on hand to hear Leonard declared the winner.

'Leonard's superior boxing ability carried him through to victory. Shapiro was aggressive enough but he seldom was able to reach the former titleholder with any degree of effectiveness. Leonard, on the other hand, hit Shapiro often with heavy lefts and rights to the head. His greatest surge occurred in the fourth round when he almost felled his Bronx rival with a left to the jaw.'[329]

Queensboro Stadium, New York, 28 July 1932; Edward J. Neil at ringside. 'The skill and guile that were the Benny Leonard of nine years ago came back in part Thursday night to dazzle rugged Billy Townsend, blond Vancouver welterweight, and carry the

328 *Joplin Globe* Missouri 17 June 1932
329 *Syracuse Herald* 23 July 1932

former lightweight champion to the most convincing victory of his comeback campaign. Leonard, now 36, plastered the Canadian with left jabs for ten rounds, staggered him a couple of times with right-hand smashes and took a unanimous decision. A crowd of 6,000 rose and howled in glee at the veteran's gallant display.

'The picture of the old Leonard Thursday night was almost a duplicate of the most spectacular moment in Benny's career – the night Lew Tendler dazed him with a left hook nine years ago in Jersey and then let Leonard talk himself out of danger. Benny had gone along beautifully for three rounds, but in the fourth Billy suddenly popped over a right that bruised Leonard's cheek. Another right smashed on Benny's chin and a terrific left hook caught him on the lower part of his jaw. Leonard's chin dropped and his eyes popped open. His knees bent and he stumbled in, desperately clutching the raging Townsend ...

Then, Benny started whispering in Townsend's ear. The youngster stopped to listen as Benny held and rested. He told Townsend what a nice punch that had been, Billy grinned back at him, pleased as a pupil congratulated by his teacher. Expansively, Benny reached out and shook Townsend's hand. But by that time, as the crowd howled with delight, Benny's head had cleared. Billy realised too late he had been outgeneralled. He tore into the old champion and Benny smacked him with lefts and a right cross that set the youngster back on his heels; his big chance gone.

'Bring on young Jackie Fields, your Jimmy McLarnins. Benny Leonard is ready for them. Through ten of as tough rounds as he has been asked to go since he came back, he beat young Paulie Walker to a ten-round decision at Ebbets Field in Brooklyn last night. He finished like a gamester, almost knocking out the New Jersey lad in the tenth round, but Walker weathered the storm.'[330]

---

330 *New Castle News* Pennsylvania 12 August 1932

Boston welterweight Mike Sarko had another go at Benny, to no avail. Leonard took the decision in six rounds. New York welterweight Phil Rafferty turned up at the Long Beach Stadium, bringing a savage body attack with him, but Benny had seen it all before and sent Phil off home with a loss added to his record. For the second time in the year, Jimmy Abbott tried his hand with Mr Leonard, and for the second time Mr Leonard spanked him, this time inside three rounds. Still another guy in Mike Sarko turned up in the opposite corner for the third time and Benny gave Mike another trouncing in six rounds at Manhattan's Starlight Park …

The comeback added up to 12 months, 20 bouts, 19 wins and one draw. Five bouts on the road; Boston, Vermont, Baltimore, Philadelphia, Paterson and Newark in New Jersey.

'Now that I have made good in my comeback, I can look back on the year I spent getting back. It was a tough grind. Hard work in the gymnasium after years of idleness is enough to make a fellow quit unless he grits his teeth. Then there is the mental strain. What will the friends who saw you fight in your heyday think of you when you get in the ring again? Will they laugh or sneer or call you a sap for trying the impossible? I tell you, I did plenty of thinking along those lines.

'Some days in the gymnasium, you can't help looking badly against a boy you could have finished in a round. And what experiences in the tank towns on tour! One night my bit, after railroad fares, hotel bills etc had been paid, amounted to eight dollars. Eight dollars for a tougher fight than the one I had with Lew Tendler when we drew $450,000.

'You ask me if my comeback has been worth the effort?' Benny was talking to Wilbur Wood, noted sportswriter with *The Sun*. 'Since I started boxing again a little more than a year ago, I have put $65,000 into a savings bank account. When I was in showbusiness, part of my act was to box three rounds. That stage boxing did me a lot of good. Even three rounds of that sort of thing, if you do it two or three times a day, is good enough exercise to keep a fellow in shape. Believe it or not, I had got up to 178 pounds. When I went to Gus Wilson's place and began to work out, my only purpose was to pare myself down to a decent weight. I worked off between 25 and 30 pounds, weight that I should not have been carrying. In some ways, I'm better today than I used to be. I know more about the game. I have a better understanding of what is going on than I ever had, if you get what I mean.'[331]

'He's not as old as he looks. His legs are round and thick, like those of a burlesque queen, vintage 1890, and not at all like the flat, slender pins of the young athlete. His waist, too, is round and thickish and blends into his chest. His locks are in full retreat and are now battling against disappearance. He looks old but, again, he's far from as old as he looks because just the other day, he slapped a tough and promising young New Jerseyite, Paulie Walker, all around Ebbets Field.

'It's Benny Leonard we're talking about: Benny the one-time brilliant lord of the lightweights who may really come back if the Walker test is any criterion. Leonard's comeback has been far more successful than his critics expected it to be. In his best showing so far, the Walker affair, Benny went the route against a much younger, fast opponent and gave more than he had to take in the latter rounds. Benny also retains that rough right of his which, in his prime, was a hurdle too high for the best boys at his weight. He hasn't lost any of his brains, either.

'However, getting the decision over Walker is not taking the measure of such fellows as Jimmy McLarnin and Jackie Fields for whom Benny is now gunning. Leonard insists he is ready for them. The Walker bout and his tussle with Billy Townsend indicate he

---

331 Wilbur Wood *The Ring* magazine October 1932

may have the right idea. But Benny is 36 – and getting older by the minute.

'One thing Benny retains which has all the lustre it possessed in his regal days and that's the old box office pull. New York fight fans who followed Benny when he was Big Ben have remained quite loyal to him.'[332]

'As Leonard's comeback progressed, the boxing commission became concerned. "The commission called us down," Arcel recalls. "You know, there's always somebody that will interfere with your progress. You don't bother anybody. You go along, but there's always some SOB who can't mind his own business, who'll file a complaint. And the complaint was, why do you allow a great fighter like this to make a fool out of himself in these small clubs? So I went down and talked to the commission with Leonard. And I told them, I said, 'He's broke.' And they said, 'Look, Ben, get yourself a shot of money and call it quits. We don't want you to fight.' So he said all right. By this time he felt like he'd had it, too. 'Cause he wasn't making any headway.'"[333]

The big one, the 'shot of money' the commission had proposed, would be against Jimmy McLarnin in Madison Square Garden on 7 October 1932. 'Arcel told some reporters that Leonard's brother Willie, who had begun to take more of an active managing interest in the scheduling of opponents, was the primary promoter of a bout against prominent welterweight contender Jimmy McLarnin. "It was typical of Benny to search for the toughest and hardest road," said Arcel. "I was dead set against such a match. Not only had McLarnin smooth boxing skill, but he was strong. Fit as he was, I couldn't see Benny giving so much away in age without being hurt. But Benny was obstinate and his brother was for the McLarnin clash." What Arcel remembers most vividly about the training camp

332 William Ritt *Hammond Lake County Times* Indiana 20 August 1932
333 Ronald K. Fried *Corner Men* 1991

they set up at Pompton Lakes in New Jersey for preparing for the fight was a conversation with Leonard one evening. "He got very reflective one night and talked about how, when he was champion for eight years, the big business tycoons were falling over each other to invite him to functions where he was a drawing card for big fundraisers. 'But when I retired and the Wall Street Crash came, Ray,' he told me, 'not one of those millionaires ever asked me how I was doing, how was I handling my money. Don't ever let anybody use you the way they did me.'"[334]

Jimmy McLarnin was 24 years old, born in Ireland, raised in Vancouver and nurtured in boxing by wise old Pop Foster. When he faced Leonard that night in the Garden, Jimmy's record showed 58 bouts with eight losses, one of them to Sammy Mandell for the lightweight championship. Since hitting New York in February 1928, the feisty little Irishman had destroyed the top Jewish fighters in the city, including Sid Terris, Joe Glick, Ruby Goldstein and Al Singer. Now it was time for revenge and Leonard's fans swamped the box office to see their hero and idol put McLarnin in his place.

'What about the fight with McLarnin?' Benny was talking to Wilbur Wood of the *New York Sun*. 'Say, I'm going to surprise a lot of people that night, including Mr McLarnin. I'm sure I can beat him. In fact, he will be easier for me to fight than a lot of those rough, tough kids I have met in the last year. That's because he is an orthodox boxer. When he makes a certain move, I will know what he is going to do next and I will make the right move myself. He is a good boxer and you always can tell just about what a good boxer is going to do.

'There'll be a lot of satisfaction in beating McLarnin, not only because he stands out as one of the best boys in the game today, but from another angle. Probably you know that Jimmy knocked out Sid Terris in one round, Ruby Goldstein in two and Al Singer

---

334 Donald Dewey *Ray Arcel A Boxing Biography* 2012

in three. In a way, each of these boys was my protégé. I was always pulling for them to win because, like me, they came out of the East Side; because like me when I was a kid on the East Side, they set out to win the lightweight title. Each of them was referred to by the newspaper boys as "a second Leonard". I hated to see them flattened by McLarnin.'

'Well, Benny, the army of East Side fight fans will be there to see you make your bid,' added Wood. 'Every one of them that can beg or borrow the price of admission.'[335]

'What's in a name?' Henry McLemore of *United Press* posed the question to his readers. 'Well, Benny Leonard's was worth $65,000 to him during the past 12 months, that being the amount he accumulated on the comeback trail. You don't have to be told that Benny's name earned the 65 grand. But Benny realised that his name was more potent than his fists, so capitalised on the Leonard that used to be. You needn't try and put the old bite on Benny. He doesn't know where the money is. "I've learned my lesson," he says. "This time I've got it so well hidden I can't even find it myself."

'Now, $65,000 a year is elegant money. For a boxer who is getting bald, and whose best years are a decade or more removed, it's downright remarkable. But Leonard has set his heart on recovering that original quarter-million that went "pouf!" in the market. Whether he gets it or not depends on one person – that apple-cheeked, dynamite-socking broth of lad, Jimmy McLarnin. Leonard saw McLarnin lose to Lou Brouillard and didn't think much of the fight Jimmy put up. But Benny, we believe, forgets one thing. McLarnin hit Brouillard hard enough and often enough to drop any fighter in the business other than the Worcester bull. If McLarnin hits Leonard one-tenth as many licks, old Bennah is going out of there feet first.'[336]

---

335 Wilbur Wood *Ring* magazine Octopber 1932
336 Henry McLemore *Ames Daily Tribute Times* Iowa 26 August 1932

'The barber says "you know you are getting gray back of the ears?" Isn't Benny Leonard fighting tonight?' Joe Williams asks in his column, 'and does anybody know of a greater fighter in his or her time than Benny Leonard? I won't go for that stuff about Gans and Lavigne being better. I never saw them and thousands of others didn't. I will concede that maybe they were just as good but I defy anybody to prove that they were better. I am still trying to tie up those gray hairs with Benny Leonard. You see, he fights tonight. And Benny is an old man, too. So I must string along with him. The boys say he hasn't got a laundryman's chance. Maybe he hasn't. But even so I am going to stick with him until they count him out.'[337]

Damon Runyon ran this through his typewriter for Universal Services Inc. 'Benny Leonard is now 36 years of age, and the blaze of fistic youth is but a little ember on the far horizon of the past. It seems but yesterday that he was the prettiest, most graceful physical specimen on exhibition in these parts, a pugilistic wonder mentally, and with his gloved fists. He retired, still champion, in 1925. Now Benny Leonard climbs into the ring tonight at Madison Square Garden in a valiant attempt to defeat one of the oldest laws of athletic competition, which is THEY NEVER COME BACK. Leonard will be the sentimental favourite, but sentiment isn't worth a penny a hundredweight in the ring, and against sentiment you will probably be able to get 3 to 1. I presume Leonard returned to the ring for the same reason that has brought a lot of other citizens out of retirement these past couple of years. He thought he had enough money to last him the rest of his life. Then he suddenly discovered himself a trifle short of enough. They tell me he is very confident of giving a good account of himself tonight, and I'll say one thing for Leonard – he rarely guessed 'em wrong in the old days.'[338]

337 Joe Williams *El Paso Herald Post* Texas 7 October 1932
338 Damon Runyon *San Antonio Light* Texas 7 October 1932

CHAPTER TWENTY-SIX

'ALL NEW York was talking of the clash,' recalled Arcel, 'and the house was sold out days beforehand.' A capacity crowd of 21,893 paid a gross gate of $65,355.15, according to Fleischer's *Ring Record Book*.

'Hundreds of disappointed fans milled around the Garden as we drove up on the night. They charged one dollar to five dollars. Five dollars ringside. And Leonard got as much as McLarnin – 25 per cent. There were no guarantees in those days. Jimmy Johnston, the head of Madison Square Garden boxing, said they could draw $60,000, which they did. Sold out completely. Leonard's purse was $15,000.

'The atmosphere was tense as we walked to the ring and climbed through the ropes. For five minutes, the fans roared solidly for their Benny while he smiled and bowed his acknowledgements. He didn't seem nervous or distressed in the slightest degree, and when I came to pull his robe off I found I was trembling.

'Immediately, McLarnin tried to rush Benny off his feet. With consummate ease Benny avoided him, and brushed him rapidly with flickering lefts. Again Jimmy tore in to attack only to find his rival wasn't there. Lightly, Leonard moved around the ring, swiftly he hit, rapidly he slid out of danger. There was a baffled look in the Irishman's eyes as his thunderous blows missed their target, and the fans were howling their appreciation of a superb, scientific exhibition; Benny was working miracles of balance, timing and footwork. He was then as good as ever he had been.'[339]

Round one – Leonard neatly stabbed McLarnin's head with his left and slipped away from a two-fisted volley as the grim little Irishman tore in on him. Leonard was very fast as he boxed away from McLarnin and to the crowd's amazement he dropped Jimmy to his knees with a terrific right under the heart. McLarnin came up instantly but Leonard, the master, shook him again with a left hook to the head. McLarnin, storming in, managed to belt Benny with a half dozen lefts to the body. He shook off the left jab Leonard kept in his face and caught Benny with a terrific left hook to the chin. Leonard reeled in a corner. Another left hook to the head left him groggy as the bell ended a sensational round.

'The crowd had come to see Leonard, hoping that a veteran of 36 could defy the oldest law of the ring. They saw him muster much of his old skill and, just once, enough of his old punching power to drive the dynamite-laden McLarnin to his knees for the flash of a second in the first round. For the first two minutes of the opening round, the great crowd cheered him frantically; he was almost the old Leonard.

'In plowed McLarnin, the killer crowding the old man of 36. Benny set himself, whipped a right uppercut to the young Irishman's heart, flashed his left hook to the chin. McLarnin's knees buckled. For one startled second, he started to the floor. But he barely touched it before he was up again. Benny fended him off, but just as the round ended Jimmy reached Benny's chin with a short right hook.'[340]

Round two – Leonard bored carefully but McLarnin, trying to bring his guard down for a head attack, poked two left hooks to

---

339 John Jarrett *Ray Arcel Champ in the Corner* 2007
340 Edward J. Neil *East Liverpool Review* Ohio 8 October 1932

Benny's body and Leonard stabbed McLarnin's head with a left, but another left hook sent the old champion to the ropes. He needed all his skill and guile as McLarnin crowded after him and rights and lefts whistled inches past Leonard's chin. He took another left hook to the head but robbed another right. A left dropped Leonard for nine. He came up gamely throwing right hands to Jimmy's body. A left to the head sent him reeling to the ropes. He stabbed at McLarnin's head, tried to drive him off with rights but McLarnin kept after him, flinging left hooks after left hooks to the jaw as Benny gamely staggered through to the bell.

'McLarnin, punching at every opportunity, came close to ending matters near the middle of the second round. Leonard was bobbing and weaving in his corner when a left uppercut came steaming out of nowhere to catch him flush on the jaw. Down he went. He was up at nine, but all his fight was gone. From that point until the end he was strictly on the defensive, confining what few punches he threw to infighting. That Benny was able to last so long was due entirely to his mastery of the art of self-defence. Spent as he was, the one-time scourge of the lightweights automatically went through the motion, which in his heyday made it all but impossible for an opponent to land a telling punch.'[341]

Round three – Leonard shot his left into McLarnin's head and made the Irishman miss with both hands. Benny danced away and McLarnin's left and right batteries whistled harmlessly past his head as the veteran ducked and pulled out of danger. McLarnin buried a right in Leonard's side but Benny crossed him sharply with a right to the jaw. McLarnin drove Benny into a corner and shook him up with a left and right to the head. Benny reeled to the ropes under a right to the jaw and was content to cover his head in his arms to avoid punishment. Leonard missed wildly with a left

---

341 *Cedar Rapids Gazette* Iowa 8 October 1932

and then a right as he grew very tired and McLarnin pounded his head in a clinch. Benny rallied and flung the left hook to the body as the bell sounded.

'When Benny was good and the lightweight champion, only one fighter of that tough, hard-punching crew of 135-pounders who comprised the greatest lightweight crop since the Great War had been able to muss his hair. He used to wear it all plastered down with bear grease and shoe polish and it was a point of pride with him to enter a fight in defence of the title with his hair slicked and come out with the title intact and his hair still gleaming as though it had been painted on.

'But, of course, that wasn't the Benny Leonard that Jimmy McLarnin was fighting last night in the Garden with $67,000 in money in the place and every seat occupied and all the survivors of his old public on the ground to exult or mourn him. This Benny Leonard who tried to give away ten years to McLarnin in the new Garden, a Garden that had sprung up since he retired, was a scant middleweight of 150 pounds, 36 years old, with the outward form of an athlete, but the inward apparatus of a second-hand job. His hair was thin and weedy and it was all over his face in dark strings before the first round was over. He was using nothing but his old knowing and intuition against a fellow ten years younger and just that much stronger and resilient.'[342]

Round four – Leonard looked very old as he took a final deep breath and came up for the fourth but he bounced lightly past McLarnin's left and swung a left hook to the body. Again, Leonard banged his left hook to McLarnin's head and Jimmy was a bit befuddled. McLarnin, forcing the fighting every second, tore into Leonard with two rights to the head. He buried a two-fisted attack into Leonard's body. A left hurt Leonard's eye and he kept

---

342 Westbrook Pegler *Salt Lake City Telegram* 8 October 1932

rubbing it. McLarnin slipped to the floor as he missed a wild swing and Leonard stood smiling beside him as he bounced right up. They measured jabs evenly in the centre of the ring and Leonard tried every trick in his old book to pull McLarnin for a deciding punch. But Jimmy boxed him beautifully and they were feinting and stabbing with lefts at the bell …

'All the drama that comes down through the years at the mention of Leonard's name, once Fistiana's byword for all that was great in the ring, hung over the big battle pit as the thin-faced, thin-haired veteran gamely battled the unstoppable tide of youth and power. Some of his strength and speed came back in the fourth and the chain-lightning brain of the old warrior never dimmed as he held his own through the round.'[343]

Round five – Leonard let McLarnin's left slip over his shoulder. He nailed the youngster with a left hook to the jaw. Jimmy tried to pin the old master in a corner but Benny danced away, tapping a few times in the body. As Leonard stood in mid-ring, McLarnin fired both hands three times without laying a glove on the old champion. But in the next exchange, he took Benny with two solid left hooks and a smashing right to the jaw. Leonard bent low and McLarnin smashed his right to the side. Ferocious McLarnin tore after the veteran, nailed him with another right to the jaw that almost floored the ex-champion. Leonard was stalling, fencing off McLarnin's attack as the bell ended the round.

'Leonard stood up in his old-time style, picking dozens of punches out of mid-air and rolling with others as he successfully survived McLarnin's eager attempts to put over a final haymaker. Meanwhile, Benny's slim resources in stamina were ebbing; frequently Leonard covered up so thoroughly that all McLarnin had for a target was the bald spot on top of Benny's head. A glancing

---

343 Edward J. Neil *Winona Republican Herald* Minnesota 8 October 1932

right opened a thin cut over Leonard's right eye. In the fifth, Leonard took a bad beating, without offering anything resembling a real counter punch, but then spat blood, stood up cooly and fenced the last few moments with a flash of cleverness.'[344]

Round six – Leonard came out carefully, made McLarnin miss and popped a left hook to the jaw. But McLarnin was on him again and a left hook to the jaw spun Benny around. McLarnin tore at Benny's body, drew his guard down then dropped a hard right on the old-timer's chin. Jimmy popped Benny's head with a right hook but Leonard rallied, stabbed Jimmy with his left and again dodged marvellously away from a volley of McLarnin's punches. He nailed McLarnin with a fine left and right to the head but Jimmy drove him to the ropes and hammered his head with both hands. A left and right sent Benny reeling. As the ex-champion swayed helplessly, covering his head with his elbows, referee Arthur Donovan stepped in between them and stopped the fight, with only five seconds left in the round …

'The end came after 2.55 of the sixth round when Leonard, once the greatest of them all, tottered about helplessly in the centre of the ring, merely a bruised target for Jimmy's thudding lefts and rights. More than two minutes of the round had elapsed when the 24-year-old Vancouver Battler staggered his 36-year-old opponent with an overhand right to the jaw. McLarnin followed this with a barrage to head and body that almost doubled Leonard up. Unwilling to keep pounding away at the helpless old fellow whom he had regarded as an idol years ago, Jimmy turned to the referee and motioned for him to stop the affair. The 21,000 fans breathed with relief when referee Arthur Donovan threw his arms about the staggering, semi-bald man in black tights to save him from further punishment. They had believed for some time that Benny couldn't turn back the clock.'[345]

---

344 Alan Gould *Twin Falls Daily News* Idaho 8 October 1932
345 Jack Cuddy *Huntingdon Daily News* Pennsylvania 8 October 1932

'A ring philosopher sat upon the bare rubbing table that was his throne, a ragged dressing gown his royal robes. "It's nice," said Benny Leonard, once one of the greatest of all lightweights, "to lose occasionally. All your pals come in to see you. They don't bother when you win."

'So it was that the new Leonard, a shadow of the old, shrugged away the first defeat of his comeback campaign, a six-round technical knockout at the hands of fiery young Jimmy McLarnin in Madison Square Garden last night. "I wasn't badly hurt at all," he said smilingly as friends crowded around him. "I'm going to keep right on. I was timid. I couldn't get started. I can lick a lot of fellows, maybe even McLarnin, before I'm through."

'Just as the first round ended, Jimmy reached Leonard's chin with a short right hook. "And that punch," said the philosopher, as his trainer rubbed his neck with ice and smoothed the swelling from a spot above his right eye, "was the punch that really did all the damage. I could feel it all the way down my back. As I pulled away, something seemed to give at the base of my spine. I'd better see a bone doctor today. He fooled me," said the master strategist brightly, "rushing me like that. I thought he'd try to box. In general, I'm pretty well satisfied. I recouped quickly. My mind always was clear. I feel very good indeed. And did you see that house? They were here to see me, weren't they? I'm not going to leave that. I'm still Jewish." And so, philosopher to the end, the old fellow put on his clothes and went home.'[346]

'Every now and then Benny would pull me into a clinch and whisper, "Listen kid, let's not have anybody getting hurt around here." "I didn't say anything," Jimmy recalled. "But I was glad when Arthur Donovan threw his arms around Benny just before the end of the sixth."

---

346 Edward J. Neil *Winona Republican Herald* 'Minnesota 8 October 1932

'"Was it a hard fight?" Jimmy was asked some weeks after the bout. "Leonard was old," he replied in a tone of reverence one employs for the departed.'[347]

'When Benny Leonard retired as lightweight champion of the world in 1924,' reported *Time* magazine, 'only one man [Richie Mitchell] had mussed his sleek brown hair in many a long battle. Last week in Madison Square Garden, Benny Leonard was wiping stringy thin hair out of his eyes 30 seconds after tough Jimmy McLarnin began to hit him. The pudgy Canadian welterweight shook his head at the hardest blows Leonard's bow arms could deliver. What was left, at 36, of the cleverest boxer the lightweight division ever knew was knocked down in the second round. In the sixth he could not hold his paunch in, found his legs behaving like Leon Errol's. McLarnin hit him on the side of his head with a straight right-hand blow. The Errol legs sagged. McLarnin hit right-left-right-left. Leonard tried to back away, could not move: tried to hold, could not lift his arms. McLarnin looked at the referee, who put an arm about Leonard's shoulder, led him to his corner …

'Two minutes later ex-champion Leonard, his hair smooth again, was congratulating his master, grinning about the $15,000 (plus $65,000 he had made during his 14-month comeback) he would take home to his mother, whom he once promised that he would never fight again.'[348]

Writer and boxing aficionado Budd Schulberg was finally going to see the man idolised in his family as the Great Benny Leonard. 'At the age of 35, he announced his comeback to the ring. After beating a string of nobodies, he was matched with Jimmy McLarnin. Back home in Los Angeles, I had watched "Baby Face" Jimmy fight his way to the top of his profession, from bantamweight

---

347 Andrew Gallimore *Babyface Goes To Hollywood* 2009
348 *Time* magazine 17 October 1932

to welter, against top fighters like Fidel LaBarba, Bud Taylor and Joey Sangor. He seemed to specialise in destroying illustrious Jewish lightweights; Jackie Fields, Sid Terris, Al Singer, Ruby Goldstein.

'From Dartmouth College, where I was then a freshman, I phoned my father in Hollywood for an extra 50 dollars to get to New York to see the Great Benny Leonard, at last, against our hometown sensation, the still baby-faced 24-year-old hailed by western sportswriters as a coming champion. With excitement building in me, I promised to phone B.P. at the studio after the fight. But when I got back to my hotel from that chill October fight night, I didn't have the heart to place the call. I felt like getting in my Chevy and driving the long, winding miles back to New Hampshire. The Great Benny Leonard, when I finally caught up with him ten years too late, was a rather paunchy, over-the-hill lightweight with thinning hair, a tentative jab, and uncertain footwork, no match for the fast, young and lethal Jimmy McLarnin, who toyed with him before knocking him out in six of the saddest rounds I ever saw.'[349]

A couple of weeks after the fight, Damon Runyon was writing, 'Mr Benny Leonard, one-time champion of the world, has never tried to tell me how to run my business. So I am not going to try to tell Mr Leonard how to run his business. I am told that, in spite of his defeat by Jimmy McLarnin not long ago, Mr Leonard proposes continuing his pugilistic career. Well-meaning friends say, "Don't do it, Bennah!" But it is quite all right with me. A boxer boxes as long as he can for the same identical reason that a sportswriter continues sportswriting as long as he can – to make a living.

'I have had several hundred queries asking me what I thought of Mr Leonard in his last stand against Jimmy McLarnin. I find I didn't think much of him. He merely demonstrated what he

---

349 Budd Schulberg *The Ring* magazine May 1980

might have done to Jimmy McLarnin some years back. He could make McLarnin do anything he wished, then having made him do it, Mr Leonard couldn't go any further in the matter. His legs wouldn't respond to the urging of his nimble brain. Only his hands functioned briefly …

'McLarnin would have laid hands on Mr Leonard when Mr Leonard was at his best, just once. That would have been when they shook hands. The old Leonard would scarcely have failed to flatten McLarnin after nailing him that right hand uppercut in the first round that buckled McLarnin's knees. If Mr Leonard continues boxing against the advice of his well-meaning friends, I presume it will be because he didn't make enough money out of the McLarnin fight to suit his current needs. He had a lot of money when he retired. He hasn't got it now.'[350]

---

350 Damon Runyon *Medicine Hat News* Alberta Canada

CHAPTER TWENTY-SEVEN

'THE GLORIOUS trail of Benny Leonard's fistic career came to an end in Madison Square Garden recently when the lightweight king of a decade ago was stopped by Jimmy McLarnin, youthful Vancouver welterweight, in the sixth round of a scheduled ten rounds affair. The superb showman, just one year and a day after he had come out of a seven-year retirement to try for a comeback, bowed to the inevitable. Old age, so far as an athletic career is concerned, took its toll and Benny was on the verge of being knocked out when Arthur Donovan, the referee, humanely stepped between the wizard of old and his Irish rival and stopped proceedings with only ten seconds left for the wind-up of the sixth round.

'He stood in mid-ring, a tired old man, bald-headed old man, who had given a remarkable demonstration of his old wizardry, but had found Father Time against him. It was a remarkable exhibition of gameness that Leonard gave – cool, calculating fighting against a terrific assault of a 12 years-younger opponent, and none in that vast gathering of 21,000 persons who paid $67,000 to see Benny's attempt to break the comeback hoodoo begrudged him the big purse which he took as his share of the gate. Benny earned it. He gave the crowd a thrill for its money. New York's pride did far better than had been expected. In fact, at times, though weary, he made his rival miss so often that the fans were reminded of the days when the stars of the lightweight class were scarcely able to land a glove on him. His defensive work was a treat. He should venture no further, unless he wants to go the way of other former lightweight kings who are now engaged in the pastime of cutting paper dolls.'[351]

From this dispatch out of Albany, New York, on 26 January 1933, it looked as though Benny had not taken heed of Mr Fleischer's well-meaning words. 'Benny Leonard, former world's lightweight champion, said today he hopes to meet Jimmy McLarnin in a return bout on the coast. McLarnin technically knocked him out in the first meeting, at New York City several months ago. Leonard, here for a vaudeville stage appearance, asserted, "I expect to fool around in vaudeville for a few weeks, but don't let anyone tell you I have given up boxing." His act calls for several rounds of boxing.'[352]

Benny knew sadness in 1933. His beloved mother died, aged 62. Her obituary was in the New York newspapers on 29 April. 'Ex-champ's mother dies. Funeral services will be held tomorrow for Mrs Minnie Leiner, 62, mother of Benny Leonard, former lightweight champion. Mrs Leiner died yesterday at Park West Hospital from a complication of heart trouble and other ailments. The burial will be at Mount Carmel Cemetery, Glendale, Queens County, New York.'

'Old "Bennah" Can't Get Excited at Present Day Lightweight Crew', headed an *Associated Press* dispatch out of New York in July 1933.

'Benny Leonard, one old fellow who came at least part of the way back, sat behind me the other night at a ringside where a couple of lightweights were toiling, old Billy Petrolle and young Bep Van Klavaren. And strangely enough for a fellow who has been in there where the firing is hottest, he seemed barely interested. Perhaps it's the calibre of the lightweights today that leaves Leonard just

351 Nat Fleischer *The Ring* magazine December 1932
352 *Middletown Times Herald* New York 26 January 1933

a trifle cold. Leonard was as smart as any man who ever stepped down from a prize ring realising his career was over.

'He said at the time, back in 1923, when he was signed for a match with Mickey Walker, that he was retiring the undefeated lightweight champion because his mother did not want him to fight any more. He fooled few people with that explanation, himself least of all. He was quitting because he knew he was through, because he knew the next tough fellow he met would lick him. So he stepped down gracefully with lots of money, fine friends, an established place in the community. He dabbled in real estate, ran a hockey club, played the market. He could not gauge the latter as he did his fighting ability. He did not realise that the time to hang up his gloves in that game was in 1928. He was still in there swinging in 1929. And he came out broke.

'So he started a comeback. Jimmy McLarnin finished it. So he picked himself up off the carpet, took his $200,000 for a year of effort and went back to peaceful living and wiser investing.'[353]

A couple of months later, veteran cartoonist/writer Robert Edgren was writing, 'They are beginning to say that lightweight champion Barney Ross looks like another Benny Leonard, just as they used to say that Benny was "another Joe Gans". As a matter of fact, Barney does look like another Benny. There are several very marked points of resemblance in fighting style. When Barney Ross stood toe to toe with Canzoneri in the New York fight, disdaining to use his superior long-range skill and showing New York that he could stay in there giving blow for blow until even the fiery Canzoneri was forced to back up, he did what Benny Leonard did in many hard fights. If he keeps this up, he'll be as popular a champion as Benny was.'[354]

---

353 *Salt Lake Tribune* 30 July 1933
354 Robert Edgren *Moorhead Daily News* Minnesota 30 September 1933

'Not all boxers are as fortunate as Benny Leonard,' observed the *Bluefield Daily Telegraph* … 'Benny, one of the most intelligent fighters the ring has ever produced, left it at the peak of his career, a wealthy man. The panic swept away his fortune and he was forced to take the mittens down from the wall, where he had hung them five years before, and punch out another bankroll for himself. In a little over a year, Benny had earned about $200,000 again and the venture was well worth the beating he took from Jimmy McLarnin in his final bout.

'Today, Benny is embarked on a new career in radio, with his nest egg salted away so it won't be wiped out by a falling market.'[355]

You can't keep a good man down, well not in the boxing ring anyway. Benny Leonard was still in there punching away in May of 1934, his photograph in newspapers across America, captioned, 'Showing the same confidence in his political acumen that he displayed in his ring ability when world's lightweight champion, Benny Leonard plans to seek the political leadership of the ninth aldermanic district in New York. Here's Benny looking over a sheaf of telegrams wishing him good luck in his venture.'[356]

A few months later, in December, Benny had a new cap to wear. 'LEONARD A BASKETBALL MAGNATE' heralded the *Chicago Sentinel* with Haskell Cohen writing, 'Many sport followers will be pleased to learn that Benny Leonard, fistic idol of other years, has returned to the professional fold again. This time, the rotund and likeable Benny has purchased a 25 per cent interest in the New York Jewels basketball team. Leonard, it will be remembered, was at one time financially interested in the Pittsburgh Hockey sextet, a deal that resulted disastrously for the embryonic magnate from a mercenary standpoint. Critics claim that the former champ cannot go wrong in his latest venture as the Jewels are rapidly usurping the

---

355 *Bluefield Daily Telegraph* West Virginia 12 October 1933
356 *Madison Wisconsin State Journal* 7 May 1934

Original Celtics. Every time this crew performs on its home court, it draws 6,000 spectators and turns away many more.

'Benny has not lost his punching ability, as one young Princeton gridster will attest. Last week upon the conclusion of his training season, said football player visited a Manhattan nightclub and proceeded to imbibe of the liquid that soon inebriates and very shortly began to use harsh and bitter language that met with the strong disapproval of the ladies seated at an adjoining table. Their escort warned the dazed husky to refrain from the continuance of such vile talk but it was to no avail and the escort was forced to speak to the young man again. By this time, the boy was well gone and so made a pass at the stocky man confronting him.

'The blow glanced harmlessly over the man's shoulder and he in turn swung to the midsection of the football player and knocked him out. When the youngster was brought to, he asked who had clipped him and was informed that Benny Leonard had put him away.'[357]

'Benny Leonard is one fighter who continues to grace the spotlight long after his fighting days are over,' wrote John J. Romano. 'Benny was a great champion in his day. He is often ranked the equal, if not the superior, of the old master Joe Gans. A fighter is soon forgotten after he ceases to dazzle an opponent with a display of boxing wizardry or fails to punch them senseless. Not Leonard. He does not seek the spotlight. It is his natural kindness to young fighters which makes him the idol of fighters and fans alike …

'Last summer, Leonard took a liking to Barney Ross. This was before the first McLarnin fight. Benny had gone six rounds with the Vancouver-Irishman and undoubtedly learned many little things a youngster needed to know to whip the veteran. You all know how well and masterfully Ross fought to capture the welterweight title.

---

357 Haskell Cohen *Chicago Sentinel* 27 December 1934

Something happened to cool the ardour of counsel for Leonard and the result was that Ross did not fight as he did three months earlier and lost to McLarnin.

'Speaking about present-day lightweights, Leonard gave it as his opinion that they are no better or worse than those of his day. Poor handling and failure to study and put into practice the fine points of the game is all that is holding them back. Smart advice from a strategist of the ring and good enough for the budding youngster to follow. A word to the wise is sufficient.'[358]

'Benny Leonard, the former lightweight king whose jolting fists spread a profusion of lacerations and contusions in his heyday, has mellowed with the passing years and become a professional soother – a "Medicine Man," it was learned tonight,' reported Jack Cuddy from New York. 'Belting Bennah was cornered in a downtown tavern and questioned about his reported right-about-face.

'"Yes, it's true," the somewhat pudgy, semi-bald chap in the brown suit admitted ruefully. "I'm opening a liniment factory. Good for man or beast, etc."

'The admission was hesitant and rueful because all Broadway has been kidding the "Medicine Man" about his ointment. "I've got a couple hundred letters and postcards from wise guys and smart alecs during the past week," Benny grumbled. "They give phony addresses and ask to have a bottle sent collect. It's not right, because this is a serious business." What led Benny into the liniment business?

'"When I was fighting, a friend of mine fixed up a special rubbing lotion for me. I used to get hit on the ears a lot, and every time they started to swell I'd rub the stuff on them – and I never had a cauliflower ear. And I'd rub it on any other part of my body when it got stiff or sore. It was so good that a lot of other fighters

---

358 John J. Romano *Moorhead Daily News* Minnesota 28 January 1935

– and then wrestlers, too – started asking me for it. Since I retired, I've had so many requests for it that I figured I'd save a lot of time and money by selling it. That's what I'm doing and it's going over big."

'Between the liniment and his real estate, would 39-year-old Benny have enough money to get married soon? Benny had been thinking about that very thing, he admitted, but hadn't found the right girl yet.'[359]

(Benny's first girl friend was his mother, Minnie 'Min' Leiner. It was her failing health that made him retire as undefeated champion in 1925, and she died in 1933, aged 62.)

This was a night in August 1935 and one of the local fight clubs in the Massachusetts town of Lowell was staging a boxing show, advertising that former lightweight champion Benny Leonard would appear in person and give an exhibition.

'The fighter, who had made no such agreement, heard about it and attended in a rage. He found that the ticket sellers still were assuring fans that Leonard would be there. Following the preliminaries, the announcer began an apology to the crowd. At the last minute, he said, Mr Leonard had sent his regrets. By this time, the ex-titleholder had climbed through the ropes. "You crooked, double-crossing so-and-so. I'm Benny Leonard and I'm gonna knock your ears off right now!"

'The announcer, no dullard, turned and lifted his arms for silence. "Ladies and gentlemen," he bellowed, "exactly as advertised, Benny Leonard has come here tonight. And for the boxing exhibition that we promised as part of the programme, Benny has promised to knock my ears off!" The applause was thunderous, and Leonard was licked. Took a couple of playful swings at his swindler, shook hands, bowed to everybody, and went away from there.'[360]

359 Jack Cuddy *Nevada State Journal* 28 April 1935
360 Paul Harrison *Lowell Sun* Mass. 7 August 1935

It used to be Leonard the fighting man, now it was Leonard the travelling man. From Lowell, the former champion journeyed to Syracuse, where he was to help his friend Roy Simmons stage the police benefit amateur boxing tournament. Benny would referee the bouts on Thursday night in Municipal Stadium. 'Accompanying Leonard was Kid Herman, one of the good lightweights back in 1910–1913 and one of the few men to ever put the once-lightweight champion on the floor for a long count. Benny laughingly recalled the incident today. A green youngster, he met Herman in a ten-round bout at a small New York club and ran flush into a right in the second round. Badly hurt and dazed, Leonard slumped to the canvas. At the count of eight, he arose and managed to back pedal until his head cleared. He then went on to win the decision …

'Leonard is convinced Joe Louis is the greatest fighter in the heavyweight ranks today and should win easily over Max Baer in their September bout in New York. "The negro has everything in his favour," Benny stressed when quizzed by the local press. "He has rhythm in his punching. The blows are tossed naturally and Louis' timing in the Carnera and Levinsky bouts was perfect."

'Benny is engaged in radio work, serving as sports commentator for a New York station and also lends a hand in the dramatising of bouts of bygone days. Among the men who stopped in at the Hotel Syracuse to renew acquaintanceship with Leonard and his pal Herman was Eddie Risko, East Side Polish boy, one of the leading challengers for the middleweight crown.'[361]

Benny spent a week in Chicago as a guest of Bishop Shell's Catholic Youth Organisation (CYO) and had high praise for the CYO activities, providing sport for hundreds of boys. The ex-champ was particularly impressed with Jimmy Christy, a local featherweight who was matched with world champion Freddie Miller in a non-

---

361 *Syracuse Herald* 29 August 1935

title bout. Jimmy's only defeat was by Baby Arizmendi in a match for which the weight was four pounds below the youngster's best fighting weight, and he had beaten guys like Mike Belloise and Lew Feldman. This night he couldn't beat Miller, the veteran world traveller, but Leonard was still impressed with the kid ...

Then Benny was back to New York. He had a wedding to arrange!

'On New Year's Day, 1936,' Fleischer recorded in his Leonard biography, 'the romance between Benny and his beautiful secretary culminated in their marriage in New York. Jacqueline Stern had been Leonard's secretary for ten years and it wasn't long after she started working for the retired champion that their relationship grew into love and had it not been that shortly after they had met the depression hit Benny as it had millions of others, they would have taken their marriage vows long before the knot was finally tied. It was largely through Jacqueline Stern that Benny made good his financial comeback. Her faith in him never wavered and his love for her grew.

'Their married life was one of joy and bliss. She passed judgment on many of the talks Leonard prepared for the father-and-son dinners at which Benny was the guest of honour and in later years she was the guiding spirit behind Benny's new business ventures. He often remarked that whatever success he had was due to the guiding hand of his ma when he was a youth and to the devotion of his wife in the years of his retirement from the ring. Jacqueline was a talented girl and Leonard was mighty proud of her.'[362]

'Benny Leonard was married New Year's Eve to Miss Jacqueline Stern, who has been his secretary seven or eight years, with Benny finally admitting that the romance "began the minute I set eyes on her". Leonard, who is 39, and Miss Stern were married quietly

---

362 Nat Fleischer *Leonard The Magnificent* 1947

in the study of Dr Joseph Zeitlin, rabbi of the Temple Ansche Chesed. Miss Stern's sister, Mrs Mack Joseph, and Leonard's brother, Joseph, attended. The newly-weds plan to honeymoon at Atlantic City before taking up residence in New York.'[363]

'As well as taking a bride unto himself, Benny had taken under his wing a young Irish lad named Eddie Dunne, son of old-time lightweight Eddie Dunne Snr, who fought Kid McPartland and other former greats. Benny thinks his protégé can't miss winning the lightweight title within two years.'[364]

As March 1936 started slipping off the calendar, there was a new sporting role for Mr Benny Leonard to engage his spare time, besides managing a drinks manufactory, whatever that was. Starting Monday at Quincy, Massachusetts, and on successive nights in Boston, New Bedford, Attleboro and Brockton appearing in the role of wrestling referee.

'What does Benny Leonard know about the wrestling game? "I liked wrestling and went quite frequently to matches," said Benny. "I attended one in New York. A couple of meanies were slugging each other. The ref was knocked out. They called for volunteers. Someone shouted, "There's Benny Leonard, let him ref." What could I do? I accepted and here I am."

'Not much from a practical standpoint. But before he would accept the offer, Benny sat in on a good many exhibitions and diligently studied the rules. He knows all the holds. He practised them and can distinguish one from the other. But not to the extent that he wants to turn wrestler at this time.'[365]

'Leonard had one experience as a wrestler he is not likely to forget. When he was lightweight champion, he was in a New York

---

363 *Ames Daily Tribune* Iowa 2 January 1936
364 *Tyrone Daily Herald* Pennsylvania 15 January 1936
365 John J. Romano *Moorhead Daily News* Minnesota 28 March 1928

restaurant owned by his manager Billy Gibson. A large, beefy German was stowing away a big meal of turkey, washing the bird down with a good many seidels of beer. Came a call from Miner's Theatre in the Bowery asking Gibson to furnish a substitute for a wrestler who had failed to appear, and to bring Leonard along as the referee. The turkey-eating Teuton agreed to wrestle the head-liner.

'Knowing little about the game Benny used his legs to good advantage, keeping out of the way while the head-liner manoeuvred his opponent until he could wrap his legs around the body of the heaving German. The scissors was applied and when pressure was put on the grunts of the turkey and beer consumer were audible to those sitting back 20 rows. He appealed to Leonard to make his torturer break the hold. Thinking the German wanted to quit, Benny tapped the head-liner on the back, declaring him the winner. The Teuton jumped to his feet and made a dive at Leonard.

'Not knowing what to do under such a circumstance, Benny reverted to type and lashed out with one of the prettiest rights in his repertoire and Mr Wrestler went head over heels into the orchestra pit. It was the first and last victory Leonard scored in a wrestling match. The latter grew old in the game, but not so much that his right cross has lost any of its effectiveness. Fans of New England cities where Leonard is scheduled to appear may see the punch which brought him world renown in the ring. It is a nifty!' [366]

This was 4 July 1937 and *United Press* sportswriter Jack Cuddy opened his column accordingly. 'This being Independence Day, I am forced to break out the flag and start cheering for one of our "minute men" – Benny Leonard. Benny, former lightweight champion, doesn't know what minute they're going to take him to the cleaners – again. Benny Leonard earned more than $1,000,000 with his fists from 1912 to 1925, but after that unfortunate real

---

366 Stubby Currence *Bluefield Daily Telegraph* West Virginia 31 March 1936

estate investments and his Pittsburgh ice hockey team draped him over the ropes – financially. Since that walloping, "Bennah" staged a comeback pugilistically and financially. Jimmy McLarnin ended his comeback and Leonard retired permanently after that, but he retired with $82,000. This money salvaged some of his real estate and put him back on his feet financially.

'Leonard is 40 years old now. And he says, "Life begins at 40 – the life of a restaurateur." Benny is going into the restaurant business. I hope Benny does well. You've got to admire him for his confidence and courage. He has stuck about $47,000 into his new tavern at 72nd Street and Broadway. His partner, Max Engler, a New York restaurateur, put up a similar amount. They've risked $94,000 in rebuilding and redecorating a three-storey building in the heart of the uptown residential hotel and Tenderloin district …

'Leonard says, "We will do well here. I am a native New Yorker, I know everybody that amounts to anything in the five boroughs by their first name. Max knows food, service, liquors etc. All I'll have to do is climb into a tuxedo and say hello to my friends. And I'll be here morning, noon and night to extend the glad hand. And I know the people will come."'[367]

The people did come, but when the United States got into World War II, in 1941, Leonard enlisted in the U.S. Maritime Service and the restaurant was unable to stay afloat without his presence.

'Joe Louis wasn't the first fighter to risk his title for nothing in a war charity bout,' wrote Whitney Martin, 'which is taking nothing away from a great champion and sportsman. After all, a four-year-old kid isn't thinking much about such things, and that was Joe's age when Benny Leonard was making the grand gesture back in 1918. Benny did it not twice, but six times, and although they all were short bouts and three of them are in the record book

---

367 Jack Cuddy *Dubuque Telegram Herald* Iowa 4 July 1937

as exhibitions, if any of the opponents had landed a weekend punch to put Benny out, Benny's lightweight title would have gone right out with him.

"'Don't think they were just exhibitions," he says. "Why, Mike Golondo put a lump under my right eye at San Diego you could hang your hat and coat on."

'The 47-year-old Leonard has turned the calendar back 25 years to engage in the same type of war work he engaged in in 1918 – teaching service men to box. Only this time he is Lieutenant Benny Leonard of the U. S. Maritime Service. When this war came along, Benny looked around to see what he could do to help. He approached the army officials concerning an instruction job, but before anything came of that the maritime service offered him a full lieutenancy. And he looks right smart in his gold braid. A little on the plumpish side, maybe, as he weighed 165 compare to his fighting weight of 135, but even at that he's shrunk from the over-inflated 185 he weighed before taking over his duties.

'And he loves the work. He's stationed at Hoffman Island off Long Island, where the head man, Commander Malcolm Crossman U.S.N.R., is enthusiastic about boxing as a means of self-preservation. "The commander thinks boxing teaches a man to be calm under fire," Benny explains. "If a ship they are manning is hit, their boxing experience teaches them to keep to their posts and not go haywire, to keep their eyes open and their heads high, and carry on. They've been hit in the nose before and know what it means."'[368]

Lowell, Sunday, 21 January 1945 – Lieutenant Commander Benny Leonard of the Maritime Service received the Edward J. Neil plaque as the man who did the most for boxing in 1944. In presenting the plaque, former mayor Jimmy Walker termed Leonard

---

368 Whitney Martin *Titusville Herald* Pennsylvania 26 October 1942

"always a showman, but never a show-off". A crowd of 300 jammed the hunter room at Ruppert's Brewery for the annual presentation of the award by the New York Boxing Writers' Association.

'Lt Comdr Benny Leonard of the Maritime Service said, "I rode one post-war boxing boom for more than a million dollars, and I expect to do very well on the next one," recorded Jack Cuddy. Leonard made this significant statement last night as we rode back from a Brooklyn bond-selling show that honoured the 28th anniversary of his winning the lightweight championship of the world.

'Leonard said, "I'll remain in service until after the war. Then, when I get back into civvies, I'll gather a stable of fighters who can cash in on the greatest boxing boom the world has ever known – a boom which will make the one that followed the last world war look like small potatoes."

'Bennah – slightly plump and slightly bald, but quite dapper in the maritime blue and gold – emphasised that the approaching furore over fisticuffs would be terrific because of 1) the war-stimulated interest in boxing and 2) television. Leonard said he regretted soulfully that he wasn't "a young punk" now who could hammer his way up through the great boxing days ahead. The smell of leather was sweet to his nostrils as we rode back from the very successful war-bond show at Brooklyn's Broadway Arena. More than $3,000,000 worth of bonds had been sold at the show.

'The money he had made from his ring comeback enabled him to invest in a dress-manufacturing concern that now yields him rich dividends. "Old Benny is okay financially now," he says, "Some of the boys I've trained will come back to me as fully fledged fighters after the war, and we'll ride the boom for plenty."'[369]

---

369 Jack Cuddy *Pittsfield Berkshire Evening Eagle* Mass. 29 May 1945

CHAPTER TWENTY-EIGHT

NEWS FROM New York, 5 February 1946 – 'Benny Leonard takes off his sailor suit on Tuesday. The retired former lightweight champion, who set up the army physical training programme in World War I, returns to civilian life after three and a half years as a director of physical fitness, recreation and morale for the Maritime Service. Benny, who was transferred from Hoffman Island, N.Y. to the Maritime service station at Sheepshead Bay in Brooklyn in September 1944 – and has been there ever since – retires as a full commander. He plans a lecture tour soon in an effort to impress on Americans the need for a comprehensive physical education programme, since millions of youths were found unfit for military service in World War II. Besides his lecture tour, Benny will resume refereeing in various parts of the country.'[370]

In May 1946, Benny was off to Kingston, some 90 miles north of New York City, where he was getting involved with Ben Becker, who had been around the local amateur boxing scene for 15 years. The two Bens had almost completed plans to open a gymnasium in the town and hoped to develop the local amateurs with the intention of sending them into the professional ranks when they had learned enough to compete with the best ring athletes in the country. A

---

370 *Somerset Daily American* Pennsylvania 5 February 1946

few weeks later, Benny was into basketball, having received the Kingston franchise to compete in the New York State professional league. Becker and a group of Kingston businessmen would be associated with the ex-champ.

Benny had been a licensed boxing referee with the New York State Athletic Association since 1942, working mainly in New York and Philadelphia and as far afield as Toledo, Ohio, Milwaukee, West Virginia and Quebec and Montreal in Canada. His presence was always advertised on the fight bills, which brought the local fans in to see the "Great Bennah" in person. He always received a standing ovation, bearing in mind that he was sharing the ring with such names as Bob Montgomery, Ike Williams, Lew Jenkins, Rocky Graziano, Sugar Ray Robinson, Tippy Larkin and Marty Servo.

A regular at Madison Square Garden, Benny was working 'down the bill' at the St Nicks Arena on a warm April night in 1947. 'When professional boxing flourished throughout the city, from the 1920s to the early 1950s, the oldest and best known of the dozen or so neighbourhood fight clubs was St Nicholas Arena. It was located on the north-east corner of 66th Street and Columbus Avenue, a few steps east of Broadway. As late as the 50s and 60s, St Nick's was still referred to from time to time, because of its origins, as the St Nicholas Rink or St Nicholas Palace.

'It was built as an ice-skating rink in 1896, one of the first indoor ice skating facilities in the country. For a while in the 30s, it was called Windsor Palace, for reasons no one seems to remember. Boxing matches did not start at "the rink" until 1906. In the early days, around 1910, whenever flamboyant Diamond Jim Brady was in the house, he and buxom actress Lillian Russell, often his companion, would present a diamond stick pin to the winner of a particularly hard-fought main event.

'St Nicholas Arena had a capacity of about 4,000 for boxing and wrestling and drew a rowdy, smoke-filled house. Its balcony

– rare for a neighbourhood club – was usually occupied before the main floor and not only because of price. (In 1960, tickets cost $5 for ringside, $3 for the balcony, $1.50 for general admission.) "The overhanging balcony was wonderful," an old-timer reminisced. "You could see great from anywhere up there. Looking down on the ring was sensational. Those seats were *better* than ringside."[371]

Don Dunphy had broadcast over 2,000 fights, including 200 title bouts. In his 1988 autobiography, Don recalled, 'On 18 April 1947, Bill Corum and I were doing a Friday night fight at the St Nick's. Benny Leonard was the referee that night, and he was the only referee for the entire card. It was hot in the old fight club that night, and under the ring lights it had to be worse. Between the ninth and tenth rounds of the feature bout, I looked at Leonard as he stood in a neutral corner. I remember we smiled at each other. Now the main bout was over, but there was still another four-round bout. Corum and I were still on the air and Benny was the referee for this final contest.

'I looked at him again. Now, apparently feeling the heat, he had taken off his tie. The extra bout got under way, and Leonard circled the fighters. Suddenly he seemed to slip, and went down. The remaining crowd laughed at the spectacle of a referee on the canvas. We all waited for Benny to get up, but he didn't. Now the crowd, sensing something unusual, became very quiet.

'The fighters stopped fighting and went to Leonard, who just lay there. Dr Vincent Nardiello of the boxing commission staff quickly jumped into the ring and ministered to the fallen referee. After a few moments, the doctor looked over at Bill Corum and me, shook his head, and said, "I'm afraid he's out." It was a sad moment. Benny Leonard, born Benjamin Leiner on 7 April 1896, had passed away in the ring. His hair was still unmussed.'[372]

---

371 Lawrence S. Ritter *East Side, West Side* 1998
372 Don Dunphy *Don Dunphy at Ringside* 1988

The *Pittsfield Berkshire Evening Eagle* (Massachusetts) had the story on 19 April. 'Benny Leonard's sudden death last night at the St Nicholas Arena was one of those ironies of fate. Early this week, Nat Fleischer, editor of *The Ring* magazine and the unofficial statistician of world ring records, told Attorney Maurice B. Rosenfield, treasurer of the Shire City A.C., that Friday (yesterday) would be the 30th anniversary to the day when Leonard won the lightweight championship of the world.

'As a matter of fact, Fleischer and Leonard appeared on a National Broadcasting Company programme yesterday noon. They were guests on a programme which was designed to give an up-to-the-minute story of the ring today. Last January, Leonard appeared here under the auspices of the local B'nai B'rith. He made quite a hit because he not only was well versed "ringwise" but he had some vaudeville experience which he used to good advantage.

'Leonard, in his later years, made many visits to Syracuse and had many acquaintances here to whom his death Friday night came as a great blow. Leonard's wife, grief stricken, explained yesterday that Benny had been in perfect health and within a week had passed a physical examination to increase his insurance. Mrs Leonard, who seldom attended boxing bouts, was following her usual procedure, listening to the fight over the radio, when she heard Bill Corum announce, "Benny Leonard, the referee, has collapsed in the ring." She heard details of his being carried out of the ring and the announcement that he was dead.'[373]

'Death is no respecter of persons,' wrote Fleischer in his 1947 Leonard biography. 'It strikes everywhere. But it is only when the Grim Reaper's hands remove from our midst one dear to us that death comes as a tremendous shock. So it was when Benny Leonard passed out of the picture. So wide an acquaintance did he have

---

373 *Syracuse Herald Journal* 21 April 1947

that his passing received the same recognition that is given to a national figure.

'Benny died while refereeing a fight in the St Nicholas Rink. It was all over in a few minutes. Leonard sank to the canvas shortly after the last fight of the night had gotten under way. He collapsed and Dr Vincent Nardiello of the New York State Commission, who was sitting in Benny's corner, rushed into the ring to aid the stricken man. Dr Nardiello called for a stretcher and in about five minutes Benny was carried back to the dressing room, but he had passed away before he got there.

'Sitting at the side of her radio in the Bretton Hall on upper Broadway, Mrs Jacqueline Leonard listened intently to Bill Corum's report as he described over the radio the start of the semi-final bout. Suddenly, Corum's voice took on a new note. Something seemed to choke his voice as he hesitated then said, "Something has happened. Benny Leonard has collapsed in the ring." Mrs Leonard prayed, waited tensely for the next bit of information. Within a few minutes, the dreaded word came over the air.

'"Benny Leonard is dead. Dr Nardiello has just announced." The shock to Mrs Leonard was too great. Many times she had listened to Corum's broadcast while waiting for her husband to come home. Now she would wait in vain.'[374]

As soon as it was evident that Leonard was unable to continue to officiate, John Christensen, secretary of the boxing commission, ordered the bout between Mario Ramon and Bobby Williams stopped after Leonard was carried from the ring.

'RITES SCHEDULED FOR BENNY LEONARD' headed an *International News Service* report from New York on 20 April 1947. 'The body of Benny Leonard lay in state at Riverside Memorial Chapel tonight while admirers began to pay their respects. Leonard,

---

374 Nat Fleischer *Leonard the Magnificent* 1947

while refereeing a fight last night, died in the ring he loved so well. Death was due to haemorrhage of the brain. Funeral services will be held tomorrow. Mrs Leonard, who was listening to a broadcast of the boxing show at which her husband was refereeing all bouts, still was in a state of collapse tonight.

'One of Leonard's two surviving brothers, William, who lives in Miami, Florida, now is on his way to New York. Also surviving the boxer are the other brother, Joseph, his father and three sisters. Benny had no children.'[375]

'Benny Leonard, who often said that "I'll be in boxing until I breathe my last", collapsed and died in the ring at St Nick's Arena Friday night. Funeral services will be today at 11am with burial in a Long Island cemetery. To him, being in good condition was a constant rule. He neither smoked nor drank. Today the followers of boxing gathered, primarily along Jacob's Beach, to talk of Leonard. They remember how he entered Mike Jacobs's office during the final days of the recent war wearing the uniform of a lieutenant commander of the Merchant Marine and a pair of badly battered lips!

'As athletic director of the Merchant Marine camp, Leonard had lined up 100 of his cadet-boxers, had instructed each to jab his face. Leonard "caught" all the blows on his gloves, of course, but the constant pounding of his own gloves against his own lips had bruised them to a deep purple mass. But Leonard just sat in the office and repeated again and again, "Just think, every one of those kids will go home and tell how he sparred with Benny Leonard."'[376]

Sid Feder reported for the *Associated Press*, 'Little Benny Leonard, the greatest lightweight of them all, came to the end of the trail Friday night – just as you would expect him to – in a fight ring, with the smell of resin in his nostrils and the slide of the canvas

---

375 *Phoenix Arizona Republic* 20 April 1947
376 *Sarasota Herald Tribune* Florida 20 April 1947

under his black boxing boots. The smooth little fighting machine from uptown died while refereeing a fight in St Nicholas Arena. This was the neighbourhood club on 66th Street, just off Broadway, where he'd put on some of his own classy clouting exhibitions in his heyday. It was all over in minutes for the 51-year-old master of the ring.

'He had refereed the entire St Nick's card, as referees do in the small clubs, had finished handling the main bout in which Eddie Giosa, Philadelphia lightweight, outpointed Julio Jiminez, a Mexican mauler. Then Mario Ramon and Bobby Williams came on for the semi-wind-up. Two minutes of the first round went by. Suddenly, Benny staggered into the ropes. He fell, face forward, with such force that later a bruise was found on his forehead.

'One of the fighters stumbled over Benny's body. Dr Vincent Nardiello, the state commission physician, hurried into the ring. A stretcher was brought and Benny was carried to a dressing room. But he already was dead. Dr Nardiello called it a cerebral haemorrhage. In the death certificate, Dr William Benenson, an assistant medical examiner, gave the cause as coronary thrombosis. Thus ended one of the most brilliant careers in fistic history.'[377]

Ten days later, Dave Lewis was writing in his column, 'Benny Leonard, one of the finest champions ever to set foot in a ring, was laid to rest just a week ago. He suffered his first "knockout" at the age of 51. His death was a great shock to the fight game. Boxing men still find it hard to believe what happened in that New York ring ten days ago when Benny slumped to the canvas while refereeing a bout and the Grim Reaper tolled the count of ten.

'Everywhere I've gone the past few days, the talk always has turned to Benny Leonard. From these conversations came many great stories about the former lightweight champion, who retired

377 Sid Feder *Mason City Globe Gazette* Iowa 19 April 1947

undefeated. These stories will stand as monuments to one of the greatest little guys who ever came out of professional boxing.

'He was a gentleman throughout and loved the fight game to the very end. He was grateful to boxing with a humble, appreciative gratitude. "I've made more than a million dollars out of boxing," he stated a few years ago, then sincerely added, "but even if I'd never made a cent from it, I'd be thankful to the sport for what it's done for me. It's given me a strong body, a world of friends and what little education I've had. I'll be grateful to boxing for the rest of my life." And he was!

'Incidentally, Benny's devotion to his mother was genuine. Mother worried about him all the time and Benny never fought anywhere when he didn't rush to the phone afterwards to say, "Hello, mama, I won and I'm not hurt a bit." On that score, he rarely had to stretch the truth. He always won and usually he wasn't hurt a bit.'[378]

* * *

In the July 1947 edition of *The Ring* magazine, editor Nat Fleischer wrote in his column, 'The death of Benny Leonard should set all commissions on guard. It should serve as a warning. I was happy to learn from New York commissioner Eddie Eagan on his return from Europe that because of the St Nicholas Rink fatality, hereafter two officials will be assigned to handle the bouts at each of the smaller clubs and three at the Garden, and all outdoor shows staged in a ball park.

'Thus the penny wise and pound foolish policy in vogue in the Empire State for many years has been done away with through the martyrdom of Benny Leonard.'

---

378 Dave Lewis *Long Beach Independent* California 28 April 1947

CHAPTER TWENTY-NINE

'NEW YORK 20 April (*Associated Press*). The fight gang said a last farewell today to Benny Leonard, the retired and undefeated lightweight boxing champion of the world, who collapsed and died Friday night while refereeing a fight at the St Nicholas Arena – scene of many of his fistic triumphs. More than 600 mourners, most of whom had been associated with the boxing master when he wrote fistic history in the golden 20s, jammed the Riverside Memorial Chapel for the simple funeral services and thousands of other persons lined the streets.

'Among the fight figures who paid their last respects to Leonard was Billy Gibson, who managed the East Side ace. They were a famed team in the days when the sport was taking a firm hold and coming up with its first big gates. They were together up to the time Leonard retired as king of the lightweights in 1925 after fighting himself out of opponents in a seven-year reign.

'Also present were Maxie Baer, the former heavyweight champion, Abe Attell, Soldier Bartfield, Young Otto, Leach Cross, Harry Lewis of Philadelphia and a delegation of Philadelphia boxers.

'There were representatives of various boxing commissions, boxing judges and referees, ushers, policemen and boxing writers. The latter acted as honorary pall-bearers.

'The services were conducted by Rabbi Maurice Goldberg of Temple Shaare Zedek. In his eulogy, Rabbi Goldberg said that Leonard was "always the perfect gentleman".[379]

Benny Leonard was gone. So, as all great champions when they pass into Valhalla take their place in the various halls of fame, so the ring experts sat at their keyboards to make sure that the 'Great Bennah' would not be forgotten in the far distant future.

Grantland Rice was one of the most versatile and prolific sportswriters of all time. A few weeks after Leonard died, Rice wrote, 'The recent death of Benny Leonard revives the old argument concerning the best lightweight from a long and able parade. No other ring division has sent out as many fine fighters. The list includes such boxers and punchers as Joe Gans, Benny Leonard, Jack McAuliffe, Frank Erne, Kid Lavigne, Bat Nelson and Ad Wolgast …

'In various debates and arguments that have been under way for 40 years, there are generally two names that finish out in front – Leonard and Gans. Some time ago, Harry Smith, the veteran San Francisco expert who has been covering championship matches for more than 50 years, who goes back deep into ring history, put this selection up to many of those who had seen both men in action. In the vote that followed, Gans, the old master from Baltimore, had a slight lead. Both were rated headline artists as boxers and punchers. Leonard had much the better ring record. But Gans, to make a living, had to take orders more than once that included a dive …

'Gans finished his career in the last stages of tuberculosis, but even when a sick man he outlasted Bat Nelson, the durable Dane. No one ever knew just how good Gans might have been under cleaner handling plus better health. In addition to being

---

379 *Pittsfield Berkshire Evening Eagle* 21 April 1947.

a brilliant boxer, one who had no wasted motion, he also was a murderous puncher.

'Leonard was smart, game, one of the ablest of all the boxers and a hard puncher on the side. He was one of the greatest of the lot, and many rank him in front.'[380]

Arthur Daley of the *New York Times* was big on Leonard, writing, 'That suave and polished Leonard was a distinct credit to the game. Had it not been for boxing, he might have been just another East Side youngster lost among the swirling millions of New Yorkers. Perhaps he would have forced his head above the crowd but never would he have emerged as dominant and as praiseworthy a figure as he was to become by flashing along the fistic trail. Benny's pounding fists made him a fortune and made him a man. They brought a shy, self-conscious lad who was the original "mama's boy" to the peak of fame. He was smart not only in the ring but out of it, too. Constant association with celebrities and public figures was not only stimulating but educating. He made the most of it, which is more than anyone can say for the vast majority of those who also have been confronted by similar opportunities.'[381]

Veteran Jersey Jones of *The Ring* magazine recorded, 'In this writer's book, Leonard was one of the all-time greats of the ring. A magnificent boxer, a deadly puncher, a brilliant ring strategist and an extraordinary showman. Benny had to be a real champion, in every sense of the word, to rule over the most formidable array of challengers in the annals of the lightweight division. And what an array! Lew Tendler, Charley White, Willie Ritchie, Irish Patsy Cline, Willie Jackson, Rocky Kansas, Richie Mitchell, Johnny Dundee and Joe Welling to list only the better known of the many.

'And through those glamorous years, Benny not only dominated his own division but he knocked out Johnny Kilbane, a great

---

380 Grantland Rice *Polk Progress* Nebraska 15 May 1947
381 Arthur Daley *The New York Times* 25 April 1947

featherweight champion, and stepped up a notch to mingle with the talented welterweight titleholders Ted 'Kid' Lewis and Jack Britton. An amazing fighting machine, far and away the greatest lightweight this reporter ever has seen in nearly 35 years of active association with the rugged leather-pushing profession. But there is one thing of which we're definitely certain – pound for pound and inch for inch, Benny Leonard was the most superb ring artist these eyes of ours have ever been privileged to see in action.'[382]

Author Franklin Foer wrote, 'Leonard's conduct in and out of the ring and his impeccable public image stood as the refutation of the immigrant's anxiety that boxing would suck their children into a criminal underworld or somehow undermine the very rationale for fleeing to the Golden Land. Benny Leonard legitimised boxing as an acceptable Jewish pursuit – and even more than that, he helped make sports a perfectly kosher fixation.'[383]

---

[382] Jersey Jones *The Ring* magazine July 1947
[383] Franklin Foer and Mark Tracy *Jewish Jocks, An Unorthodox Hall of Fame* 2012

THE STATS

Benny Leonard (Benjamin Leiner)
World Lightweight Champion 1917–1925
Born: 7 April 1896
Died: 18 April 1947 (Age 51)
Hometown: New York
Professional Career: 1911–1925, 1931–1932
Total Bouts: 219
Won: 89 (70 by KO)
Lost: 6 (5 by KO)
Draw: 1
No Decision: 119 (96-16-7)
No Contest: 4.

Charley Rose ranked Leonard as the greatest lightweight of all time in 1968.

Herb Goldman ranked Leonard as the greatest lightweight of all time in 1987.

The Ring ranked Leonard as the greatest lightweight of all time in 1975.

The *Associated Press* ranked Leonard as the eighth best fighter overall in 1999.

INDEX

INDEX

INDEX

Also available at all good book stores

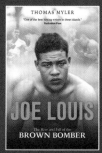

9781785315367

9781785315527

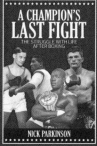

9781785311642

9781785315374

9781785314551

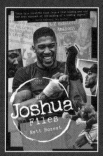

9781785313912

9781785311437

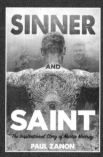

9781785313851

9781785313196